Quilting
FOR
DUMMIES®
2ND EDITION

by Cheryl Fall

WILEY

Wiley Publishing, Inc.

Quilting For Dummies® 2nd Edition

Published by
Wiley Publishing, Inc.
111 River St.
Hoboken, NJ 07030-5774
www.wiley.com

WILEY

About the Author

Cheryl Fall, a professional designer since 1986, is the author of 12 how-to books and over 2,500 how-to articles in various publications. Magazines featuring her work over the last 19 years have included *The Quilter, Quilt World, Quick and Easy Quilting, Family Circle, Woman's Day, Country Living, Craftworks,* and *Sewing Savvy.*

Cheryl is also the host of *The Creative Life with Cheryl Fall,* a nationally distributed PBS 'Plus' program that features lifestyle-enhancing projects, ideas, and useful information for women. She has also spent years creating quilting and sewing projects and teaching for various manufacturers, including Coats & Clark and Singer. As an accomplished fine artist, Cheryl has created and licensed designs for use in the textile, giftware, table top, and home furnishings markets.

Quilting can be an all-consuming occupation, but Cheryl still finds the time to goof around. Residing near Portland, Oregon, she's been happily married for more than 20 years to husband Tony and has two college-age daughters and one spoiled-rotten cocker spaniel named Buster, who thinks he rules the roost.

Dedication

I dedicate this book to would-be quilters the world over and to those who are learning this art. May all your quilts be terrific!

Author's Acknowledgments

I would like to thank my wonderful family because without their support, this book may have never made it to press. I can't thank my hubby and daughters enough for all the cooking, cleaning, and laundry they did while I was putting this book together (okay, sometimes I milked it, but it sure was fun!).

My deepest gratitude to Stedman Mays, agent extraordinaire; Chrissy Guthrie, Stacy Kennedy, and Elizabeth Rea at Wiley; and Carol Owens. These wonderful people helped make the revision of this book possible, and their help has been very much appreciated. You're all absolutely outstanding in your profession and pleasures to work with.

Originally, much of the art for this book was done by the late Phyllis Barbieri, whose help was invaluable and whose loss is deeply felt. She and technical reviewer Laurette Koserowski, both from Traditional Quilter magazine, made a great team. For the new edition of the book, I must thank artist Connie Rand for her illustrations. Many thanks, too, to all the companies and individuals who contributed time or product for this book, including:

> Coats & Clark for the use of some past projects that I'd done for them as well as their terrific assortment of threads and bias tape. (Thanks for the occasional pep talk, Meta and Lynn!)

> P&B Textiles, VIP Fabrics, Springs, RJR Fabrics, and Marcus Brothers for the delectable fabrics used in these quilts. Your catalogs offer such temptation to a fabric-phile like myself!

> Handler Textile Corporation and Pellon for their fusible products and stabilizers, which make machine appliqué a joy.

> Nolting Manufacturing for professionally machine quilting several of the larger projects in this book, saving me tons of time. Your generosity is very much appreciated.

> Fairfield Processing for the batting, pillow forms, and stuffing used in the projects.

I would also like to express my heartfelt gratitude to my assistant and photographer, Mary Nevius. No matter how daunting the task, she always stepped up to the plate and got it done.

Last but not least, I want to thank an inanimate object that I just know has a soul hidden somewhere in its gears — my trusty sewing machine. It has seen its share of quilts pass over its throat plate; it takes a lickin' but keeps on stitchin'!

Publisher's Acknowledgments

We're proud of this book; please send us your comments through our Dummies online registration form located at www.dummies.com/register/.

Some of the people who helped bring this book to market include the following:

Acquisitions, Editorial, and Media Development

Project Editor: Christina Guthrie

Acquisitions Editor: Stacy Kennedy

Senior Copy Editor: Elizabeth Rea

Editorial Program Assistant: Courtney Allen

Technical Editor: Carol Owens

Editorial Manager: Christine Meloy Beck

Editorial Assistants: Hanna Scott, Nadine Bell, David Lutton

Cover Photo: © Abbie Enneking, 2005; Quilt Designed by: Shirley Shedron

Cartoons: Rich Tennant (www.the5thwave.com)

Composition Services

Project Coordinator: Jennifer Theriot

Layout and Graphics: Carl Byers, Andrea Dahl, Lauren Goddard, Joyce Haughey, Melanee Prendergast, Heather Ryan

Proofreaders: Jessica Kramer, TECHBOOKS Production Services

Indexer: TECHBOOKS Production Services

Publishing and Editorial for Consumer Dummies

Diane Graves Steele, Vice President and Publisher, Consumer Dummies

Joyce Pepple, Acquisitions Director, Consumer Dummies

Kristin A. Cocks, Product Development Director, Consumer Dummies

Michael Spring, Vice President and Publisher, Travel

Kelly Regan, Editorial Director, Travel

Publishing for Technology Dummies

Andy Cummings, Vice President and Publisher, Dummies Technology/General User

Composition Services

Gerry Fahey, Vice President of Production Services

Debbie Stailey, Director of Composition Services

Contents at a Glance

Table of Contents

Introduction

*E*verybody loves quilts. They're soft, cozy, and comforting, and they've been around since man decided layers were the way to go. What more and more people have been realizing over the years, though, is that making quilts is fun and a wonderful way to express one's creativity with a practical bent.

Quilt making provides a wonderful opportunity to experiment with color, design, texture, and shape even if you're convinced you don't have an artistic bone in your body. Let your imagination guide you in choosing your fabrics and projects. Making quilts today is easier than you may have ever imagined; what's more, quilt making doesn't require any special skills, just a general knowledge of sewing and the desire to try! If you can sew a button or mend a hem, you can make a quilt. With just a few basic tools, a small amount of fabric, and a little time, you can create your own piece of comfort. This book shows you how. (And don't worry about mistakes — they add to the charm of your finished project.)

And speaking of projects! The range of quilted objects you can create is limitless! Think beyond the traditional bed quilt, and consider making quilted place mats, hot pads, or a table runner for your kitchen or to give as a host or hostess gift. You can even create quilted wall hangings as art for your home.

About This Book

This book guides even the beginningest-beginner through all the steps necessary for creating a first quilt. Although most people interested in quilting have sewn a bit, you can use this book even if your sewing experience is limited to threading a needle. If you're in the shallow end of the experience pool, you can simply start small, build experience and confidence, and eventually move on to tackling your grand design.

I show you how to select fabrics and materials, create a design, and then cut, piece, quilt, and finish your creation — all within the covers of this book. And to kick-start you in putting the skills covered in the book to actual use, I include 17 projects to fit any skill level. All are easy to create when you follow the illustrated and detailed step-by-step instructions.

Conventions Used in This Book

I used a few conventions when writing this book. Here they are:

- ✔ Each time I introduce a new quilting term, I *italicize* it.
- ✔ Step instructions and keywords that you should pay attention to in lists appear in **boldface.**
- ✔ Web sites and e-mail addresses appear in monofont to make them stand out.

What You're Not to Read

Of course, I'd love for you to read this book from cover to cover. After all, I've worked pretty hard on it, and it includes some great tips and tricks I've learned over the years! However, I do live in the real world, and I realize that you may be pressed for time and just want the bare-bones facts. If that's you, you can safely skip the sidebars, which appear in gray boxes, and any paragraphs that have the Technical Stuff icon attached. Reading these tidbits will enhance your quilting knowledge, but you can get by just fine without them.

Foolish Assumptions

I hate to assume anything about anyone I've never met, but when writing this book, I did have to make a few assumptions about who may be reading it. If you fit into any of the following categories, this book is for you:

- ✔ You're someone who has admired the art of quilt making from afar, but until now, you've been too skittish to try it.
- ✔ You're already in the process of learning to quilt and want a good, basic guide to help you build your skills.
- ✔ You've discovered that you're a fabric junkie and want to figure out what to do with all the great fabrics you've accumulated.
- ✔ Your favorite auntie is insisting you learn to quilt so that when you inherit her fabric stash, you can actually do something with it.

How This Book Is Organized

For logic and ease of use, this book is organized into six parts, the chapters of which progress from the most basic definition of a quilt and its parts through various skills and techniques that will help you create your quilt. This section gives you a brief description of each of these parts.

Part I: Gathering Your Tools and Getting Ready

A quilt may be made up of fabric, batting, and thread, but those aren't the only things you need to produce the final product. In this part, I go over all the basics of a quilt's components and talk a lot about the necessary supplies and tools you need to get started. I also share my hints about fabric selection and choosing the right batting for your project.

Part II: Planning Your Masterpiece

Quilts break down into a variety of elements, from blocks and strips to borders and appliqués. In this part, I introduce you to all these design elements and guide you through the general processes of creating quilt blocks and using templates. Here, you find out how to make templates, transfer markings to your fabrics, and design your own quilts either from your doodles or using your computer.

Part III: Sharpening Your Sewing Skills

Quilting gives you lots of creative flexibility, but it's important to remember that creativity doesn't trump precision. Careful measuring, cutting, and pressing are crucial if you want your quilt to lay crisp and flat. This part tells you what you need to know to stay on the straight and narrow with your quilting skills. I also give you a primer on appliqué, a potentially challenging technique that really pays off by giving you even more decorative and creative options.

Part IV: Ahead to the Finish: Quilting the Pieces in Place

Ultimately, your quilt is a creatively stitched-together sandwich of fabric (the bread) and batting (the filling). This part helps you build the coziest of quilt sandwiches, getting all your creative juices flowing. When you've read through these chapters, you should know enough to get started on a project of your own (if you haven't already). Basting, stitching, and binding are all covered here, so you're sure to finish your masterpiece in style.

Part V: Completing the Circle: Projects to Try

If you're anxious to start quilting but don't have any of your own projects or designs in mind, this part provides 17 projects to get you started. These projects are all suitable for rank beginners and cover a wide range of styles and techniques, so you're sure to find something that gets your quilting fingers twitching.

I provide patterns for the appliqué projects, but for some you need to run to your trusty copy center and enlarge them to full-size. (They're reproduced here at 50 percent; my ideas are clearly bigger than this book.)

Part VI: The Part of Tens

In the grand *For Dummies* tradition, the Part of Tens is a patchwork part — a little of this, a little of that, and lots of information and inspiration as you become absorbed into the quilting world. Practice timesaving techniques that give you time for more quilts, try out some suggestions for displaying your works of fabric art, and find out what judges look for in a prizewinning quilt show entry. I also created an Appendix to the book, which is full of ways you can meet fellow quilters and shop for quilting supplies and such in cyberspace.

Icons Used in This Book

Sprinkled throughout this book are cute little pictures called *icons* that highlight important information. Here's the decoder key:

This icon highlights important quilting basics. Whenever you quilt, whether by hand or machine, you need to remember and apply this information — these are the eternal truths of the craft.

This icon indicates information that you don't absolutely have to know in order to work on a quilting project — but it can be helpful.

This icon points out time-tested great ways to do things regardless of how you're quilting or how long you've been doing it.

Whatever you do, don't skip information that has this icon attached to it. It points out things that could wreck your project and maybe even put your love affair with quilting on the rocks.

Where to Go from Here

Use this book in the way that makes the most sense for your situation: You can read it cover to cover or just skip around to specific chapters that interest you. If you already wield some sewing abilities, you'll probably progress through this book somewhat faster than true novices, adding new skills and developing new techniques. Think of this book as your own little quilting bee, with me as your friendly, down-to-earth mentor who presents the information you need in a way that's easy to understand and inspiring to try.

As soon as you piece your first block, I have no doubt you'll be hooked on quilting, as thousands of people all around the world are. You'll suddenly find yourself unconsciously setting aside time from your own busy schedule to collect fabric (most quilters are true fabri-holics), cut, and stitch. Pieces of fabric will unexpectedly appear in your hands each time you sit down, whether you're watching television, riding the bus, or taking some time for yourself. You'll find that quilting somehow helps you relax after a hard day. Oh, to shut yourself off in your own wonderful, colorful world of fabric and thread!

Although I've attempted to include everything a beginner could want in a quilt book, keep in mind that there are as many ways of making a quilt as there are quilters and far more additional techniques, hints, and tidbits than this book's space allows. So in addition to gathering a nice stash of fabric, I encourage you to start building a library of quilting reference materials; I include some of my favorite reference works and supply sources in the Appendix to nudge you along. Happy quilting!

Part I

Gathering Your Tools and Getting Ready

In this part . . .

This part explains what makes a quilt a quilt and tempts you with the wonders of fabric. Every quilt is made from the same basic ingredients: fabric, thread, and a filler. In this part, I tell you everything you need to have on hand to make a quilt from beginning to end. I also share with you the must-have gadgets and tools and offer advice on how to select materials — including batting — appropriate for your project. By the time you get through this part, you'll be on your way to becoming a true fabric-holic, greedily stuffing fabrics into every spare nook and cranny in your home in anticipation of the next project

Chapter 1

The Art of Quilting

In This Chapter

▶ Deconstructing the quilt

▶ Exploring the history of quilt making

▶ Appreciating quilting today

For centuries, quilts have played an important role in people's lives, providing their makers and recipients not only with warmth and comfort but also with colorful, attractive works of art. Traditionally, quilts also have been showcases for the talents and skills of their creators.

Throughout history, most households, regardless of income level, had certain quilts used only for special occasions or when honored guests visited. Quilt makers put their greatest efforts into these quilts, using the best quality fabric they could afford and covering them with miles and miles of beautiful quilting stitches. Many of these rarely used "best quilts" survive today as a testament to the history of quilting and the talents of their makers and are highly coveted by quilt collectors.

In this chapter, I explain what a quilt is and document the quilt's rich role in the texture of human life. I also share some of the newest developments in quilting and talk a bit about how quilting has become a modern form of artistic expression.

Following the Recipe for a Fabric Sandwich

A quilt — that soft, cozy, comforting hunk of fabric and filling — in its simplest sense is a textile *sandwich;* in fact, that's how the quilt layers are traditionally described. This simple sandwich is what distinguishes a quilt from any other sewn object.

All quilts — whether intended for use on a bed or as a simple potholder — consist of three layers:

- ✔ Pieced or appliquéd quilt top
- ✔ Filling (called *batting* or *wadding*)
- ✔ Fabric backing

The top, batting, and backing layers are held together, or *quilted,* using a series of basic running stitches. You can also tie the layers together by stitching yarn, narrow ribbon, or pearl cotton through the layers at regular intervals and tying off the ends. However you do it, your goal is to prevent the layers from shifting during regular use and washing. You can see a cross section of a quilt in Figure 1-1.

Figure 1-1:
The layers
are what
make a quilt.

Quilt top

Batting

Backing Fabric

Some folks call various types of bedcoverings "quilts," but if it doesn't consist of three layers (top, filling, and backing), it isn't really a quilt but rather a coverlet, bedspread, or throw. Also, although the word "quilt" is casually used to refer to a quilted bedcovering, many other objects — such as place mats, vests, wall hangings, and diaper bags — can be quilted.

The quilt top

The topmost layer of the quilt sandwich is the *quilt top,* which is typically made of fabric blocks that are pieced, appliquéd, or crafted using a mixture of both techniques. Quilt tops can also be devoid of individual blocks, made instead of whole cloth.

Piecing things together

A *pieced* (also called *patchwork*) quilt top can be made up of tens to hundreds of small pieces of fabric joined together by hand or machine to create a pattern or repeating design. Modern cutting and stitching techniques make the work of piecing both fun and easy to do. I discuss these techniques in Chapters 8 and 9.

Patchwork is the most recognized form of quilt making and was devised as a way to turn a bunch of fabric odds and ends into one cohesive unit, eliminating waste by using any fabric available. Over the centuries it evolved into the art form we know today. Patchwork uses basic shapes such as squares, triangles, rectangles, and hexagons to form patterns ranging from simple to complex. To create a patchwork top, you piece various patterns together into one block and then piece each block to another to create the overall quilt design. I talk more about patchwork in Chapter 4.

Layering up with appliqué

Appliqué is another method of creating quilt tops. To create an appliquéd top, you stitch various fabric shapes onto a base fabric. In the past, appliqué was used mainly for "best quilts" — the quilts used when company was expected — because of the money and time involved in making them. Stitching a piece of fabric on top of another piece wasn't a very frugal use of precious fabric, making the quilts more expensive to create than patchwork ones. Appliqué also takes a bit longer to stitch than piecing, but the appliqué method allows you to create interesting patterns that can't be pieced, such as dainty flowers with gracefully curving stems.

You can do appliqué work either by hand or by machine. Machine appliqué provides a variety of creative possibilities and is easy enough for even the rank beginner to master yet can be done intricately enough to produce a masterpiece worthy of a blue ribbon at the state fair. Chapter 10 covers appliqué in more detail.

Working with the whole top

Whole cloth quilts are one more branch of the quilt tree that bears mentioning. These were the fanciest of quilts, often created by wealthy women for only the most distinguished guests. In whole-cloth quilting, the quilt top consists of one large piece of fabric without seams (wide fabric widths were uncommon and very costly before the invention of modern fabric looms in the 18th century). This single piece is intricately quilted with delicate, closely-spaced stitching designs. One of the unique features of a whole cloth quilt is that it's reversible, with the front being identical to the back. In France, these types of quilts are known as *boutis.* Today, whole cloth quilts are often referred to as *white work* or *bridal quilts,* and due to their intricacy, they're still reserved for the best occasions.

The batting

The middle layer, or filling, of a quilt consists of cotton, wool, silk, or polyester *batting* (also referred to as "wadding" in some parts of the world).

Batting is a very important component of a quilt; in fact, it's the batting that makes a quilt truly a quilt. Without that wonderful, soft inner layer, you have a coverlet rather than a quilt. Batting adds depth and dimension to the quilt in that it buffers the quilt top and bottom, and it gives quilts the loft and coziness that make them so special.

Before the invention of commercial quilt batting, quilt makers used whatever they could find as filler. Wool was usually the filler of choice because it could be fluffed, laid out, and felted by dampening, pounding, and rolling the fibers until they meshed together. Quilt making got a whole lot easier when the first commercial quilt batting was produced from cotton in 1846. Cotton is still one of the favorite choices for quilt batting today.

I talk more about batting options and selection in Chapter 3.

The backing

The bottom layer of the sandwich, the *backing,* is a large piece of plain or printed cotton that may or may not be pieced together from smaller pieces to create the proper size. I talk more about the backing in Chapter 3.

After you assemble the three layers that make up a quilt, you have a sandwich of sorts: the quilt top and backing fabric enclose a layer of batting. The next step is to *quilt* the sandwich, meaning that you secure the three layers together by hand or machine stitching them into one cohesive and cozy unit.

"Quilt-thropology:" A Brief History of Quilt Making

Quilt making isn't just an American pastime; it has roots in Europe, South America, and Asia as well. Quilts were essential articles in households of the past, but they weren't used only as bedcoverings. You may be surprised to find out that quilts were used as curtains to keep out drafts, draped on supports and used as tents, used to cover doorways when no door was there, and used as petticoats and waistcoats to keep the body warm. Really thick quilts were even used as armor! Need proof? Head out to a Renaissance fair with a battle reenactment and you'll see something very similar to the quilted armor of our historical past.

Because quilts were so useful, quilting lessons began early in life. As soon as a young girl was able to manipulate a needle, she began her quilting and sewing career. Historic records show quilts included in a bride's dowry, and no self-respecting bride's family would allow her to marry without a certain number of quilted items in her hope chest.

The power of patchwork

Patchwork quilting evolved from the frugality of homemakers in times when fabric wasn't very plentiful; it was a way to use up fabric odds and ends, ensuring nothing went to waste. Necessity truly was the mother of invention. Women saved every scrap from other sewing projects, and they often recycled worn out items into patches for quilts. Most patchwork quilts were intended for everyday use and were simply patched up when they became worn. If they became too worn, these tattered quilts were often used as fillers for new quilts.

During the U.S. Civil War, patchwork quilts also served another purpose: Many quilts featured special blocks or combinations of colors that made them function as maps of the Underground Railroad, guiding America's slaves from one safe house to another during this tumultuous time in history.

Leaving a social legacy

Quilt making has always been an important social activity. The *quilting bee* was one of the few opportunities women had to retreat from the backbreaking chores of farm life and spend time with one another. These groups of ladies (and sometimes men) often worked together on special presentation quilts to commemorate weddings or births or to express appreciation to members of their communities. These presentation quilts — which often included the signatures of the many makers, either written poetically on the blocks in permanent ink or embroidered in thread — became known as *autograph* or *album quilts.*

Proof that quilting goes way back

The oldest quilted object found thus far, which may date from around the first century B.C., is a rug taken from a Siberian tomb. Quilting may also have been practiced by the ancient Egyptians: Carvings at some ancient sites show the use of objects that have a quilted appearance. As well, many ancient nomadic peoples created quilted fabrics to use as tents, insulating them from the cold.

The oldest known quilted objects from Europe include armor, saddle blankets, and whole cloth quilts from Sicily.

The secret of Granny's petticoats

Have you ever wondered what granny wore under her billowing skirts to keep warm during icy-cold winters? The answer is a quilt! Garment exhibits at museums often display fine examples of quilted petticoats, corset covers, and waistcoats.

Quilted petticoats for everyday wear were very simple and usually made of wool, serving mainly to keep their wearers warm. The filler material in many of these old petticoats was wool wadding, but some more frugal gals actually used horsehair — sounds like an itch-fest to me!

Other petticoats served decorative purposes only. These were elaborately quilted and were probably reserved for special occasions or for times when skirts were pinned up to show underskirts and petticoats, depending on the fashion rules of the day. (Showing more petticoat than the rules of proper conduct allowed may have been considered scandalous!) In the 1800s, these fancy petticoats were made of quilted silk or taffeta.

Some quilted items, such as corset covers, had both form and function. They were designed to be supportive but were also highly decorative.

Autograph quilts became popular around 1840 and were made in a variety of styles: Some were constructed of identical pieced blocks, and others consisted of individual appliquéd blocks. Commemorative autograph quilts in elaborate red and green appliqué were quite popular on the east coast of the United States during the 1800s and are known as the Baltimore Album style. From a style that originated in the Baltimore, Maryland, area, these quilts were often made to welcome a new minister to the community, to celebrate a wedding, or to give as a gift on a young man's 21st birthday.

Quilting bees were an established community tradition by the mid-1800s and were even introduced to the Hawaiian Islands by missionaries during this time. The Hawaiian tradition of whole-cloth quilts appliquéd with whole cloth appliqués (basically one huge appliqué centered on one large piece of background fabric) evolved from this point into the unique art form it is today.

Today, community-created quilts are made to honor the fallen (such as the quilts made after 9/11); bring hope to the sick and those afflicted with AIDS, cancer, and other illnesses; and bring comfort to premature babies and the homeless. Quilting is still bringing people together to stitch, chat, and enjoy each other's company.

A Persistent Pastime: Quilting Today

Although they continue to add warmth to many a household, today's quilts are no longer a necessity but rather a means of self-expression. Today's quilt makers have a dizzying array of fabrics to choose from and decorative threads and other great items to incorporate into their designs. Quilts stores are popping up everywhere offering quilters seemingly boundless choices of fabrics and patterns as well as inspiration. For quilters who enjoy making the quilt tops but aren't too keen on doing the actual quilting, many shops offer quilting services for a fee to their customers and keep a long-arm sewing machine in the back room just for this purpose.

Quilt making today is a hobby enjoyed by men and women alike (although women, with their needle-nimble fingers, still predominate). In many cases, machine techniques have replaced tedious hand piecing and appliqué, but modern quilt makers still take inspiration from quilts of days past, adapting those designs and techniques to today's lifestyles. For example, although some quilts are still made from fabric scraps, the maker is more likely to use the patchwork approach to recreate the charming look of old quilts or to commemorate a life or an event than for reasons of necessity.

Quilting as an art form has become very chic. I'm always amazed at the number of museums here in the United States and abroad that feature art quilt exhibits, and you can even find museums dedicated solely to the art of quilting. Quilting has certainly come a long way throughout the centuries — it has become *fiber art.*

Artistic quilters are dyeing their own fabrics and block-printing unique hand-made designs on fabric to create custom textiles for their art quilts. These artists create their own patterns inspired by nature (such as watercolors or landscapes), geometry (such as kaleidoscopes and *tessellations,* those nifty interlocking block designs that are all identical and fit together neatly and go on into infinity), or life in general (such as portrait quilting, life stories, or dedications). They also mix traditional and unusual fibers with other media, such as paint, beading, embroidery, and even plastic.

Exhibits of gorgeous quilted art at local art museums are fairly common. To find one near you, check your local paper, visit your local art museum's Web site, or check with the local quilting guild. You'll be amazed by what you see on display!

New technologies are also inspiring new generations of quilters. Software allows quilts to be designed, viewed, and altered before a single cut is made or stitch is taken, and special products now make it possible to print fabric using a computer and printer. An ancient art form has gone high-tech.

Talented, dedicated quilters have elevated the art of quilting to an entirely new level, creating a veritable fiber revolution (if I sound excited, it's because I am!).

Do quilting bees still buzz?

Great-granny probably didn't get out all that much, considering the lack of transportation available to her and the fact that she may have lived out on a farm in the middle of nowhere. This is why a quilting bee was so important to her — it was one of her main means of socializing with other women and staying in touch with her community.

Although the quilting bees of days past served a very important purpose, they no longer exist in the same capacity. Society is considerably more mobile now, and a quilting bee is no longer a necessity for social interaction. But before you panic, consider what has replaced it — the *quilting guild.*

These days, most quilters are members of or have attended some form of a quilting guild. Most guilds meet for a few hours on a monthly or bimonthly basis to share news of quilting, show off finished projects, and work on projects in-progress. Some also work on community service projects, such as quilts for the homeless or house-bound, quilts and layettes for premture babies, and memorial quilts for AIDS victims and their families, to name just a few.

Many guilds have special programs that bring in top teachers from all over the country, and they often host yearly quilt shows, which are an excellent opportunity to check out what other quilters in your area are working on!

Finding a quilting guild is easy. Simply ask at the local quilting supply store or fabric retailer, or check with your local library. Be sure to find out what the "visitation" policy is ahead of time; some guilds allow one or two visits before requiring membership and a nominal fee, and others may charge a per-visit fee (a buck or two). To find out what types of events are being planned by your local guild, contact their program chairperson.

Don't think you have the time for a guild but like to spend hours surfing the Web? Consider a cyber-guild. The Internet is full of great places for quilters to interact with each other without ever leaving their homes!

Chapter 2

Threads, Needles, and Gadgets — And All That Jazz

*Y*ou may think that fabric selection, which I cover in Chapter 3, is the most important part of prepping for your quilting adventure, but I've got news for you: Gathering the right equipment — threads, needles, gadgets, and gizmos — is just as critical. Unfortunately, as with most things, no one choice is right for every situation.

For example, suppose you want to buy a simple spool of thread. Well, there's no such thing. Step into any sewing supplies store and you'll find yourself facing an endless array of little spools of every thickness and color imaginable. If you choose a spool of thread just because it matches your fabric, there's a good chance you aren't making the right choice.

In this chapter, I explain all you need to know in order to select the right thread for the task at hand and assemble your team of tools, including both the essentials and the fun — but optional — toys.

A Thread for Every Occasion

Just as there are different sizes of nuts and bolts for almost every purpose, so is the story with thread. You can choose from all-purpose, buttonhole-twist, rayon, cotton, and silk. How about woolly nylon? Do you need monofilament, extra-fine, or metallic? Do you want basting thread or darning thread? And to make things even more complicated, consider color. Cotton, mercerized cotton, and nylon thread all come in a wide range of colors. So which thread is the best thread for your project? This section helps you figure that out.

For help with thread selection at-a-glance, see Table 2-1. I explain the uses of the different threads in the sections that follow.

Table 2-1	Finding the Right Thread for the Job
For...	*Use...*
Piecing, hand or machine	All-purpose thread
	Mercerized cotton thread
Appliqué, hand	All-purpose thread
	Silk thread
	Cotton thread
	Six-strand cotton floss
Appliqué, machine	Buttonhole-twist thread for blanket or buttonhole stitches
	Nylon monofilament thread for invisible appliqué
	Rayon or polyester machine embroidery threads for satin stitch or other decorative stitch appliqué
	All-purpose thread for satin stitch appliqué
	Metallic thread for special appliqué effects
Quilting, hand	Extra-strong hand quilting thread (polyester core)
	Cotton quilting thread
Quilting, machine	Nylon monofilament thread for invisible stitches
	All-purpose thread for general machine quilting
	Buttonhole-twist thread for prominent-looking stitches
	Metallic or specialty thread for special effects

As for the other threads you may find in the store, ignore them — they're not quilt-worthy.

Assembly threads

For small-scale assembly, such as when you're stitching together the pieces of fabric in a quilt block, or large-scale assembly, such as when you're sewing the quilt blocks together to form a quilt top, choose an *all-purpose thread* to coordinate with your fabrics. I know what you're thinking: It's pretty unlikely that one thread color will coordinate with all the fabrics you use in a particular project. You may use many different colors of fabric in one project, making it impractical (if not impossible) to select a thread to match every fabric and change thread each time you stitch two pieces together. So here's my advice: When in doubt, select a thread from the mid-color range — one that falls somewhere between your darkest and lightest fabric colors.

All-purpose thread is the most commonly used thread and is available in nearly every color in the spectrum. It's strong and durable because it's made from mercerized (treated) cotton with a polyester core (called *poly-core*). The great thing about all-purpose thread is that you can use it for both hand and machine stitching.

Some quilting "purists" prefer to use nothing but 100 percent cotton in their quilts because they really like the idea of all-cotton quilts. This thread choice is perfectly acceptable, too. Like all-purpose thread, 100 percent cotton thread is also available in a reasonably nice range of colors,

If you decide to go with 100 percent cotton thread, be sure to select one that has been *mercerized,* or treated with a caustic soda; this treatment adds strength and durability to the thread. After all, you want your project to eventually become an heirloom, right?

Machine-quilting threads

For machine quilting, which I cover in Chapter 13, you have several thread options: all-purpose, monofilament, buttonhole-twist, variegated, and metallic.

For standard, everyday machine quilting, all-purpose thread is a safe bet. Some manufacturers market *machine quilting thread,* but in some instances, the thread is really just repackaged all-purpose thread. This isn't an attempt at deception but rather the manufacturer's way of helping you select the right thread for your needs. The thread choice for standard machine quilting is really up to you.

If you prefer to end up with "invisible" stitches, choose a nylon *monofilament* thread. Monofilaments are available in clear and smoke colors; the clear is great for bright fabrics mixed with white or off-white fabrics, and the smoke is best for darker fabrics. No matter the color, monofilament thread is durable and hides all manner of mistakes.

For a fun and more noticeable effect, try using buttonhole-twist, variegated, or metallic thread for machine quilting.

- **Buttonhole-twist** is a heavier version of all-purpose thread and has a thick, dramatic effect. For extra pizzazz, use buttonhole-twist in a color that contrasts with your fabric!

- **Variegated** threads contain banding of several colors in one thread. These threads are wonderful for quilting on patterned fabrics because the color bands tend to get lost in the pattern, so they don't stand out awkwardly.

- **Metallic** thread looks . . . well, metallic. The added sparkle is beautiful in holiday projects in particular.

Metallic thread is notorious for breaking easily during stitching, so you should try different brands whenever possible. If you change brands but still have breakage, look for a metallic thread with a softer feel to it. Also, using metallic threads in machine quilting will dull your needle quickly (just like you'd end up with really dull scissors if you used them to cut metal). In order to keep your machine in tiptop quilting shape, be sure to insert a fresh needle after using metallic threads.

Hand-quilting threads

Hand-quilting thread is available in two different forms, both of which are slightly heavier than all-purpose thread:

- Polyester-core, cotton-wrapped thread with a polished finish
- 100 percent cotton thread with a polished finish

The polished finish on hand-quilting threads provides abrasion resistance, making it easier to stitch with, and helps keep the thread from tangling. If you run into knotting and tangling problems during hand quilting, however, run your thread through a beeswax cake before threading your needle. The beeswax acts as a lubricant and helps prevent any handling problems. You can find beeswax in the same departments as needles and quilting supplies in most fabric stores.

Appliqué threads

For machine appliqué, all-purpose thread is a fine option, but it's not your only one. You can also choose from a number of other types of threads, many of which add visual interest to your final product.

- ✔ **Rayon and polyester threads** are very fine and have a beautiful luster. They're especially good choices if you're doing satin stitch appliqué (see Chapter 10 for details).

  Rayon and polyester threads' sole purposes in life are to be decorative, so don't use them for assembly.

- ✔ **Metallic and textured specialty threads** add special visual effects that catch the eye. Try using a wooly thread to appliqué a teddy bear, giving it a touchable texture, or experiment with a textured multi-colored thread for a bit of pizzazz.

- ✔ **Buttonhole-twist thread** is very thick and used mainly for topstitching, which is regular old straight stitching. However, I recommend you use buttonhole-twist thread for appliqué because this thread makes buttonhole-stitch appliqué look like time-consuming hand embroidery! The thickness of the thread is what does the trick.

- ✔ **Nylon monofilament** is the thread of choice for invisible machine appliqué.

For hand appliqué, all-purpose and silk threads are good choices because of the wonderful range of colors they come in (your appliqué thread often needs to match your appliqué fabric) and because of the way they handle in a hand-sewing needle. Thick (such as buttonhole-twist) or fine threads (such as monofilament) don't handle well in a hand-sewing needle.

If you find yourself in a pinch, you can use a single strand of embroidery floss for hand appliqué work.

Stocking Up on Sewing Basket Essentials

So you've got a great sewing basket . . . now what do you put in it? This section runs through the basic supplies that should be in every sewing basket, whether you're ready to start quilting or just thinking about it.

Scissors — One pair won't cut it

Read carefully: You need *at least* two pairs of scissors, with one pair reserved for fabric cutting *only*. Nothing dulls an expensive pair of fabric scissors faster than cutting paper or cardboard, so get a really good pair of fabric scissors and tag them with a skull and crossbones if necessary! Hide them if you have to, or lock them away. Do whatever it takes to protect your precious snips, and be sure to tell family members about your scissors rules. Let the would-be scissors-snaggers know that if you catch them using your fabric scissors to cut anything other than fabric, they'll face some severe consequences (I'll leave the punishment up to your imagination). Relegate your second pair of scissors to all other tasks. Use these all-purpose scissors to cut templates or clip patterns.

Whether for cutting fabric or general use, if your scissors become dull, getting them sharpened is easy enough. Most fabric and craft stores contract with local sharpening services that pick up and deliver freshly sharpened scissors to the store within a few days. If you have the sneaking suspicion that your fabric scissors are going to be commandeered for other uses, cheapies are okay too as long as you cycle them out of your sewing basket (toss them or relegate them to the kitchen junk drawer) as soon as they become dull. Cheap scissors really aren't worth the expense to sharpen — you're better off just investing in a new pair.

You may also want to get small, sharp scissors for cutting appliqués or *thread snips* for trimming threads. Thread snips are little trimmers with a squeeze handle that make snipping small threads a bit easier because all you have to do is grab the snips and pinch the thread. Although neither is truly necessary, they're nice to have (and we quilters do love our gadgets). If you decide to expand to your scissor repertoire, reserve these additions for cutting fabric and thread only. Figure 2-1 shows three types of scissors.

Figure 2-1:
Fabric scissors, scissors for general use, and thread snips (left to right).

Needles for sewing by hand

When it comes to needles, you need them for two different purposes: general sewing and quilting. Because some needles work better than others for some tasks, a "household assortment" of needles is handy because it usually contains a variety of needle lengths and widths.

Household needles are called *sharps;* they're fine (very narrow) needles with small, round eyes. These needles are called "sharps" simply because they are — they penetrate fabric (even multiple layers) easily. Sharps are suitable for hand piecing and appliqué.

When selecting needles, remember this: The *smaller* the number, the *larger* the needle. Sharps in size 8 or 9 work well for quilting, but you should always choose a needle that you're comfortable with. Some folks prefer a small needle, and others like 'em big! If your hands are large, you certainly don't want to struggle with a teensy-weensy needle — it'll feel more like a splinter than a sewing tool. If your hands are small, choose a smaller needle rather than one that feels like a metal toothpick with a thread hanging out one end.

If you have trouble threading general-purpose needles, look for easy-threading needles with slotted eyes.

For hand quilting, select needles called *betweens.* Like sharps, betweens are fine needles, but they're generally shorter than sharps and are made especially for quilting or other detailed handwork. Size 8 is a good size for the beginner, but many long-time quilters prefer size 12, which is really tiny; its diminutive, narrow size allows the quilter complete control and enables the quilter to take quite a few very small stitches onto the needle before passing it completely through the quilt. With a longer needle, you have less control while quilting because your fingers are further from the fabric.

Seam ripper

Unless you're one of those lucky people who never, ever makes a mistake, you definitely need a seam ripper, shown in Figure 2-2. As my own grandmother used to say, "As ye sew, so shall ye rip!" Mistakes are a common aspect of quilting. Get used to it.

Practice using your seam ripper on a few scraps of fabric sewn together, making sure that you cut only the thread without ripping into the fabric. Keep your seam ripper handy when sewing, and be sure to replace it now and then — seam rippers dull with use. Seam rippers are cheap, so don't fret about replacement. And you may want to keep several on hand because they tend to get lost easily.

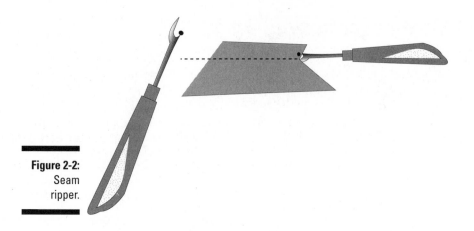

Figure 2-2:
Seam
ripper.

Measuring tape and marking implements

Measuring tapes are handy for a number of things: checking seam allowances, creating patterns, measuring fabric, and so on. I like to use a retractable fabric tape measure, but any small measuring tape does the job — even a dressmakers tape. Figure 2-3 shows a retractable measuring tape.

Figure 2-3:
A retract-
able
measuring
tape is
handy for
quick and
precise
measure-
ments.

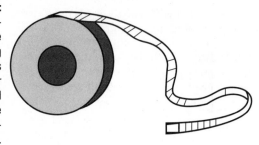

A standard #2 pencil, the kind of pencil you needed in grade school to fill out those standardized tests, is a useful addition to your sewing basket, but don't use it to mark fabrics. For that job, you need an assortment of water-soluble marking tools. At your sewing supply store, look for pencils and pens specifically designed for marking on fabrics — they're guaranteed to wash out and not harm your fabrics.

Personally, I don't use pens of any kind — not even those meant for use on fabrics. I prefer to stick to fabric-marking pencils or tailor's chalk. Both wash out beautifully and never soak through fabric to the other side. My favorites are EZ Quilting Washout Pencils, which are available in blue, white, and yellow. I also like the Berol Marking Pencils available in silver, white, blue, yellow, rose, and #4 graphite.

Never, never, never ever, ever, ever use a standard pen or marker on your fabrics. The ink may become permanent, especially after pressing, and the dark lines show through to the other side of fabrics, making unsightly marks in your finished quilt. Also, beware of anything that says "fade-away" or "vanishing fabric marker." These marks fade rapidly (usually within about 48 hours, or quicker if you leave the fabric in direct sunlight), and you may have to re-mark your fabric when you least expect it.

Needle threader

A needle threader (see Figure 2-4) is a great tool to have in your sewing basket because you never know when you'll have trouble with a particular thread or needle or will simply be trying to thread a needle in low light. (The best of the best needle threaders has a magnifier on one end.)

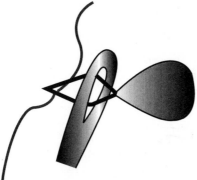

Figure 2-4:
A needle threader eases the task of joining needle and thread.

Thimble

Eventually (maybe even at first!), you're going to prick your finger with a needle. Seeing as you probably don't want blood on your quilt top (although I tell you how to remove blood spots in Chapter 13), invest in a thimble or two.

Thimbles help protect your fingers from needle pokes and sticks. You wear a thimble on the finger that pushes the needle through the fabric, but you may also want to wear a finger protector on your other hand as well. Several different types of thimbles are available, including varieties made of metal, plastic, and leather (see Figure 2-5). Others are adjustable or fit around long fingernails, so there really is a thimble out there for everyone.

Get a thimble that fits your finger snugly without being tight. Because thimbles are inexpensive, try a few different styles to find the one that's most comfortable and most effective for you. You may find that you like certain thimbles better for different applications.

Most right-handed quilters wear their thimbles on the middle finger of the right hand, using it to help push the needle through the fabric without piercing the skin of the "pushing" finger. It's also helpful to wear a leather protector on the "receiving" finger — the one positioned under the work to help guide the needle (either the middle or index finger on most folks). If you're a lefty, reverse these tips!

Figure 2-5:
Let your thimble get the point so you can quilt in comfort.

Pins and pincushions

Quilters can never have too many pins. Straight pins are indispensable for holding pieces of fabric together and holding appliqués in place. And you can't have lots of pins without a pincushion, which prevents the pins from rolling off your work surface and onto the floor — and later finding their way into someone's foot!

I prefer magnetic pincushions because they're an easy target to hit when you're pulling pins with one hand and guiding fabric through the machine with the other (you only have to get the pins close enough for the magnets to attract them). Magnetic pincushions also work great when you accidentally knock the whole shebang off your work table and your pins scatter all over the floor. Simply hold the empty or near-empty pincushion a few inches above the floor in the spill-zone and watch your pins fly back to the pincushion!

Be wary of pin spills on carpet, however. If pins are lodged in the carpet fibers, the magnet may not pull them out, and you'll most certainly end up with one sticking right through your house slippers. (I know what you wear while sewing — don't play coy with me!)

If you decide not to thread baste your quilt sandwich (see Chapter 12), safety pins are a must-have for holding the layers of your quilt together for machine quilting. To prevent potential rust stains, choose large, nickel-plated brass finish pins, often labeled "quilting safety pins," at the fabric store.

Glue stick

A glue stick may not sound like a typical sewing basket staple, but it's a neat and tidy way to hold small appliqués in place in areas when pins are just too large or cumbersome. You can use either a standard glue stick from an office supply store or one specifically designed for fabrics, which you can find at a fabric store. Both work and wash out equally well.

More Basics and Nice-to-Haves

Some supplies don't fit into a sewing basket but are essential for successful quilting nonetheless. Other supplies are just plain nice to have — sure, you could do without them, but why should you? In no particular order, here's a list of large essentials and portable nice-to-haves:

- Sewing machine and extra all-purpose machine needles
- Iron and ironing board
- Traveling quilting pad, with a rotary-cutting and marking surface on one side and an ironing/pressing surface on the other side
- Pressing cloth to protect specialty fabrics such as metallics, lamé, or anything that could potentially melt during pressing
- Rotary cutting supplies, specifically a rotary cutter with extra blade, a plastic see-through ruler, and a cutting mat
- Assorted plastic quilting templates, such as squares and triangles
- Quilting frame and hoops
- Graph paper and tracing paper
- Colored pencils for layout design ideas
- Masking tape
- Spray bottle of ouchie-fixer (you're bound to go "Ouch!" at least once) and a supply of bandages

The following sections zone in on some of these supplies.

Rotary cutting supplies

A *rotary cutter* is kind of like a pizza wheel with a very, very sharp blade. With a rotary cutter, you can quickly and accurately cut through multiple layers of fabric, drastically decreasing the time spent cutting out strips and patches. Rotary cutters are easy to use regardless of whether you're right- or left-handed. Cutters come in a number of different sizes, but I recommend that you purchase a larger cutter with a 45 mm blade one because it's more comfortable to handle than the 28 mm size.

To protect your cutting surface, purchase an 18- x 26-inch or larger *self-healing rotary cutting mat.* Choose a cutting mat that's marked with 1-inch grid markings and bias lines.

Don't attempt rotary cutting without the proper mat! You're guaranteed to destroy your cutting surface and dull or possibly even ruin your rotary blade if you don't have the right kind of protective mat.

To get neat, accurate fabric cuts with your rotary cutter, a 6- x 24-inch clear plastic ruler and other sizes of clear plastic rulers and templates are especially helpful. These rulers and templates are clear so you can see your fabric and the cutting mat grids through them, ensuring accuracy. In Figure 2-6, you can see a variety of rotary cutting supplies. For more on rotary cutting, check out Chapter 8.

After you get the hang of rotary cutting and are thoroughly hooked (trust me, you will be!), consider investing in a rotary cutting system for quilters. These systems have everything you need to cut quilt patches compiled into one tidy parcel. You get a mat with attached guides, and rulers that pivot in every direction, virtually eliminating the need for loose rulers and templates. All you have to add is your favorite rotary cutter. I like the QuiltCut2 fabric cutting system from Alto's; it has a pivoting cutting guide that will cut everything from blocks and stripes to triangles and hexagons. The system saves tons of time and means I have less equipment to knock off the table.

Quilting hoops and frames

Quilting hoops and frames hold the layers of a quilt taut for hand quilting (see Figure 2-7). A *quilting hoop* consists of two circles of plastic or wood that are nestled together; a screw eye on the outer circle allows you to tighten and loosen the tension of the hoops as necessary. If you're a beginning quilter, you may want to stick to small projects that can be quilted easily in a hoop. Although you can quilt large projects in hoops, doing so is usually a heavy and cumbersome undertaking — after all, the weight of the project sits in your lap when you use a hoop! (I talk more about quilting with hoops in Chapter 13.)

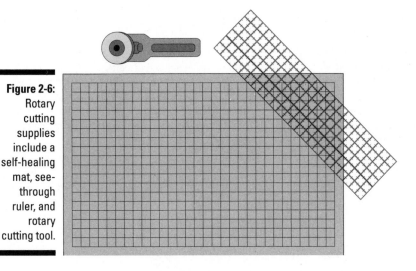

Figure 2-6: Rotary cutting supplies include a self-healing mat, see-through ruler, and rotary cutting tool.

Hoops of varying sizes are available in any quilting or fabric store. A 20-inch hoop is a good all-purpose hoop. You may also want a larger hoop — up to 30 inches or so in diameter — for large-scale projects such as a bed quilts. Remember, the smaller the hoop, the more you have to unfasten it to move around and work on different areas of your quilt.

When you really fall victim to the quilting bug and start quilting regularly and working on larger or more advanced projects, you may choose to invest (and I do mean invest — they can be quite expensive) in a floor-standing quilt frame, which you can see in Figure 2-8. Your local quilting or fabric store is likely to sell quilting frames, and they're also advertised in the backs of quilting magazines. (For your convenience, I provide the names and phone numbers of quilting frame manufacturers in the Appendix of this book.)

Paper and colored pencils

Graph paper, tracing paper, and colored pencils are great tools for sketching ideas and working out designs. With colored pencils and graph paper, you can experiment with different color combinations and ways of setting the blocks in your quilt, and tracing paper allows you to trace patterns you like directly from books and magazines.

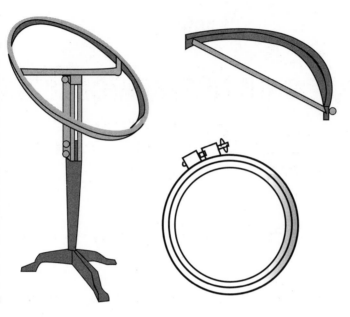

Figure 2-7:
Quilting hoops are easy to transport and are available in large sizes, some with optional floor stands that work almost like free-standing frames.

Masking tape

Masking tape is an indispensable tool because it sticks without leaving any sticky residue. I keep masking tape on hand in a variety of widths, including ¼-, ½-, 1-, and 2-inch sizes. The narrow widths are great as straight-line quilting guides, and I use the wider widths to securely hold a quilting project in place as I baste the sandwich together. (*Basting* is pinning or stitching to keep the layers in place while quilting.)

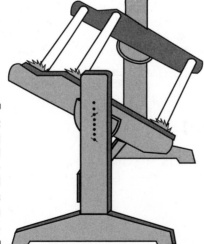

Figure 2-8:
Quilting frames hold large, bed-sized projects while you quilt.

Chapter 3

The Pièce de Résistance: Fabric

*F*abric is to the quilter what paint is to the artist — you just can't work without it. So you want your fabrics to be beautiful, durable, and work well together. Fortunately, fabrics suitable for quilting are very easy to find. Most fabric stores have entire departments devoted to quilting fabrics, where you can find fabrics in every color of the rainbow — enough to dazzle the mind!

You also may want to expand your fabric search to stores that cater specifically to the needs of quilters (these are also great places to find all the fun gadgets I describe in Chapter 6). Simply look up "fabric" or "quilting" in the phone book, and you're bound to find several promising listings for your area.

It's not uncommon to be dazzled by the swirl of colors and patterns when you visit one of these fabric fantasies or page through a glossy catalog from one of the mail-order houses described in the Appendix. However, this chapter can help you keep a level head long enough to choose the right fabrics for all the layers of your quilt. (And then, feeling proud of your carefully made decisions, you can get impulsive and buy six yards of that sale-priced zebra fun fur that you'll never use.)

Quilting in Tall Cotton

For the best quilt results, cotton is king. I recommend using only 100 percent cotton fabric for quilting because it's light but sturdy and cool to the touch.

Cotton also holds a crease well, making it ideal for those turned-under edges of hand appliqué. (I discuss appliqué in Chapter 10.) Best of all, it's not slippery or otherwise hard to manage.

I could go on and on about the wonders of cotton for quilting, but we have more important things to get to, so I'll just summarize a few more of cotton's pros:

✔ It's easy to sew through by hand or machine.

✔ If you make a slight mistake, cotton can be somewhat forgiving in that you can often stretch it back into shape.

✔ If you have to rip out stitches, the cotton fibers obligingly work themselves back into position when moistened, and the needle holes magically disappear!

✔ It washes well and comes out looking fresh as a daisy.

✔ It can take a lot of love, which you know is important if you've ever watched a child drag around his favorite blankie. Cotton's durability helps it stand the tests of time. In fact, nearly all antique quilts are made of cotton, with the exception of a few wool quilts.

You can use fibers other than cotton to add special effects to quilts, but be sure to use them only as accents. A little bit of gold tissue lamé in a holiday quilt is a nice touch and adds sparkle. But if you choose a special-occasion fabric for use in your quilt, be sure to check the care label on the end of the *bolt* (you know, the cardboard thingy the fabric's wrapped on in stores) to make sure that you don't include dry clean–only fabrics in a quilt meant to be laundered at home. Otherwise, you run the risk of having your special fabric shrink and buckle, ruining the entire project — now that would be a real bummer!

Recognizing quality cotton

Although cotton is *the* choice for quilters, not all cottons are created equal. Keep the old adage "You get what you pay for" in mind when buying cotton fabrics.

The cotton fabrics you find in most fabric store quilting departments and shops devoted to the art of quilting usually are just fine, but you may often come across tables loaded with bolts of bargain fabrics, sometimes priced as low as a few dollars per yard. Although you certainly can find bargains (and when you do, you should definitely jump on them in a fabric-buying frenzy), some so-called bargain fabrics aren't all they're cracked up to be.

Avoiding the two evil sisters, Poly and Ester

Fabric pack rats tend to purchase fabrics on impulse, and these impulse purchases often come from the bargain bin or remnant section, where fiber contents are questionable. Everybody loves a good deal, but even the best bargain is no good if you're getting shoddy material. No matter how good the price, always avoid polyester and poly-blend fabrics. They're a poor choice for quilts because they slip and slide as you stitch. Avoiding polyester sounds easy enough, but determining a fabric's fiber content can be tricky at times. Here are a few pointers for differentiating between a polyester (bad!) and cotton (good!) fabric:

✔ **Read all about it.** If the fabric is still on its original bolt (ask if you're in doubt), consult the fiber content information printed on the end of the bolt.

✔ **Get in touch with your feelings.** Polyester is slippery! Rub a double layer of fabric between your fingers. Does it slide easily, or does one layer grip the other? A fabric that's 100 percent polyester has no grip, but a poly-cotton blend sometimes has a slight grip because of the cotton in it. Polyester fabrics and poly-cotton blends also tend to

have higher *luster* (meaning the fabrics reflect light or have a bit of a sheen to them) than 100 percent cotton fabrics. Finally, fold a piece of the fabric in question and *finger-press* it by running your nail along the fold. Does it hold a crease well? Cotton tends to hold a nice sharp crease whereas polyester and poly-blends have a weak crease.

✔ **Burn it, baby!** Okay, this isn't an acceptable tip to follow while shopping, but it's a great way to determine the fiber content of hand-me-down fabric. The technique is very simple: Cut off a small section of fabric, and use tweezers to hold it over a piece of waxed paper. Ignite the fabric with a match or cigarette lighter, and see what happens. Polyester fabric burns, melts, and shrinks away from the flame. It also has a sweet smell, gives off black smoke, and leaves behind a hard bead on the waxed paper. Cotton, on the other hand, may smell like burning leaves or wood and leaves behind a fine ash when it burns.

The best advice of all: If in doubt, don't buy it. Find something else.

Some fabrics, bargain or not, feel like good choices because of the *sizing* applied during the manufacturing process. Manufacturers use sizing to stiffen the fabric before wrapping it on the bolt. Its purposes are to make the fabric easier to handle in the manufacturing process, make it look nice, and keep it from slipping off the bolt. But after you wash some of these sized fabrics, they become limp and flimsy and aren't suitable for quilting. You may even find that they resemble cheesecloth!

When in doubt about the quality of a particular fabric, always check the thread count. Unfortunately, that's easier said than done; thread count is rarely, if ever, listed on the sticker at the end of the bolt, so you have to eyeball it. Remember, the more threads per inch, the better suited the fabric is for quilting; 90 threads per inch is a good number, but higher is even better!

(Counting threads is a daunting task, and I don't really expect you to physically count them — that's where the eyeballing comes in.) If trying to estimate thread count is just too overwhelming, compare the fabric to a more expensive piece of fabric. Store personnel shouldn't mind too much if you drag around a bolt of good quality fabric to compare with their quilting fabrics — they may look at you funny, but that's about it.

Some manufacturers try to reduce the cost of their textiles by reducing the thread count and adding heavy doses of sizing. Don't buy anything that resembles glorified (meaning colorfully printed and well-stiffened) cheese-cloth. Trust me when I say that stuff so thin, with threads so far apart, that you can strain cottage cheese through it! Also, avoid anything with polyester; see the sidebar "Avoiding the two evil sisters, Poly and Ester" for details.

Staying in style and getting a good (color) value

When searching for cotton fabrics to use in a particular project, keep in mind the look you want to achieve. Is the project a casual country quilt or a more formal Victorian design? A simple pieced block can take on many different moods depending on the style of fabric you choose. Soft pastels in tiny prints can give a project a feminine feel, whereas deep browns, rusts, and blues may give the quilt a country flavor.

For a high-end, decorator look, choose *coordinates* for your quilt. Coordinates are a group of fabrics that complement each other, or coordinate. They can be as diverse as a large-scale floral with a wide matching stripe or as similar as a softly shaded, sweet little calico with matching solids and tiny little prints. Most fabric stores display coordinate fabrics together (usually on end-of-the-aisle displays), making it easier to pick and choose the fabrics that best fit together . . . and best fit your style. You can also find bundled selections of coordinating fat-quarters and fat-eighths in many stores. I must admit, these bundles are my favorite weakness — I often purchase them on a whim or to fill out my fabric stash.

To get started on matching your quilt style to your fabric selection, use Table 3-1 as a guide.

Table 3-1	Fit Your Fabric to Your Style
Quilt Style	*Fabric Suggestions*
Victorian or feminine	Realistic florals mixed with small- to medium-scale coordinates
Cottage	Bright pastels in small- to medium-scale prints mixed with solid off-white
Lodge	Medium- to large-scale deep, woodsy-colored solids and plaids, all in shades of brown, green, rust, red, ochre, tan, navy, and sometimes black
Country	Muted, dusty-toned prints in all scales, plus solids or two-color schemes such as red with white or blue with off-white
Scrappy	Go crazy, pal! Anything goes here!
Traditional Amish	Deep jewel-tone solids and black; no prints
Contemporary	Colorful novelty prints, especially geometric prints
Juvenile	Bright crayon colors in solids and prints

Pay close attention to the *color values* of the fabrics you select (see Figure 3-1). Your projects need some contrast so they don't look washed-out, so for the best results, gather an assortment of light-, medium-, and dark-valued prints. In a well-designed quilt, light-value fabrics recede, dark-value fabrics pop out prominently, and medium-value fabrics hold the whole thing together. Without this variety, your quilt doesn't look like much from a distance — just a lump of fabric with batting in between the layers!

Light, medium and dark values   Small, medium and large-scale prints

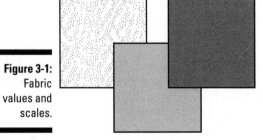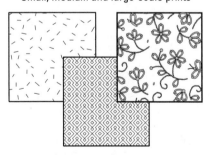

Figure 3-1:
Fabric
values and
scales.

Storing your stash

Collecting fabrics is half the fun of quilting. Sooner or later, though, you'll need to organize those haphazard piles you stuffed in the closet and under the bed so you can find just the right piece quickly and easily. Here are some helpful hints for organizing your stash:

✔ Purchase clear plastic, shoe box–size storage boxes. Label each box with its assigned color or group of sub-colors, and arrange your labeled boxes in a pretty armoire or hutch with doors to hide the contents. Then you can keep your fabric anywhere in your home.

✔ Stacking, four-drawer units on rollers are great for quilters who migrate from room to room, looking for a place to work. Use one unit for fabrics and another for threads, notions, and tools. You can find these rolling drawers in most office-supply stores and anywhere you find items for home organization. In addition to being functional, they're reasonably priced!

✔ Store your fabrics under your bed in cardboard or clear plastic under-the-bed storage bins.

✔ Buy an inexpensive shelf at a home center, set it up in an unused corner of the house or garage, and stack your fabric on it. Better yet, set up a worktable and storage shelves or containers and claim the garage for yourself!

✔ Take over the dresser in your guest room (assuming you have both). Guests seem to prefer living out of their suitcases anyway, so why not organize your stash in the drawers? Use shoeboxes or cardboard strips as dividers to help keep the stacks tidy so you can see what you have and grab what you need without a lot of sorting.

✔ Take over the guest closet. (This almost always follows taking over the guest dresser.)

✔ Take over the entire guest room. Send guests to a hotel!

Some fabric stores carry a nifty little tool called a *value finder,* which is simply a little rectangle (about 2 x 4 inches) of transparent red plastic that, when held over printed fabrics, allows you to see the color value without the clutter of the print getting in your way! It works by changing the color of the fabric to gray-scale, allowing you see with ease which fabrics are light, dark, or somewhere in between. The value finder's small enough to fit in your purse or pocket, so it's easy to keep on hand.

In addition to value, *scale,* which is the size of a fabric's print, is also very important when choosing fabrics for a quilt. Figure 3-1 shows a few examples of the different types of print scales. Just as with values, small-scale prints recede in a design, and large-scale prints can be real eye-poppers!

Try to avoid using more than one or two large-scale prints in your quilt. They tend to look too "busy" and are hard on your eyes when cutting, stitching, and quilting, not to mention when you're trying to enjoy your final product.

Measuring up

No matter the fiber content or design, quilting fabrics are available by the yard in 44- and 45-inch widths. At quilting supply stores and more and more fabric stores, you can also find them precut and sold in tidy little bundles called *fat quarters* and *fat eighths.*

A fat quarter isn't just a precut quarter of a yard (which, for a 44-inch wide fabric, is 9 x 44 inches). Instead, the store cuts a half-yard length of fabric from the bolt and then cuts the resulting 18- x 44-inch piece in half down the center crease, giving you an 18- x 22-inch piece of fabric. This measurement makes cutting larger quilt pieces from the fabric much easier, and you aren't limited to templates or patches that are only 9 inches or smaller.

If you only need a small amount of a particular color for your project, go with fat quarters. They save you time because you don't have to wait for store personnel to cut the fabric from the bolt for you, and you get more useable fabric for your money because of the way the pieces are cut. Fat quarters are also a great way to build your fabric stash because they're often cut from fabrics that are being discontinued and are therefore greatly discounted, which means you can stock up for less cash.

Fat eighths are simply half of a fat quarter and usually measure 18 x 11 inches. If you need a very small amount of fabric and don't think you'll need to have extra fabric on hand just in case, fat eighths are a fine choice.

When purchasing *yard goods* (another name for fabric sold on the bolt), always ask that your fabrics be cut on the grain — especially if you're buying plaids. This type of cut eliminates wasted fabric when you're cutting pieces that require *cutting on the true grain.* (For more information on fabric grain, see Chapter 5.) Also, insist that the clerk cut the fabric rather than rip it. Ripping tends to pull the entire piece of yardage off skew and out of whack, which can make it harder to line up the edges, especially when rotary-cutting.

Prewashing for project protection

Prewashing is an important step in quilting preparation. Although prewashing isn't rocket science, the task may require some willpower! There have been many times when I've brought a fabulous piece of yardage home, wanting to dive right in and start cutting it into pieces. But after years of quilting experience, I learned to control the urge to start cutting and take care of the prewashing first, knowing it's better for my finished project.

Prewashing 101

To prewash fabric, simply machine-wash it on a regular, everyday washing setting with mild detergent. Tumble dry until the fabric is only slightly damp, and then press it using a dry iron (no steam) on the "cotton" setting. Fold the fabric neatly until you're ready to use it.

I recommend washing your fabrics as soon as you bring them home so that when you pull them out to work on a project two days, two months, or even two years later, you don't have to stare at the hunk of fabric, wondering if it's been washed yet. Washing fabric as soon as you get it home eliminates any doubt!

Quilters often inherit fabrics from other *fabri-holics* or win them at quilting raffles; whether these fabrics have been prewashed is a mystery. When in doubt, wash it. Large cuts can go directly into the washing machine, but smaller pieces tend to be "eaten" by the machine. So to wash small cuts of fabric, fill a sink or basin with room-temperature water and a bit of mild soap. Slip the fabric into the water, swish it around for a few seconds, and then rinse it well. Lay the fabric flat on a terry towel and let it air dry; then press it with a dry iron when it's just slightly damp.

Benefits of prewashing

Prewashing all the fabric you plan to use in a project has a number of important benefits. First of all, it gets the fabric's natural shrinkage out of the way so it doesn't seriously warp your design later on. Keep in mind that a 12-inch square of 100 percent cotton fabric can shrink, sometimes as much as ¼-inch both horizontally and vertically. Different fabrics may shrink at different rates: One fabric may not shrink at all, but another may shrink considerably. To be safe, you should always prewash everything, no matter how much or how little you expect it to shrink. Shrinkage after you launder your finished project can have disastrous effects. Imagine that after all your effort in making a quilt, you wash it and find that the pretty blue print in the center of the block has shrunk, puckering each and every block in such a way that the pattern's unrecognizable — it can happen!

Prewashing removes the sizing from fabric, which makes it easier to handle or machine quilt because the sizing doesn't get gummy or sticky from the moisture in your hands (remember playing with starch in grade school?).

Prewashing also removes excess dye that can bleed onto other fabrics and spoil the color — not a good thing, unless, of course, you want that pretty red print to bleed and turn the entire quilt pink. Hey, some folks do strange things. If you notice that a particular fabric *crocks* (bleeds) when washed, continue washing and rinsing the fabric until it no longer loses dye. If the fabric continues to crock, discard it and replace it with something more colorfast. Imagine putting hours of work into a red and white quilt only to discover that the whole thing turns pink after washing because the red fabric bled into the white!

Hitting a Homer with Your Batting

The *batting,* or filler, for your quilt is just as important to the look of the finished quilt as the fabric. You need to decide if you want a flatter, old-fashioned-looking quilt, a soft and comfy but low profile quilt, or a thick, lofty, jump-right-in-and-snuggle type of quilt. Each look requires a different type of batt (that's quilter lingo for batting).

Battings are available in several different fibers, the most common being polyester, cotton/polyester blend, cotton, and wool (yes, poly and ester may be banned from your fabric choices, but they're safe for batting). With so many choices, answering a few simple questions about your project can narrow the field and help you pick the right batting for your needs:

- ✔ Are you planning to hand quilt, machine quilt, or tie the quilt?
- ✔ How much effort do you want to put into the quilting stage?
- ✔ Do you plan to heavily quilt the project or just stitch enough to hold the quilt layers together?
- ✔ How do you intend to use the quilt when it's finished?
- ✔ Will the quilt be laundered often?
- ✔ What size is the quilt?
- ✔ Is the predominant color of the quilt dark or light?

When choosing your batting, always read the manufacturer's recommendations printed on the wrapper or the batting bolt label. This information not only lists suggestions for using the product, but it also provides laundering instructions and any special handling tips, such as prewashing the batting before working with it.

The following sections help you sort through all the batting options and use your answers to the questions above to find the best batting for your quilted pieces.

Prepackaged or by the yard?

Batting comes prepackaged and by-the-yard. Price-wise, there's not much difference between the two, so your choice depends on your needs.

Prepackaged batting is convenient because it's already cut to standard bed sizes (see Table 3-2 for measurements), shrink-wrapped, and easy to take home. But if your project is smaller than a bed size, buying prepackaged batting means you bring home more batting than you actually need. Too much batting isn't bad, of course — you just have to stash it away somewhere until you're ready to use it for the next small project.

Shrink-wrapping may make prepackaged batting easy to get home, but the batting gets bulky and more difficult to store after you remove it from the package. To tame this wild beast of fluff, carefully remove the batting from the package and unroll only the amount necessary for your project. Cut off what you need, and then quickly reroll the batting and put it back in its bag before it has a chance to expand.

Table 3-2	Standard Sizes for Prepackaged Quilt Batting
Quilt Size	*Batting Dimensions*
Craft/Crib size	45″ x 60″
Twin size	72″ x 90″
Full/Double size	81″ x 96″
Queen size	90″ x 108″
King size	120″ x 120″

Batting by the yard is the same stuff as prepackaged batting, but you have the option of purchasing only as much as you need. It's available in both polyester and cotton and in varying widths and lofts. The downside to buying lofty batting by the yard, however, is that it hasn't been shrink-wrapped, so it may be bulky to bring home and store.

With any batting choice, after you cut the size you need, unfold the batting a few days before using it to let it breathe! Doing so allows the batting to expand and relax after spending months or even years in its tightly packaged form.

Choosing your batting's fiber content

Compared to just 20 years ago, quilters have a wide variety of batting options at their fingertips. Batting comes in different materials, sizes, weights — even colors! This section helps you figure out what batting is best for your quilting project.

100 percent cotton

Quilting through 100 percent cotton is like quilting through warm butter — smooth and easy. Because some cotton batting can shrink nearly 5 percent when washed, the "crinkled" effect achieved after this shrinkage can give your quilt a wonderful antique look. If you don't want a shrunken batt, read the label carefully to see if the manufacturer recommends preshrinking. You can purchase cotton batting that won't shrink in varying weights and lofts.

The major downside to many inexpensive cotton battings is that, if you don't use closely spaced stitching intervals when quilting, the batting bunches to all the corners, nooks, and crannies during use and laundering. Trust me on this one — you'll have lots of batting in your corners but nothing where you need it most! A minor downside is that some cotton battings require pre-washing (a step I prefer to eliminate).

Some experienced quilters — the ones who don't mind spending an entire year working on one quilt — often prefer cotton batting over any other. Perhaps it's because they like the old-fashioned look or want to stay true to traditions (polyester batting is a new-fangled invention).

Cotton/polyester blend

Many blended battings give your quilt a very traditional look and feel without the hassle of cotton. Like cotton batting, cotton/polyester blends can shrink, but not as much as 100 percent cotton — you may not even notice the shrinkage. In fact, some cotton/poly blends don't shrink at all. A nice thing about cotton/polyester batting is that you can quilt it at slightly larger stitching intervals than 100 percent cotton batting because the polyester content helps keep the fibers from migrating during use or laundering.

If you decide to use cotton/polyester blend batting, refer to the package for additional information on usage.

Polyester

Polyester battings launder well with no shrinkage and can be quilted at large stitching intervals, which means you finish the quilt quicker, freeing up more time for additional quilting projects! For this reason, polyester batting is the most popular choice among quilters.

Polyester is the only fiber available for *high-loft battings* — what you'd choose for a really thick (think sleeping-bag-thick) quilt. Because hand or machine quilting a high-loft batting is difficult at best, use high-loft battings for tied quilts (the ones held together with fancy knots of yarn or ribbon).

Polyester battings also now come in a fusible variety: Both sides of the batting are coated with the same type of heat-released glue used in the fusible webbing you use for machine appliqué (see Chapter 10). Fusible batting is great for small projects because fusing the quilt top and bottom to the batting using a hot iron (follow the manufacturer's directions) eliminates the need to baste before quilting. I don't recommend it for larger projects, though, because getting everything fully fused can be tough unless you're able to lay the project flat on a very large ironing board. Also, when working on larger projects, say larger than 30 x 30 inches, it's much too easy to cause distortion when moving the item around on your ironing board.

Colored batting?

Batting is available in a wide range of colors — as long as it's white or black you want (my apologies to Mr. Ford and his Model-T). Actually, the colors are white or off-white depending on fiber content and deep gray. As you may have already figured out, the light-colored batts go in light-colored quilts, and the dark gray batts are perfect for dark-colored quilts. Why does it matter, you ask? Because if a fiber or two from the batting migrates to the surface of the quilt (which inevitably happens), you don't notice it very much if the batting works with the colors in the quilt. Pretty simple stuff, really.

You're probably wondering why polyester is fine for batting but not for fabric. First of all, cotton fabric is traditionally used in quilt tops and backing because it feels nice against the skin — unlike polyester. Because polyester batting is completely enclosed by cotton fabrics, you don't feel the polyester at all, so the touchability factor isn't an issue. Also, polyester batting holds its shape well, especially after repeated washings.

Silk

This batting is best suited for quilted garments. Textile artists who specialize in unique, one-of-a-kind garments like to work with silk batting because it drapes well and is lightweight.

I don't recommend silk batting for bed quilts or wall hangings. Why not? First, silk batting is very expensive. Second, it's often difficult to find. Third, it usually isn't made in sizes large enough to accommodate a bed-size project, and even if it were, the cost would be quite prohibitive!

Wool

The great thing about wool batting is that it's very heavy, so it's great if you're making a quilt that's meant to insulate on cold winter nights.

Wool batting is very easy to needle through (that is, your needle meets little resistance as you stitch), but its fibers tend to migrate, so it requires closely spaced quilting (short stitching intervals), just as cotton does. Wool batting also tends to *beard,* or lose fibers, through the quilt top more than some other battings. To help prevent this problem, many experienced quilters who prefer this type of batting encase their wool batts in extra layers of lightweight fabric.

Wool batting washed in warm water and tumbled dry can shrink substantially, so hand washing and drying flat or professional dry cleaning are usually the recommended forms of laundering. Because of these care restrictions, wool batting probably isn't the best choice for a young child's bed quilt, a set of place mats, or other projects that will be subject to frequent laundering.

Batting 1000

Use Table 3-3 to help you determine which brand of batting is best for your needs, depending on the look that you're trying to achieve. If you can't find the exact brand I list here in your local fabric or quilting supply store, ask store personnel to recommend an available batt that has similar qualities.

Table 3-3		Batting Choices	
Brand Name (Manufacturer)	**Fiber Content**	**Thickness**	**Notes**
Old-Fashioned Antique Look (Low Loft)			
Soft Touch (Fairfield Processing)	100% cotton, bleached	⅛"	45" x 60" and 90" x 108" only; very low loft, excellent drape. Quilt up to 2" to 4" intervals.
Poly-fil Cotton Classic (Fairfield Processing)	80% cotton, 20% polyester	⅛" and ³⁄₁₆"	Flat, antique look; glazed to hold fibers together. Quilt up to 3" to 5" intervals.
Mountain Mist Bleached Cotton (Stearns)	100% cotton	²⁄₁₆"	Low-loft, easy to needle. Quilt at ¼" to ½" intervals.
Mountain Mist Blue Ribbon (Stearns)	100% cotton	³⁄₁₆"	Antique appearance. Quilt up to 2" intervals.
Quilters' Dream (Quilter's Dream)	100% cotton	¼", ½", ¾", 1"	Comes in natural or white colors. Quilt up to 8" intervals.
Warm & Natural (The Warm Company)	100% cotton	¼"	Manufacturer recommends prewashing to avoid shrinkage (unless you're looking for an antique look). Quilt up to 10" intervals.
Mountain Mist Quilt-light (Stearns)	100% polyester	⅛" to ³⁄₁₆"	Glazene finish allows for fine stitches; washes well.
HTC Fleece (Handler Textile Corp.)	100% polyester	¹⁄₁₆"	45" wide by the yard; best for small projects.

(continued)

Table 3-3 (continued)

Brand Name (Manufacturer)	Fiber Content	Thickness	Notes
Traditional Look			
Poly-fil Low-Loft (Fairfield Processing)	100% polyester	¼" to ⅜"	Lightweight, easy to handle, washes well. Quilt up to 2" to 4" intervals. (A favorite of mine.)
Poly-fil Ultra-Loft (Fairfield Processing)	100% polyester	3⁄16" to ¼"	Dense structure for warmth; recommended for machine quilting only; washes very well. Quilt up to 3" to 5" intervals.
Poly-fil Traditional (Fairfield Processing)	100% polyester	⅛" to 3⁄16"	Easy to needle, washes well. Quilt up to 3" to 5" intervals.
Mountain Mist Polyester (Stearns)	100% polyester	¼" to ⅜"	Easy to handle, washes well, nice drape. Great for quilts, small projects, and garments.
Quilters' Dream Polyester (Stearns)	100% polyester	¼", ½", ¾"	Comes in white or midnight colors, nice drape. Machine quilts well.
Quilters' Dream Blend for Machines (Quilter's Dream)	70% cotton, 30% polyester.	¼"	Recommended for machine quilting. Great for bed quilts.
Morning Glory, Glory Bee I (Carpenter Co.)	100% polyester	¼"	Lightweight, requires careful washing. Quilt up to 2" intervals.
Super Fluff! Traditional Weight (Buffalo Batt & Felt Corp)	100% polyester	¼" to ⅜"	Resin-bonded, requires careful washing, best used for machine quilting. Quilt up to 2" intervals.
High-loft and Tied Quilts			
Poly-fil Extra-loft (Fairfield Processing)	100% polyester	⅜" to ½"	Full and airy; wash gently and dry flat when possible.

Brand Name (Manufacturer)	Fiber Content	Thickness	Notes
Poly-fil Hi-Loft (Fairfield Processing)	100% polyester	⅝" to ¾"	Very lofty, great for crafts; wash gently and dry flat when possible.
Mountain Mist Fatt Batt (Stearns)	100% polyester	⅜"	Glazene finish prevents fiber migration; excellent choice for tied quilts. For machine or hand quilting, up to 4" intervals.
Morning Glory, Glory Bee II (Stearns)	100% polyester	½"	Nice loft; wash gently and dry flat when possible.
Super Fluff (Europa)	100% polyester	⅜" to ½"	Very dense; holds up well; machine washes and dries well.

Backing Up Your Quilt with the Proper Fabric

At one time, backing a bed-size quilt required piecing fabrics together to make a backing piece large enough to accommodate the massive width and length. Today, manufacturers make it easy to back these monstrosities: Backing fabrics are available by the yard in 90- and 120-inch widths in a variety of colors and prints as well as in traditional solid white and natural. In my opinion, these large backing fabrics are the best choice for large-size quilts because they save so much time.

Cotton bed sheets also make excellent backings and are available in an array of prints, colors, and sizes. Golly, you can even give your bed a completely coordinated look by adding matching pillowcases and a bedskirt! If you use a flat bed sheet, remember to undo the decorative hem at the top of the sheet so you don't get any strange seam lines or fabric layers.

Before you venture out to purchase backing fabric, determine the width and length of the piece you needed. It never hurts to purchase a little extra fabric, especially considering the fact that it's very difficult to cut these large-width fabrics perfectly straight at the store, so you may end up with a backing that isn't perfectly square. So allow an extra few inches along each side as a fudge factor. For example, if the finished size of your quilt is 75 x 90 inches (to fit a full-size bed), you need a backing piece that's *at least* 80 x 95 inches. In this case, you can purchase either 3 yards of 90-inch–wide fabric (which gives you a surface area of 90 x 108 inches) or a 2⅓ yards of 120-inch–wide fabric (which gives you a surface area of 120 x 84 inches).

If you really like one of the fabrics in your quilt top and want to use it as the backing, piecing isn't as terrible as it sounds. Figuring out how much 44- or 45-inch–wide fabric you need just requires a bit of planning on your part. For example, if the finished size of your quilt is 75 x 90 inches (to fit a full-size bed), you need to purchase two cuts of fabric that are each 2¾ yard.

Why purchase two lengths of fabric instead of one 5½-yard length? The answer is simple: to eliminate your margin of error. How upset would you be to get your fabric home, prewash it, press it, cut it, and then discover that you mismeasured and you're 8 inches short on one length? If you purchase your fabric in two lengths, the measuring is done for you. Plus, the folks doing the cutting at the store always allow an extra ½ inch or so when cutting, which helps you out in the long run.

To piece 44- or 45-inch wide backing fabric for your 75- x 90-inch finished quilt, you have a number of options:

- ✔ Cut one of the lengths of fabric directly down the center, making two 22-inch–wide strips. Stitch one strip to each long side of the uncut length of fabric (see Figure 3-2a), and press the seams open. This design puts the seam lines toward the outsides of the quilt, which can make it easier to center your quilt top and batting because no one will notice if you end up slightly off-center!

- ✔ Stitch the two lengths of fabric together along one long edge (see Figure 3-2b), and press the seam allowance open. With the seam running vertically, layer this backing panel with the batting and quilt top. This design puts a seam down the center of the quilt and means that you need to be fairly accurate when centering your batting and quilt top on the backing.

- ✔ Stitch the two lengths of fabric together along one long edge, and press the seam allowance open. Rotate the pieced result so that the seam runs horizontally across your quilt (see Figure 3-2c), and layer this backing panel with the batting and quilt top.

- ✔ Cut three lengths of fabric that are 40 inches wide, and stitch them together horizontally (see Figure 3-2d). When using this method to create your backing, make sure that you carefully center the fabric under your quilt and batting so that the seams are as unnoticeable as possible.

The piecing method you choose depends on the actual size of backing needed. You can use any method, but keep in mind that the more seams you have, the more difficult it is to quilt through the layers due to the extra thickness in the backing's seam areas.

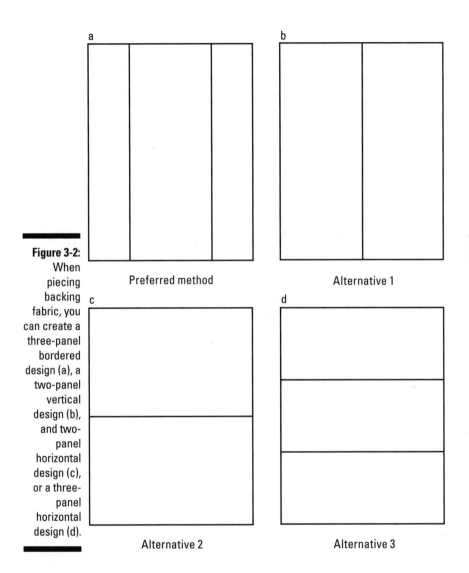

Figure 3-2: When piecing backing fabric, you can create a three-panel bordered design (a), a two-panel vertical design (b), and two-panel horizontal design (c), or a three-panel horizontal design (d).

Before you go piecing yardage together for your backing piece, cut off the selvages! The selvage edge is the manufactured edge along the length of the fabric. Never use a selvage edge, even if you think it will be absorbed into a seam allowance; it's tightly woven and doesn't shrink, which could mean big trouble for your final fabric piece.

Part II
Planning Your Masterpiece

In this part . . .

Most quilters would agree with me on this: Quilt design is the stage of the quilting process when you really get to stretch your creative muscle. It's definitely my favorite part of the process! In this part, I discuss planning and laying out your quilt, designing your own blocks, and making and using one of quilt-dom's essential tools — the template. You also get the lowdown on creating settings and arranging quilt blocks into true works of art. And don't forget about designing quilts using your computer — after all, this is the modern age, right?

Chapter 4

A Patch in the Fabric of Time: Designing Quilt Blocks

In This Chapter

▶ Appreciating tried-and-true traditional block designs

▶ Seeing the possibilities of four-patch and nine-patch block systems

▶ Experimenting with your own block designs

▶ Getting to know foundation piecing

*P*atchwork quilting is nothing more than taking individual pieces of fabric, called *patches*, that have been cut out in basic, geometric shapes and stitching them together to form what appear to be more complex patterns. The technique is a bit like putting a simple children's puzzle together, with each piece fitting into a designated spot. In the case of patchwork, the puzzle pieces are made of fabric. Sounds simple enough, right?

Only a few shapes are necessary for basic traditional patchwork designs: squares, triangles, rectangles, hexagons, and long strips. (Of course, curved shapes such as the fan or Double Wedding Ring are also possible, but they require a bit of extra handling.) The breadth of creativity available with patchwork ranges from elegant simplicity to incredibly intricate, Picasso–like fabric art. This creative aspect, combined with the practicality and eco-friendliness of recycling scraps of fabric into useful treasures, has made patchwork the most popular form of quilting.

In this chapter, I show you how blocks are built, share tips for designing your own unique quilt blocks, and discuss the latest craze in accurate quilt block-making — foundation piecing.

Would a Quilt Block By Any Other Name Feel as Cozy?

As you read through this or any other quilting book, you'll probably notice that all quilt blocks have names. Some names describe the block's motif — Maple Leaf, Turkey Tracks, Flower Basket, Flying Geese, and Log Cabin (see Figure 4-1) — but others seem to have no clear root in the design — Robbing Peter to Pay Paul, Johnny-Round-the-Corner, Corn and Beans, and Broken Dishes.

How did the creators of these blocks come up with such strange names? The answer lies both in the popular culture of the day and what was going on in the quilters' lives at the time.

Figure 4-1:
Two historical patchwork designs are Flying Geese and Log Cabin.

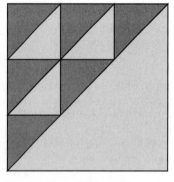

Flying Geese

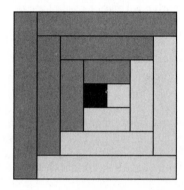

Log Cabin

Some blocks were named to honor prominent individuals or events — consider Lincoln's Platform and Road to California, which commemorates the great gold rush of the late 1800s. Others express the quilter's religious devotion, as in Jacob's Ladder, Dove in the Window, Tree of Life, and Cross and Crown.

A number of block names, such as Robbing Peter to Pay Paul (see Figure 4-2) and Drunkard's Path, may express the frustrations of the eras in which they were created. Kansas Troubles expresses the emotions experienced by farmers during the dust bowl years.

Still others blocks were named purely for fun. Consider Puss in the Corner, Wild Goose Chase, and Jack in the Box. Perhaps Old Maid's Ramble, which you can see in Figure 4-2, was named simply because Auntie couldn't stop gossiping during a quilting bee.

Figure 4-2: Unusual block names include Robbing Peter to Pay Paul and Old Maid's Ramble.

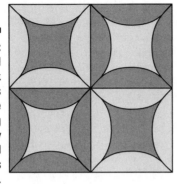

Robbing Peter to Pay Paul

Old Maid's Ramble

From one anonymous quilter to another

The following pseudo-letter is a perfect example of how seamlessly quilt names reflect the real life they're so much a part of. I've underlined the quilt block names so you don't miss them — some aren't hard to spot, but others may surprise you!

Dear Sunbonnet Sue,

It's been a rough week down on the farm. I found a hole in the barn door — the one on the same side of the barn as the weathervane. Anyway, the hens and chicks escaped through that darn hole and ate up all the corn and beans I had planted in grandmother's flower garden. After I saw what they did to my rose of Sharon, I rounded the critters up and locked them in the old log cabin, where I found a cowering puss in the corner. Since Puss looked guilty too, I locked him in there with the others.

I was going to head up the road to Kansas that afternoon but postponed my trip. Handy Andy came over for a visit instead. You know, he was actually my grandmother's choice for a husband for me because he looked better in a *bow tie* than *Overall Bill*. With all the *Kansas troubles* right now, Andy still can't afford a *wedding ring*, so he gave me a *cut glass dish* and a *Dresden plate* instead. How's that for a strange engagement gift! Too bad I dropped them — I ended up with just a bunch of *broken dishes*! And I almost broke Grandma's *cake stand* with my elbow as I swept up the *bits and pieces*!

Don't give me any lip about this; I remember when you started dating that Clay fellow. Clay's choice of an engagement gift was a cherry basket. Well, at least it wasn't breakable. You know, I never really did like him, 'cause he was always playin' with his whirlygigs or fiddlin' with the churn dash.

Well, I guess I have to go now — you know how us old maids ramble!

Love,

Edith

I could go on and on about all the strange, silly, and meaningful patchwork block names out there (perhaps someone should name a block Cheryl's Rambling Again . . .). However, my point is this: In many ways, block design names are similar to the names of constellations — they don't always look exactly like the names they're given. Sometimes you have to use your imagination to see the resemblance, if there is one. Regardless, these traditional quilt blocks continue to be the foundations quilters use today for their most beautiful and creative efforts.

Choosing Your Quilt Block System: Four-patch or Nine-patch

You may hear seasoned quilters talking about their latest projects, often referring to the blocks as *four-patch, nine-patch,* or some other number of patch. Although it sounds like Latin or Greek to the untrained ear, the grid-based system by which quilt blocks are designed is very easy to decipher — and it actually makes sense.

The system is based on a simple grid filled with the various geometric shapes used in quilting. The two most common patch systems used in block design are the four-patch and the nine-patch, but others are often used for more complex designs. In this section, I stick to the two most basic treatments.

Basic four-patch design

When a quilter refers to a *four-patch block,* she (or he — many men have taken up quilting as well) is talking about a block that's based on a grid of four squares, as shown in Figure 4-3.

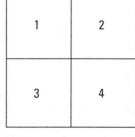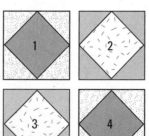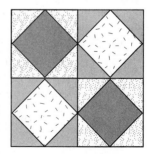

Figure 4-3: A four-patch grid and example block.

Describing a block as a four-patch doesn't necessarily mean it's made of only four pieces of fabric. Rather, four-patch describes the way the block is laid out, which is basically in four units. Each unit may be made of one or more pieces stitched together.

A four-patch block can be relatively simple in nature, like the block shown in Figure 4-3. This block is composed of four blocks, each consisting of five pieces. When you stitch together the four units, you have a completed four-patch block.

Basic nine-patch design

A *nine-patch block* is similar to a four-patch block, but its design is based on a grid of nine squares rather than four. Each of the nine squares can be broken down into additional units, but the block remains a nine-patch block. Figure 4-4 shows the basic nine-patch grid as well as a Pinwheel block created in a nine-patch design.

Figure 4-4:
A nine-patch grid and example block.

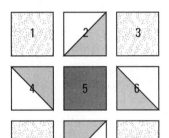
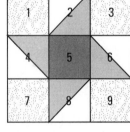

 For any patch design, the grid doesn't have to consist of equal-sized squares. For example, the Churn Dash (also known as the Hole in the Barn Door) block shown in Figure 4-5 is based on a nine-patch grid, but the center area is stretched to give it a different look. Although the nine units vary in size, the block stays true to its nine-patch origins.

Figure 4-5:
The nine-patch grid and Churn Dash block.

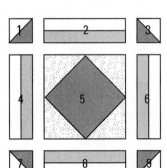
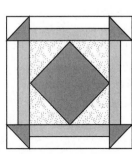

Mapping Out Your Designs

As I mention at the beginning of this chapter, only a few shapes are necessary for basic traditional patchwork designs. Now you have the chance to play with those basic shapes — squares, triangles, rectangles, diamonds, and long strips — and create a new block of your own.

Starting out small

The majority of my quilt block designs have started off as random doodles on graph paper that I fill in with colored pencils. Letting my design mind wander is one of my favorite ways to design quilts because it's easy and can be done anywhere — just keep a graph paper pad close at hand and you'll see what I mean.

To sketch your own patchwork designs:

1. **On a sheet of graph paper, mark the four-patch and nine-patch grids that appear in Figures 4-3 and 4-4.**

   I recommend paper with four, eight, or ten squares per inch, but any size graph works just as well; the only real difference is that more squares per inch mean that your doodles are smaller.

2. **Fill the grids with various shapes and discover how many quilt block designs and possibilities are at your fingertips!**

Play with as many variations of shapes as you please, and reverse the direction of the pieces for even more options. To draw the eye to certain designs within your larger layout, color in the pieces with colored pencils or felt-tip markers, or sketch in some textures to differentiate between the various fabrics you'd like to use. When you create a design you're especially fond of, name it — after all, it's your own creation.

Turning doodles into full-sized block patterns

After you design your quilt block in miniature on graph paper — assuming you don't go blind squinting at all those tiny squares and give up on quilting forever — you're ready to create a full-sized pattern of your block design to use when making templates. (See Chapter 5 for tips on creating templates and cutting out patches.)

The block's size depends on the number of blocks you need for your project, given the size of your finished project (see Chapter 6 for help choosing a layout and determining how large the finished project should be). Figuring out the size of your full-sized block is just a matter of some very simple math. For example:

- ✔ **If you're making a single-block throw pillow,** a 14- to 16-inch block is your best bet. A 12-inch block would likely require the addition of some borders (unless you want a very small pillow), and an 18-inch block might be great on the floor but could overwhelm your sofa or chair.

- ✔ **If you're planning a wall hanging or bed quilt,** use a 10-, 12-, or 14-inch block. Anything larger would just look too strange on something as large as a bed (although it has been done!). It's really all a matter of personal preference.

  - If you're using the four-patch system and your project calls for a 4-inch block, each of the patches in the block should be 2 inches square. Similarly, a 6-inch block requires patches that are each 3 inches square, and a 12-inch block uses 6-inch patches. See the pattern here? With a four-patch system, just divide your final block size in half to determine your individual patch size.

  - If you're using the nine-patch system and your project requires a 6-inch block, each of your patches should measure 2 inches square. Similarly, a 9-inch block requires patches that are 3 inches square, and a 12-inch block requires 4-inch patches. With a nine-patch system, just divide your final block size by three to determine your individual patch size.

Chapter 5

Creating and Using Templates

• •

• •

*T*emplates are the backbone of a pieced block: They're the cutting patterns that are absolutely necessary in the quilt-making process. Creating accurate templates is one of the most important steps in making a quilt. Good templates mean the difference between a well-squared block that goes together easily and a catawampus, crooked-all-to-heck one that fights you every step of the way.

Although ready-made templates are available for a variety of popular quilt block designs, making your own templates is usually cheaper, and it can even be fun. Plus, if you come up with a spectacular, intricate design that no one else has ever thought of (you clever devil!), creating your own templates is a must — otherwise your design will never be more than a pretty little sketch on paper. And if that's all you wanted, you would have bought a coloring book instead of this book, right?

In this chapter, I give you tips for everything from choosing template materials to making the special templates needed if you plan to piece your quilt by hand. Scared that you'll goof up this template stuff? If you ever traced around your hand to make a turkey in grade school, relax, little pilgrim — you're an old pro at using templates.

Paper or Plastic?

Shopping for quilting supplies can be just as overwhelming as shopping for groceries. You encounter bolt after bolt of fabric (Should you choose the vanilla, the chocolate, or the strawberry, or should you settle for the Neapolitan, which will make everyone happy?), spool after spool of thread (Who knew there were 73 different brands of spaghetti?), and package after package of fluffy batting (Who has time to do a squeeze test on all those toilet paper brands?).

At the grocery store, the easiest choice you make is probably deciding what kind of bags you want your groceries packed in. Luckily, when it comes to choosing template material for quilts, you have that same simple choice: paper or plastic.

Scrounging up some paper

Creating paper templates from a pattern you design (or from patterns you find in this book or purchase at quilting stores) is simple and cheap. You simply trace the individual pattern pieces onto tracing paper; add seam allowances if the pattern doesn't already include them (the ones in this book do); use whatever kind of adhesive you have handy to attach the traced pattern to cardboard, old file folders, heavy card-stock paper, or even empty cereal boxes; and then cut out the templates. (The section "Making Templates" later in this chapter takes you through this process one step at a time.)

Springing for plastic sheeting

So you can't make paper templates because the kids taped together all the cardboard in the house to make a 10-foot-tall robot named Zorbot. And you don't want to eat four boxes of Serious Sugar Surge cereal just so you can start your quilting project (see the preceding section). Don't despair! Many quilting supply stores carry transparent, flexible plastic sheeting that's especially designed for creating quilting templates.

With this material, you trace individual pattern pieces directly onto the plastic, add seam allowances if the pattern doesn't already include them, and cut out the templates (see the section "Making Templates" later in this chapter for detailed instructions). Plastic sheeting saves you a few steps because there's no gluing involved. Just keep in mind that this material can be a bit expensive, and you won't find a secret decoder ring at the bottom of the package either. Bummer.

If you're making a large quilt and plan to trace around your templates over and over again as you create your blocks, I suggest that you use the plastic template material or make more than one set of cardboard templates. With repeated tracings, cardboard template edges eventually wear down, making the templates inaccurate, so it's good to have fresh ones ready to swap out with the old. If you've decided on cardboard and want to protect your templates and preserve them for posterity, purchase some self-sticking laminating sheets and apply them to both sides of the templates before cutting them out.

Patterns versus templates

If you're wondering what the difference is between a pattern and a template, here's a little secret: There's not a heck of a lot of difference except that a template is cut from stiff material and a pattern is printed on paper. Both are usable, but a template can make your work easier by giving you a somewhat consistent surface to trace around, rather than pinning flimsy paper to your fabrics. If you plan on making multiple blocks from your patterns or templates, keep in mind that flimsy paper will disintegrate faster than warm cookies in a room full of children.

Going with the Grain

All woven fabrics have two grains:

- A *straight grain* that runs parallel to the *selvage edge* of the fabric (the uncut edge that appears tightly woven and often contains the name of the fabric manufacturer). The straight grain doesn't stretch at all.

- A *cross grain* that, as the term implies, runs across the straight grain of the fabric at a 90-degree angle. The cross grain has some stretch to it.

To make your life easier, I refer to both the straight grain and cross grains of the fabric as *on-grain.* And when I use the term *bias,* I simply mean on the diagonal of the two grains.

Always cut off the selvage edge before cutting out your pieces of fabric. Because of the tight weave, this area is difficult to stitch through by hand or machine (and it doesn't shrink along with the rest of the fabric).

Before you make any templates or cut into any of your fabrics, you need to mark *grain line arrows* on your pattern to help you place your template along the proper grain line of the fabric you're cutting (see Figure 5-1). These grain lines help you build your blocks in such a way that they don't stretch out of shape while they're being stitched.

Place any templates for the outside edge of a particular block pattern on-grain rather than on the bias. (In the case of triangles, proper placement is essential.) Because bias edges stretch, placing them along a block edge can cause distortion in the finished block. You should also try to avoid having two bias edges together whenever possible so that you don't have two edges of stretch stretching together!

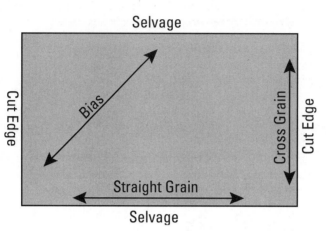

Keep in mind that there are times when, no matter what you do, you end up with two bias edges together or a piece of bias along an outside edge. There's no need to panic; just be sure you don't accidentally stretch the fabric when cutting or sewing. To be safe, you also may want to stitch those pieces first so they have the support of each other and the line of thread to help stabilize the bias edge.

Figure 5-2a shows how *not* to mark the grain lines on your patterns and templates. Notice that the shaded piece was cut with a bias edge on the outside of the quilt block. This block is a good candidate for some major distortion, whereas the pieces in the block shown in Figure 5-2b are perfectly aligned.

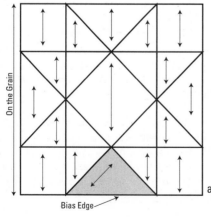
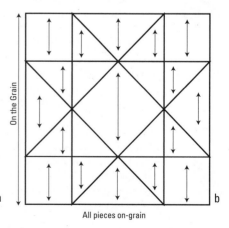

Always use care when handling bias fabric pieces. The more they're handled, the more they stretch and distort!

Making Templates

Making templates is easy, but they need to be precise. The instructions in this section will go a long way in ensuring accuracy in your patterns.

I prefer to make my templates from plastic sheeting rather than cardboard because the plastic is sturdier and because cardboard tends to wear down around the edges after you trace multiple pattern pieces.

Making templates from patterns you've created

Follow these steps for making templates from patterns that you create (refer to Chapter 4 for information about designing your own quilt block patterns):

1. **Make several copies of your pattern before you cut or otherwise permanently alter the pattern.**

   Copies ensure that you always have a spare on hand in case your kids decide to make paper airplanes out of your tax forms and quilt block patterns. Hey, it could happen.

   If you're using a photocopier to copy the patterns, be sure to measure the copies for accuracy. Some machines tend to stretch images in one direction, throwing off the accuracy of your templates.

2. **Letter or number each pattern piece, as shown in Figure 5-3, so you know where it belongs in the quilt block after you cut apart the pattern.**

   I like to mark the starting point of the block, in this case the center squares turned on point, as *A* or *1*. Then I work outwards from the center, lettering or numbering the pieces accordingly.

3. **Carefully cut out the pattern pieces.**

   Do *not* use your fabric-cutting scissors to cut templates; use another pair you have around. Fabric scissors were never meant to slice, dice, cut through tin cans, and still slice a tomato paper-thin (I've been watching too much television). You're guaranteed to dull them if you try to cut through heavy paper or plastic templates.

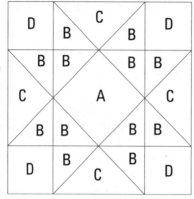

Figure 5-3:
Mark
identical
pattern
pieces
before
cutting.

Cut only around the outside (cutting) edge of the pattern. Discard any pieces that are duplicated in the quilt block pattern because you only need to make one template for each basic piece. For the block template shown in Figure 5-3, for example, you need one each of pattern pieces A, B, C, and D.

4. **Using a pen or pencil, trace the pattern pieces onto tracing paper or plastic sheeting, spacing the pieces at least 1 inch apart in all directions.**

5. **Using a ruler, carefully draw a second line exactly ¼ inch outside the outline of each pattern piece, as shown in Figure 5-4.**

   Make sure that the spacing between the lines is accurate and that all angles are sharp.

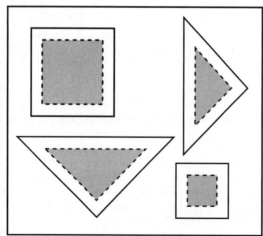

Figure 5-4:
Allow a
¼-inch seam
allowance
between
your
stitching
line (inner)
and cutting
line (outer).

This new line is the *cutting line,* the line along which you cut out the template and then later cut out the fabric patches. (The first line you drew is your *stitching line.*) The space between the two lines (¼ inch) provides the correct seam allowance for constructing your quilt block.

For rounded templates, use a flexible curve to trace curves with ease and accuracy. You can find them at most office supply or engineering supply stores.

6. **Mark a small dot on each template wherever two seams will converge when you start stitching your pieces together, as shown in Figure 5-5.**

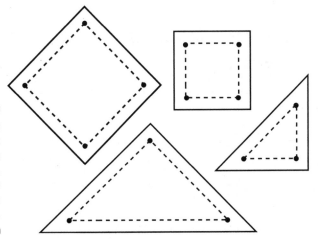

Figure 5-5: For an accurate block, connect the dots when stitching.

When piecing really intricate patterns, these dots act as guides for your stitching. And by matching up the dots on the fabric pieces, you ensure that the pieces are correctly aligned.

7. **If you traced your pattern pieces onto tracing paper instead of plastic sheeting, glue the tracing paper pieces to lightweight cardboard or other heavy paper.**

   This step adds durability and makes your templates easier to handle.

8. **Cut out the templates along their outer (cutting) lines, using old or general-use scissors, not your fabric-only scissors!**

Making templates from ready-made patterns

To make templates from ready-made patterns, including those in this book, follow these two easy steps:

1. Trace the patterns onto tracing paper or plastic sheeting.

2. Cut them out, as you would your own pattern designs (see the preceding section).

   On ready-made quilting patterns, cutting lines are always indicated by solid lines, and stitching lines are always indicated by dotted lines.

Make sure that you cut out template pieces along the cutting lines and not the stitching lines, or that king-sized bed quilt will end up looking like a place mat. (In which case you have to decide whether you still want to make the matching bed skirt and pillow shams!)

Making window templates for hand piecing

If you plan to hand piece your blocks (see Chapter 9 for more about hand piecing), you may want to make *window templates* so that you can easily mark the stitching lines on your fabric pieces. Most of the time when you're tracing a template, you're only tracing the outside cutting line. The great thing about a window template is that you're able to trace two lines on the wrong sides of your fabric: the outside cutting line and the inside stitching line. You then have a visual aid for perfect hand piecing — simply make your stitches follow the marked inside line!

A bonus to using window templates is that you're able to center a design element from the fabric in your piece. Perhaps you want to highlight a bouquet of flowers or a special emblem? Use the window to get the exact image you want. This technique is called *fussy cutting* because you carefully select the area you want to highlight in your finished quilt block.

Here's how you create a window template in two easy steps:

1. Make a template from plastic or cardboard by following the steps outlined in "Making templates from patterns you've created" and "Making templates from ready-made patterns," depending on whether you're creating your own design or using one from this (or another) quilting book.

   I know, I know; that adds up to more than two steps already, and you're still in the first step. Making that basic template is simple enough, though, right?

2. Cut out the template's center along the stitching line (the inside line you drew when you traced the pattern's shape onto the plastic).

Discard the center piece, or save it for another project if you think it's big enough to make another template out of someday. If you're using plastic sheeting for your template, you definitely want to consider saving your scraps for future use —saving a penny here and there is always good.

With your completed window template, you can mark both the cutting lines and the stitching lines on your fabric pieces. Don't believe me? Read on for details.

Putting Pencil to Fabric

After you make your templates, you're ready to transfer their shapes to your prewashed and freshly pressed fabric. (See Chapter 3 for the scoop on fabric and fabric preparation.)

Trying to trace templates onto a wrinkled piece of fabric is just setting you up for disaster. Wrinkles can scrunch and hide underneath the template, making your cut fabric pieces inaccurate. Remember, neatness counts!

Lay your template on the wrong side of the fabric (that's the back side of the fabric's design), paying special attention to match up the fabric's grain lines with the direction of the template's grain arrow (see "Going with the Grain" for grain arrow instructions). Trace around the template, using a well-sharpened water-soluble pencil. Sharpen the pencil often to keep your lines accurate. If you're using a window template, be sure to trace the inside (stitching) line, too.

To prevent templates from slipping on the fabric as you trace around them, try gluing small pieces of sandpaper to their backs (or purchase some adhesive-backed sandpaper and skip the gluing step). You can also make no-skid templates by applying a thin layer of rubber cement to their backs. (Just make sure that the rubber cement is dry before you use the templates, or you'll end up with a globby mess all over your fabric.) Rub off the rubber cement and apply a new layer as it becomes coated with fabric lint and loses its grip.

Chapter 6

Playing with Blocks and Borders: Which Way Should They Go?

*A*fter you select a block design (Chapter 4) and create the templates you need (Chapter 5), you're *almost* ready to start cutting and stitching. I say almost because first you need to determine

✔ How many blocks you need and how to arrange them

✔ The type of borders to cut

The number of blocks you need to stitch depends primarily on the size of the quilt you intend to make and the manner in which you plan to set the blocks (*setting the blocks* is quiltspeak for the layout of your design). In this chapter, I talk about the most common settings for quilt blocks and describe some border variations to help you plan your quilt.

Set 'Em Up, Sally!

The arrangement of blocks in a quilt is called a *set*. Within a set, you also have additional components such as sashing, cornerstones, and borders. You can arrange quilt blocks in literally hundreds of ways, but in this section, I stick to the most common sets. (For details on borders, skip to the section "Making a Run for the Border.")

The straight set and sashing

The most common and easiest set to put together is the *straight set.* You arrange the blocks one against the other in orderly rows that run in vertical and horizontal lines. Figure 6-1 shows a clear example of a straight set; it has nine blocks stitched together in three rows of three blocks each. You can see that the blocks are placed *block-to-block,* meaning that each block is placed square with the ones around it.

The Blue Star Place Mat project in Chapter 18 uses this set; check out the color section in the middle of the book for a photo of this project.

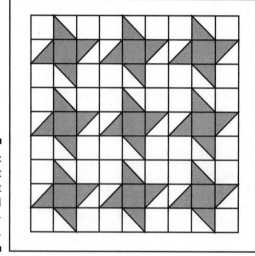

Figure 6-1: A straight set arranged block-to-block.

Figure 6-2 shows the same blocks as Figure 6-1, but the difference is that they're separated or framed by thin strips of fabric called *sashing* or *lattice strips.* Adding sashing to the set gives the quilt a completely different look, don't you think? Sashing or lattice strips can be plain, or you can jazz them up by inserting squares in the lattice, as you see in Figure 6-2. These squares are called *cornerstones* or *sashing squares.*

You can find sashing used in a straight set in Pieced Blossoms Lap Quilt (Chapter 17), Scrappy Bloomers Wall Hanging or Lap Quilt (Chapter 16), Snow Crystals Lap Quilt (Chapter 16), and several other projects in Part V (the color section shows the finished projects). Bear in mind that adding additional sashing or borders increases the size of the finished quilt.

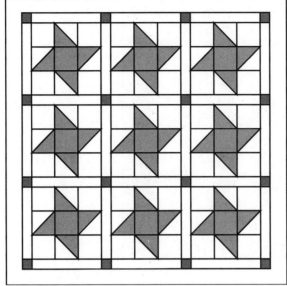

Figure 6-2:
A straight set with sashing and cornerstones.

The diagonal set

The second most common set is the _diagonal set._ In this arrangement, you place the blocks diagonally, on their points, at a 45-degree angle from the sides of the quilt. (Blocks set diagonally are said to be _on point._)

In a diagonal set, you can use all patchwork blocks, or you can alternate just a few patchwork blocks with plain squares, making great use of a minimal number of patchwork blocks. The alternating layout, which you can see in Figure 6-3, makes for a very traditional look.

If you decide to alternate your patchwork blocks with plain ones, in addition to plain squares, you need two different sizes of plain fabric triangles:

 ✔ Large triangles for the perimeter

 ✔ Small triangles at the corners

To make your diagonal set quilt even more eye-catching, add diagonal sashing strips and cornerstones to the blocks.

The Pastel Nine-Patch Wall Hanging project in Chapter 18 uses this simple but versatile set (see the color section for a photo).

Figure 6-3:
A diagonal
set gives
you a great
look with
fewer
patchwork
blocks.

The vertical or "strippy" set

Another popular set for quilt blocks is the *vertical* or *"strippy" set,* which is one of my favorites. Instead of forming orderly rows of blocks, you place the blocks in vertical strips separated by other strips (hence the name *strippy*).

Figure 6-4 shows a straight strippy set consisting of three rows and sashing. In the two outer rows, the blocks are set diagonally on their points, and in the middle strip, they're in a straight set. As you can see, you can set your blocks either way for an interesting result. You can really get creative with a strippy quilt, setting your blocks diagonally, staggering them, or keeping them straight. This set gives you a great opportunity to experiment with your graph paper and see what design ideas you can come up with!

For a different look using the same strippy set, Figure 6-5 shows an offset strippy layout (minus sashing) in which the blocks are set diagonally on their points. Putting the blocks on point really plays up the offset look and gives the pattern movement. Notice that the center strip is offset from the outer strips by the addition of partial blocks to the top and bottom of the strip.

Figure 6-4:
A straight strippy set with blocks set both diagonally and straight.

Figure 6-5:
An offset strippy arrangement with blocks on point.

The medallion set

Some quilters prefer to set their blocks in the *medallion set,* in which a single block or group of blocks acts as a central focal point. With the center in place, you have a number of different options for the empty space surrounding it. You may want to simply use different types of sashing and borders. Or if you've found a block design that complements the medallion block, you can place a number of those blocks around it. In a common design using the medallion set, you incorporate smaller versions of the medallion block, perhaps rotating them as showing in Figure 6-6.

The Traditional Basket Wall Hanging project in Chapter 15 uses this type of set (see the color section for a photo).

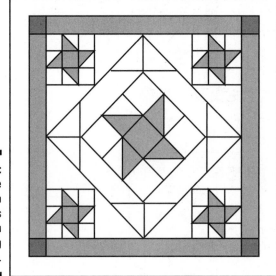

Figure 6-6:
The medallion set gives you something to focus on.

Making a Run for the Border

A *border* is a strip of fabric that frames a quilt. Usually, the entire quilt top is bordered (sometimes with multiple borders), but you can also incorporate borders surrounding your quilt blocks or as part of the quilt block design.

A quilt's borders can be wide or narrow, pieced, appliquéd, or created using a combination of techniques. Obviously, you should always try to choose a border that complements rather than clashes with your blocks.

Selecting a border type

You have dozens of border options to consider when planning your quilt, but as with the arrangement of quilt blocks (see "Set 'Em Up, Sally" earlier in the chapter), this section focuses on the most common borders you're likely to use.

The easiest and most common border style is the *plain border,* which uses solid cuts of one fabric. Depending on your expertise, you can stitch the plain border with squared corners or with mitered corners (see Figure 6-7). The squared-corner border is the simpler of the two to stitch because you simply extend two border strips to the very edge of the quilt. A *mitered corner* is stitched at a 45-degree angle to the sides of the quilt, producing a picture frame effect.

Figure 6-7:
A plain border can have squared or mitered corners.

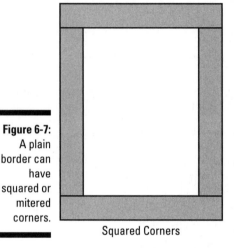

Squared Corners

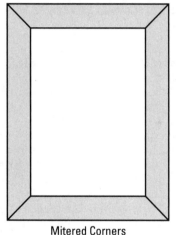

Mitered Corners

You may want to add cornerstones to your plain border (see Figure 6-8). The cornerstones can be complementing or contrasting fabrics, or you can use pieced or appliquéd blocks that complement the center area of your quilt.

For a more striking effect, make checkered borders by piecing small squares of fabric together into strips and stitching them to the quilt center in the same manner as you would a plain border.

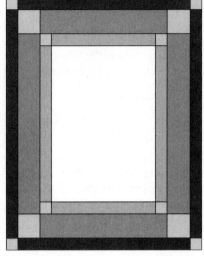

Figure 6-8:
Multiple
borders with
corner-
stones.

Calculating border size

After you decide what you want your border to look like, you need to figure out how much border fabric to cut. Sometimes your first quilt can be, well, a little off-kilter. The following steps guide you through a simple method for cutting your borders while squaring up the quilt top at the same time, making those uneven measurements jive once again! (The instructions in this section work even if your quilt top is perfectly square, too.) To keep things simple, assume that you want a border width of 10 inches.

1. **To determine the length of your side borders, measure the length of the quilt top down the center (see Figure 6-9).**

2. **Round off the measurement to the nearest inch.**

   If, for example, your quilt center is 33 inches long at the center, you have a finished border size of 10 x 33 inches.

3. **Add ¼-inch seam allowances to all four sides of the side borders.**

   The cutting size of your side borders is 10½ x 33½ inches.

4. **To determine the length of your top and bottom borders, measure the quilt from the middle of one side to the middle of the other side, including the side borders (see Figure 6-9).**

   Assuming that the width of the quilt is 22 inches across the middle and your side borders are 10 inches wide, the finished size for your top and bottom borders is 10 x 42 inches.

5. **Add ¼-inch seam allowances to all four sides of the top and bottom borders.**

   The cutting size of your top and bottom borders is 10½ x 42½ inches.

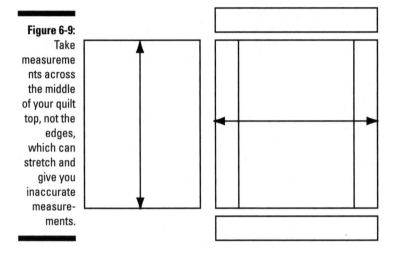

Figure 6-9: Take measurements across the middle of your quilt top, not the edges, which can stretch and give you inaccurate measurements.

Stitching the borders to your quilt

Before you attach borders to your quilt center, you need to prepare the border strips so that everything (hopefully) comes out just right. Essentially, you don't want to end up with too little border fabric in proportion to your quilt top.

1. **Fold each of the four border strips in half width-wise to find the center of the strip, and either press the fold to form a crease or place a pin at the halfway point to mark it.**

2. **Find the center of each side of the quilt top and mark it in the same manner (fold and press or mark with a pin).**

   After you mark the centers of the border strips and the quilt perimeter, you're ready to stitch.

3. **Align the center fold of the border with the center fold of the quilt top, having the right sides of the fabrics together.**

4. **Pin through the layers at the center marking and at each end.**

   The pins will hold the layers together during stitching.

5. **Stitch each border to the quilt along its length, easing in any excess border fabric (eliminating puckering and helping to square up the quilt again), using the following technique:**

   1. Place the side that has the excess length (whether it's the border or the quilt top) down against the *feed dogs* of your machine — those are the ridged teeth under the plate of the machine that move the fabric along as you stitch. These feed dogs help ease the extra length for you because they tend to feed the bottom layer of fabric through at a faster rate than the top layer, making it easier to take up the slack. (This trick won't work if you're using an even-feed foot, which I discuss in Chapter 13.)

   2. Start stitching, holding back the top (shorter) layer slightly and allowing the feed dogs to do their job of feeding the lower layer of fabric.

6. **After stitching the borders to the quilt top, press the seam allowances toward the border fabric.**

Chapter 7

Using Your Computer as a Crystal Ball

In This Chapter

▶ Exploring design software for quilters

▶ Designing quilt blocks with digital tools

▶ Playing with your final product before you start working

*Q*uilt design has come a long way since the days of horses and buggies. Did you know you can easily design quilts on your home computer? Designing blocks and entire quilts is fast and easy if you use software created specifically for quilt design. In fact, computer-savvy quilters have an advantage in that they can design quilts, test sets, and select fabrics for their masterpieces before they even leave the house to get their materials.

With design software, you can do the following without cutting a single bit of fabric:

✔ Design your own blocks

✔ Sample blocks from a block library

✔ Test different block layouts

✔ Sample different border styles

✔ Play with different fabric arrangements

✔ Print accurate patterns

✔ Print fabric shopping lists

Golly, who would have ever thought that handmade quilts and computers would some day become a great team?

In this chapter, I walk you through the quilt-planning process using quilting software, highlighting special features and timesavers along the way.

Software for Soft Quilts: Checking Out What's Available

Several companies currently produce quality quilting software. Some even offer free trial software, but you should be aware that trial software is usually very limited. To best design quilts on the computer, you need to purchase the real thing. A good software program will keep your fingers creatively tapping and stitching for years!

To find a software program, enter the key phrase "quilting software" in any search engine on the Internet. Your search should reveal plenty of options to investigate further. Some of the most popular quilting software programs are:

- ✔ QuiltSoft
- ✔ EQ5
- ✔ PC Quilt
- ✔ QuiltPro
- ✔ SewPrecise
- ✔ Quilting Studio

Quilting software can be pricey, ranging from $50 to over $100, but *not all software is created equal*. Some programs have more features than others, so you need to shop carefully. Some of the less expensive programs limit your design options to pieced designs only, making it difficult to design an appliqué block. Others have limited block or fabric libraries. In many cases, spending a little extra money upfront is a good idea because once you're hooked, you'll want all those extra bells and whistles, believe me! It's a blast skimming through dozens of fabrics or sample blocks!

I like to use EQ5, the Electric Quilt Company's software program, as well as its fabric updates, which are called Stash. EQ5 is easy to use thanks to tutorials that are so helpful even a child can master the software. After you purchase the EQ5 software, you can go to the Electric Quilt Company's Web site (www.electricquilt.com) to download lots of freebies, including fabric palettes and quilt blocks to add to your library; newsletters to help you better use the software; and lots of tutorials. My favorite aspect of this software is the frequent updates and tips found on the Web site — there's always something new to discover. Electric Quilt Company also makes another software program called BlockBase, which features over 4,000 block designs, ensuring that a quilter never runs out of blocks to play with!

You can purchase quilting software directly from the manufacturer via the Internet, pick up a copy at a consumer sewing show, or inquire at your local quilt shop (many quilt shops now carry software in their stores and may even let you take a program for a test spin).

The vector inspector

Design software — including quilting software — uses technology known as *vector graphics*. To make a long story short, vector graphics allow you to take simple elements such as points, lines, curves or arcs, and geometric shapes and combine them to create an image on your computer screen. These various design elements can then be flipped, rotated, stretched, turned, skewed, copied, and mirrored to create any design your mind can imagine.

While you're busy in the sketching phase, each element of your design is layered, one on top of the other. To prepare the design for printing by the computer, it's flattened or compressed into one image. This compression is called *rasterizing*. In a nutshell, rasterizing squashes the whole shebang and turns the finished drawing into pixels — those billions of dots that make up a picture on your computer screen.

Beginning Your Quilt Design: Building Blocks

I love designing quilts by using software! I don't have to think much, and I don't get hand cramps from endless sketching. I may complain once in a while about a cramp in my mouse-clicking finger, but I'm just joshing. One of my favorite things to do before actually putting mouse to design pad is to browse through the software block libraries, which are full of inspiring ideas just waiting for me to tap into them.

All quilting software programs come with *block libraries*. By opening up a library, you can select blocks, both pieced and appliquéd, based on existing quilting designs. Some software programs have separate libraries for pieced and appliquéd blocks, so check with your owner's manual to be sure you're seeing it all. With a click of the mouse you can add blocks you like to an assortment of layouts and then, like a kid with a box of crayons, color the blocks and transform the design into your own unique masterpiece.

You can also build your own unique blocks, using block-building tools. Standard options for new blocks include pieced blocks, appliquéd blocks, blocks using mixed techniques, foundation piecing patterns, and stencils for quilting (I explain quilting stencils in Chapter 11).

Another really cool feature in some quilting design programs is the ability to trace a bitmap image, such as a sketch you scan and save to a file. If you find a picture or drawing you want to convert to an appliqué design, you simply scan it, import it into your design software, and follow the instructions in your owner's manual, of course!

For all the tasks I cover in this chapter, I give you general directions that apply to most software programs. For more specific instructions and trouble-shooting, turn to the owner's manual that came with your program.

Selecting or creating your block

To work with a ready-made block, open a block library, select the block you want, and add it to your workbook or your favorite quilt layout. Repeat this process for each block you want to use in your quilt design.

To design your own blocks, you open a sketchbook of sorts — a blank screen with a grid layout similar to graph paper (see Figure 7-1). You can select the number of grids in your block, usually by selecting a Layout Options tab (or something similar) from the toolbar in your program.

I like to use a grid that matches my desired block size. For example, if I'm creating a quilt based on 12-inch blocks, I set up a 12- x 12-square grid. If I want a 10-inch block, I use a 10- x 10-square grid. When designing more intricate blocks, I like to double the grid size for more flexibility and to make the design easier to see and break down into individual pieces. For example, I may use a 20- x 20-square grid for a 10-inch block and a 24- x 24-square grid for a 12-inch block.

Perfecting your block design

With a blank design grid on your computer screen, you can use the tools available in your design program to draw your block. These tools typically consist of lines and arcs and include options to copy, flip, and resize anything you draw. Playing with the different tools in your software allows you to layer appliqués on your block, rotate, resize, and reshape any element of your design.

After you click on the desired tool and place it on your design grid, you'll notice that the shape appearing on the screen has something akin to handles (see Figure 7-2). These are your grabbing points for resizing, reshaping, or otherwise altering the shape or entire block. Different programs have slightly different handles, but they function in the same way: Just click on one of the grabbing points with your mouse and drag your mouse until you achieve the desired effect.

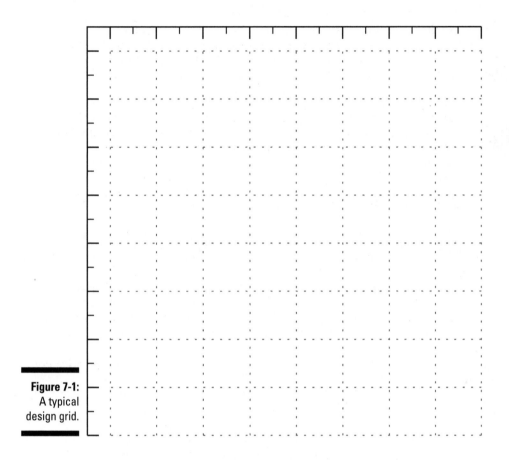

Figure 7-1:
A typical
design grid.

When you have your block design the way you want it, save it to your project file, or start adding fabrics to your design using your software's fabric libraries. (I like to wait until all the elements of my "sketch" are complete before I start trying on fabrics, but it's just a matter of preference.)

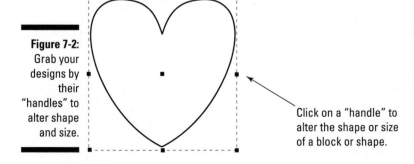

Figure 7-2:
Grab your
designs by
their
"handles" to
alter shape
and size.

Click on a "handle" to
alter the shape or size
of a block or shape.

Even though you create specific sized blocks in your block sketchpad, you can easily resize the blocks when laying out the final quilt. All you need to do is revise the size block you desire in your quilt layout (see the next section) — the software does the rest!

Don't know what size blocks you need for a quilt that fits your king-size bed? The software does! Just enter the size you want your finished quilt to be, and the design program works out your block measurements so they fit your desired quilt size. You can also specify the number of blocks and borders you'd like to have in your finished design. The software considers these preferences and produces a layout you can manipulate until it's just the way you want it.

Glimpsing Your Quilt's Future

Every quilter wishes he or she could see what a quilt will really look like *before* purchasing or cutting into expensive fabric. Thank goodness for quilting software — it's like a peek into the future. You can see what works and what doesn't work before you invest any more time or money in a project!

With design software, you can see if your blocks look better in a straight set or on point, need narrow or wide borders, look better with or without sashing, and you can easily *try on* various color palettes for size. (For color palette and fabric information, check out Chapter 3.)

Playing with layouts and borders

Quilting programs come with layout libraries, so all you have to do is select a layout and add your quilt blocks. You can choose from straight sets, strippy sets, medallions, blocks on point, free-floating blocks, charm quilt layouts, and more, all of which can be arranged horizontally or vertically. (For examples of these layouts, flip to Chapter 6.) You can also create your own custom layouts.

With your set selected, you can add sashing strips between the blocks in any size, add one or more borders, and choose the perfect style of border for your quilt.

After selecting your layout and border design, you'll see a skeleton of your quilt on your computer screen. This skeleton is ready to be filled with the blocks you designed or selected from the block libraries. Simply click on the thumbnail of the desired block and then the area of the quilt where you want the block to appear, and voila! It's there!

Trying on fabrics from fabric libraries

Quilting software is equipped with libraries full of fabrics that you can apply to your quilt without ever having to make a single cut. Fabrics of various colors and prints arranged in different themes or collections help take the guesswork out of selecting fabrics that work well together.

To colorize a block with a sample fabric, simply open the desired block in your sketchpad, select your fabrics, and click on the individual elements of your block to add the fabrics. After you get the hang of it, this is really easy stuff.

When you have the block and fabric the way you want it, save the block to your file, and add the colorized block to your quilt layout. After arranging your colorized blocks, select the fabrics for your borders and add them to the layout. When you're done, your quilt mock-up is ready to go.

If you can't find just the right fabric for your quilt in your software's existing fabric libraries, add-ons and updates should be available through your software's manufacturer. I like to order the updates each year so I can always have the latest and greatest fabric choices on hand when I'm designing.

Calculating yardage and printing patterns

With your quilt designed and the perfect color selections made, you're ready to shop for fabric. Yet again, you're not on your own; let the program print out a shopping list for you. The process is fast and simple, and you end up with a very accurate to-buy list. Best of all, you know you don't have to guess when buying fabric or worry that you'll end up with too much or too little of something.

When it comes time to think about actually cutting out your quilt block pieces, your quilting software can print accurate pattern templates with a simple click of your mouse.

To help them hold up better and give you more consistently accurate cuts, glue these templates to cardstock or cardboard as recommended in Chapter 5.

Part III

Sharpening Your Sewing Skills

The 5th Wave   By Rich Tennant

By the way, I quilted this hood myself.

Stop it! You didn't! What is that, a blanket stitch?

In this part . . .

*I*n this part, I explain all the skills necessary to get you happily stitching along on your first quilt. Starting with cutting basics (including using the quilter's dream tool, the rotary cutter), I share my tips for pressing the pointiest points, stitching the sharpest seams, and indulging your passion for appliqué.

Chapter 8

Cuts and Creases: Pressing Matters

In This Chapter
▶ Thinking before you cut
▶ Familiarizing yourself with rotary cutting
▶ Turning to pressing matters

You may be thinking, "Why bother with a chapter on cutting and pressing? Everyone knows how to use a pair of scissors and an iron, right?" Well, although everyone certainly knows how to use a pair of scissors, few may realize the importance of cutting accurately, especially when it comes to quilting! Accurate cutting is just as important as accurate piecing if you want your project to turn out well. Also important to the cutting process is laying out pattern pieces efficiently to avoid wasted fabric; fabric can be expensive, and you want to be certain you have enough to complete your project.

Finally, proper pressing, just like accurate cutting and stitching, can mean the difference between a well-made block and a crooked, misshapen one. Smooth seams make the stitching process much easier and give your quilt its crisp neatness.

In this chapter, I review basic techniques of cutting and pressing that are sure to make this part of your quilt-making adventure go smoothly.

Creating a Cutting Game Plan

I know you're eager to dive into your lovely fabrics and cut, cut, cut, but you need to restrain yourself just a little while longer. Cutting is a crucial part of the quilt-making process, and if you don't take your time to get it right, you're sure to have problems later on. (The information in this section applies to general preparation and cutting; for details and instructions specific to rotary cutting, see the section "Slicing through Rotary Cutting Basics" later in the chapter.)

The first thing to consider is what pieces you're going to cut first. Most quilting instructions tell you to cut the largest pieces first — usually the borders and sashing, and that's a good rule to follow even when the directions don't specify a cutting order. Cutting the borders and sashing first makes more efficient use of a large length of fabric and saves you from having to piece them together or buy more fabric later. With the large pieces out of the way, you then cut the smaller pieces of your pattern from the remaining fabric.

Before cutting into any fabric, take a close look at the block you want to make and figure out which way the fabric grain should go on each piece (refer to Chapter 5 for information about grain lines). When you've determined the direction of the grain, lay your templates on the wrong side of the fabric, placing as many similar pieces together as possible. For instance, as Figure 8-1 shows, place triangles together with their longest sides facing, and neatly line up squares. Rearrange your templates as many times as necessary to make them all fit. You haven't marked or cut anything yet, so now's the time to play around.

Figure 8-1:
Neatly line up your templates for triangles and squares: Straight edges can touch, or you can leave a little space in between.

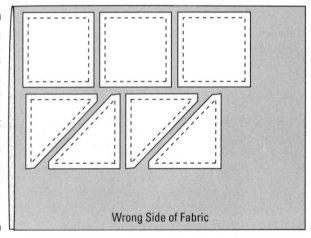

Wrong Side of Fabric

To keep your templates from slipping as you trace, glue a piece of fine-grain sandpaper to their back sides, or brush a thin layer of rubber cement onto their back sides and allow them to dry before placing them on your fabric.

With your templates firmly in place, trace lightly around them with a washable pencil or tailor's chalk. Don't use a regular pencil or pen — they may stain the fabric.

Keep in mind that if you're using a window template, the inner (broken) line on the templates is the stitching line and the outer (solid) line is the cutting line. For more on templates and how to use premade ones or make your own, check out Chapter 5.

With the pieces of your quilt block traced and ready to take shape, you have two cutting options: fabric scissors or a rotary cutter. Fabric scissors are best suited to cutting through just one layer of fabric at a time. A rotary cutter, which I explain more in the section "Slicing through Rotary Cutting Basics," gives you better precision when cutting one or multiple layers of fabric.

 If you decide to use scissors, make sure they're sharp to the very tip of the blades. (Nice sharp tips make it easier to trim appliqués and those hard-to-reach places!) If you've kept your fabric-cutting scissors hidden away from those who dishonor their sacredness by using them to cut paper, cardboard, or other taboo items, your cutting line should be sharp and clean. If you have any difficulty cutting fabric, *your scissors aren't sharp enough!* You can either have them sharpened or skip the delay and just purchase a fresh pair. Keeping scissors sharpened is smarter and easier than risking the ruin of your fabric and your project by cutting inaccurate or sloppy-looking pieces.

Slicing through Rotary Cutting Basics

Using a rotary cutter with a see-through ruler and rotary cutting mat (see Chapter 2 for information about rotary cutting supplies) is by far the quickest and most accurate method of cutting fabric. I urge you to get acquainted with this tool — you'll love it!

 You may find this method of cutting referred to by other quilters as *template-free cutting* because instead of tracing around your templates with a pencil and cutting the pieces out one-by-one, you cut multiple pieces of a specific size simultaneously.

This section covers the very basics of rotary cutting. So many different rotary cutting tips and techniques are available that it's impossible to cover them all in this chapter. If you want more detail, consult any of the many wonderful books that have been written on rotary cutting methods. Check out the booklist in the Appendix for some of my favorites.

Prepping your fabric for rotary cutting

Because you don't use templates and trace your pieces out first, rotary cutting requires a straight edge on which to base your shapes. To prepare your washed and pressed fabric for rotary cutting, fold the fabric along the center with right sides together and the tidy selvage edges (not the ragged, cut edges) together. Press along the crease. Then place the folded fabric on your cutting mat and square up one end by placing the ruler along one of the lines on the mat, as shown in Figure 8-2. You don't need to remove a large strip to square-up your fabric — just enough to make the edge even.

Slice off the uneven edge of the fabric with the rotary cutter, placing the blade against the ruler and cutting away from you in one continuous motion. If you're right-handed, the waste fabric will be on the right of your ruler; if you're left-handed, the waste fabric will be on the left of the ruler.

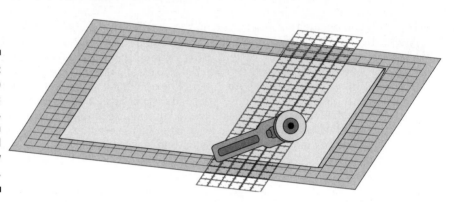

Figure 8-2: Square up your fabric with a mat, see-through ruler, and rotary cutter.

Cutting strips, squares, and rectangles

With a rotary cutter, you can breeze right through strips, squares, and rectangles. To make things really easy, squares and rectangles start out as strips.

Follow these instructions to cut strips of fabric (no matter the width):

1. **Align the newly squared edge of your fabric (see the preceding section) with the line on your cutting mat that gives you the strip width you want.**

   For example, if you want 2½-inch strips, find the 2½-inch mark on the mat and place your ruler along this mark. (Depending on how long your folded fabric is, you may only be able to see the mat lines at the very top and bottom of the mat.)

3. **Slice off the strip with the rotary cutter, cutting away from you in one continuous motion.**

As I mentioned earlier, squares and rectangles start out as strips. After you have a strip the width of the squares or rectangles you want, you use the same basic measurement instructions listed above to cut your strip into individual pieces, as shown in Figure 8-3.

Cut as many squares or rectangles as you need. Just remember that you're cutting through a double thickness of fabric (because the fabric is folded when you cut the strips); therefore, you get two pieces for each cut.

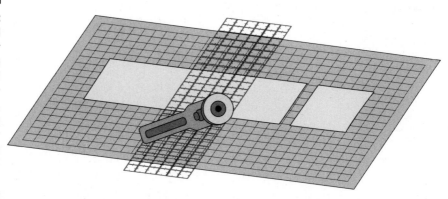

Figure 8-3: Mark and cut your strip into individual squares (or rectangles, depending on your desired measure-ments).

Cutting triangles

Cutting triangles with a rotary cutter may stir up long-lost memories of your high school geometry class, but I promise that it's much easier than your class ever was — and much less stressful. For simple, template-free triangles with 45-degree angles, cut squares first (refer back to the preceding section for square-cutting instructions), and then cut each square in half diagonally, as shown in Figure 8-4.

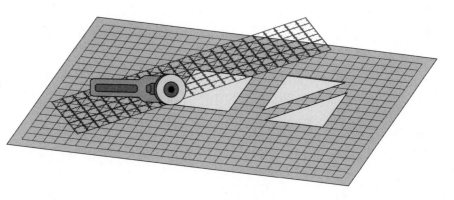

Figure 8-4: 45-degree triangles start out as squares.

To cut other types of triangles, such as the 60-degree triangle shown in Figure 8-5, you can use a triangular ruler, which is available in a variety of different sizes. Like your regular ruler, these rulers are also see-through and heavy-duty plastic, so they're easy to use in conjunction with your regular ruler and rotary cutter.

When cutting triangles, take into account that the longest side of the triangle also needs a seam allowance! If the finished size of the triangle will be 2 inches, don't cut a 2½-inch square in half to make triangles; you'll have seam allowances on the short edges but not on the long edge.

Addressing Pressing

Properly pressing your fabric pieces and your seams (after you start stitching pieces together) is crucial to making your work look "just right." The pressing tips and techniques that I share in this section aren't difficult to perform or remember.

You may have noticed that I use the term *pressing* rather than *ironing* — there's a critical distinction. With pressing, you don't slide your iron across the fabric as you would when ironing. Instead, you lift the iron to move it to a new location and then lower it down, as shown in Figure 8-6. You don't need to press down on the iron — let the weight of the iron do the job.

Sliding the iron across the fabric tends to distort bias edges and can really stretch your pieces out of place.

Figure 8-6:
Lift, rather
than slide,
your iron
when
pressing
fabrics.

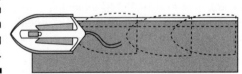
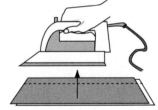

Keeping track of cut pieces

Neatly organizing cut pieces of fabric not only helps keep your work area clean and the pieces from getting mixed up but also shows you at a glance what you've already cut and what still needs to be done.

To keep all those little pieces neat and organized, stack them by color, shape, and so on. Then store them using one of the following methods:

- Place individual stacks of cut pieces in clear plastic zip-top bags to keep them tidy and contained.

- Thread a needle and insert it into the top of a stack, pulling the needle through the entire

stack of pieces at once, as shown in the figure below. Leaving a 3-inch tail of thread at the top of the stack, insert the needle through the stack again, going from the bottom up. Without knotting it, cut off the thread, leaving another 3-inch tail. When you need to use a piece from the stack, simply pull one off the top. The thread will hold the remainder in place!

Store your bags or threaded piles in a pretty basket or box, or better yet, if you're working on more than one project at the same time, store the pieces in separate baskets or boxes.

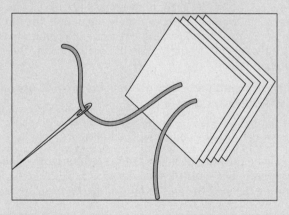

 As for equipment and setup, don't use an iron with an automatic shut-off feature if you plan on doing a lot of quilting. The iron is guaranteed to shut off at the most inopportune times, so you'll find yourself resetting it constantly. Also, keep your iron within easy reach of your cutting and sewing area so you can easily press as you stitch. (I always keep my ironing board just a few steps away.)

Pressing seam allowances

After you stitch pieces of fabric together, you need to press the seams to ensure that everything lays neatly when you add more pieces and assemble everything together. You should always press a seam before stitching across it with another seam.

To press your seam allowances, set your iron for cotton with no steam and then follow these easy steps:

1. **With the right sides of the sewn fabric still facing each other, press the seam to set the stitching.**

2. **Open up the fabric pieces along the seam, and with the right side facing up, press along the seam.**

3. **Flip the opened piece over so the seam is facing up, and press both the seam allowances toward the darker fabric.**

   Pressing to the darker side prevents dark shadows from showing through the lighter fabrics in the finished quilt.

   Be sure to press the seam allowances together in one direction rather than open. When you press a seam open, only the stitching thread keeps the pieces together. Pressing the seam allowances to one side provides an added layer of fabric across the seam, making the seam stronger and more durable.

4. **Wherever multiple seams meet, press them in opposite directions to avoid bulk (see Figure 8-7).**

   This technique may mean that sometimes you have to go against Step 3 and press toward a lighter fabric, but that's okay.

   When you need to press toward the lighter fabric, hand trim a small bit of the seam allowance from the darker fabric to avoid a strong shadow showing through the lighter fabric.

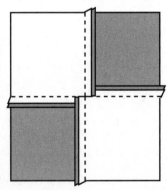

Figure 8-7:
Pressing seam allowances in opposite directions prevents bulk.

When pressing the seams of long strips such as borders, change the direction of the tip of the iron each time you lift and lower it, as shown in Figure 8-8, to ensure that your strip doesn't favor one side and stretch out of whack. If you forget to press and accidentally slide the iron along the strip, the seam may curve, resulting in a less-than-straight strip of fabric. To correct the minor disfigurement, dab a little water onto the seam line (just a dab!), realign your edge, and press again the correct way. The seam should stay in shape as long as you press and don't slide.

If you're having trouble getting a seam to lie flat, apply a bit of water with your fingertips where you need it and press on. Don't spray or dampen an entire block — use the water only where needed.

Figure 8-8:
Lift, turn, and lower your iron to ensure that you're correctly pressing long strips.

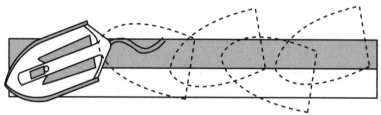

Blowing off steam

Throughout this chapter I've talked a lot about pressing, but I've never mentioned steam because water and steam are rarely ever used when making a quilt — and for good reason.

The long and the short of it is that steam can result in distortion by causing the quilting fabric to swell and dry again. It can also permanently set a seam before its time. For example, suppose you steam-press a block that you later discover is a little off-kilter. You decide to take the block apart and restitch it for the sake of accuracy (what a good quilter you are!). Because your block was steam-pressed, you'll notice that the creases won't release without using more water, which only makes the fabric swell and shrink even more, distorting your cut edges a bit and causing some hairy-looking fringing. You end up scrapping the block in favor of recutting and stitching.

Never press a finished quilt. Pressing — either wet or dry — flattens the batting, therefore defeating the purpose of quilting through three layers. No one wants a flat quilt! If your finished quilt needs a little face-lift after being folded, pop it in the clothes dryer and select a delicate or fluff setting. After a few minutes of tumbling, the creases release and your quilt's fluffy and cozy once again.

Chapter 9

Positively Perfect Piecing

*P*erfect piecing doesn't require profuse preparation, but some preliminary planning (placing pieces together in pairs) will better prepare you for producing perfect patchwork.

Did you get that? Essentially, accurate piecing requires preparation. A little work upfront not only ensures piecing success but also makes the job proceed more smoothly and quickly.

In this chapter, I guide you through all the piecing techniques you need to know to make accurately pieced blocks. I also share a few tricks for speeding up the process and repairing the inevitable mistake. Well-formed points and perfectly square blocks are well within reach if you follow just a few basic rules, so don't be shy — dive on in!

Perfect Machine Piecing for the Impatient Quilter

Your grandmother may have spent her free time painstakingly piecing her quilt squares by hand, but today, you have the good fortune to be able to piece by machine. As a self-described "machine queen," I prefer to do everything I can with the aid of my sewing machine. Elias Howe, the wonderful wizard who patented the very first sewing machine in 1846, is truly my hero.

Although the rules are basically the same for both hand and machine piecing, machine piecing dramatically reduces the time it takes to complete a quilt top. (If you like to stitch on the go or simply don't want to use a machine, see "Hand Piecing for the Purist" later in this chapter.)

Chances are good that if you're attempting to make a quilt (even if it's your first), you already know something about the basic workings of a sewing machine. So this section simply covers some setup details and techniques that are specific to machine piecing.

Setting up your machine

Piecing by machine is a breeze. It's fast, accurate, and easy. But before sewing a single stitch, make sure that your machine is set up properly by following the basic steps I outline in this section.

Loading your thread

Thread both the upper part of the machine and the bobbin with an all-purpose thread. Select a thread color that coordinates with the fabrics you're stitching together. If you're working with different colored fabrics, select a thread from the mid-color range — one that falls somewhere between your darkest and lightest fabric colors.

Using the presser foot

Your *seam allowance,* the area of fabric taken up by the seam, is probably the most important factor to keep in mind when piecing, whether your block is simple or elaborate. And unless you're quilting in miniature, your seam allowance is always exactly ¼ inch.

Some machines come with a special patchwork presser foot that measures exactly ¼ inch from the needle hole to the outside edge of the foot. To stitch an accurate seam allowance every time, simply keep the edge of your fabric aligned with the edge of the foot (see Figure 9-1).

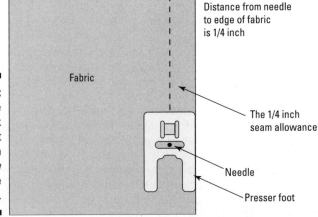

Figure 9-1: The patchwork presser foot aligned with the raw edge of the fabric.

Distance from needle to edge of fabric is 1/4 inch

Fabric

The 1/4 inch seam allowance

Needle

Presser foot

Taking advantage of tape

If you prefer not to bother with a patchwork presser foot, or if you discover that your patchwork foot isn't accurate, you can make your own stitching guide with a piece of masking tape.

Without any fabric in the machine, simply measure ¼ inch from your needle and place a piece of tape on your sewing machine's *throat plate,* that slab of metal with the hole in it that the needle goes up and down, and up and down through, so that the right edge of the tape is at the ¼ mark. This tape is your seam guide, meaning that you align the right-hand edge of the fabric you're piecing with the tape line as you sew and end up with a straight, exact ¼-inch seam. *Tip:* You may need to replace the tape often if you do a lot of stitching.

If your machine didn't come with a patchwork presser foot, you may be able to purchase one from a sewing machine dealer. Dealers usually carry machine feet for specific brands of machines as well as "generic" feet that fit a number of different machines. When you go shopping for a patchwork presser foot, be sure to take along one of the feet that came with your machine. Otherwise, you may get home and find that your new presser foot doesn't fit your machine's specifications. What a bummer!

Before you start piecing with the new presser foot, check the accuracy of its ¼-inch measurement by placing a lightweight piece of paper in your machine and lowering the presser foot. Make a few stitches, and before you remove the paper from the machine, mark a pencil line along the edge of the presser foot. Remove the paper, and measure the distance from the needle holes to the pencil line. If this measurement is exactly ¼ inch, you're in great shape! If the measurement isn't accurate, use the tape trick described in the sidebar "Taking advantage of tape" to help keep your seam allowances accurate.

Checking stitch length and tension

Set your machine's stitch length to its default setting (usually 12 to 14 stitches per inch, depending on the machine). Then make sure your machine is stitching properly before you attempt to machine piece anything. A machine with an improper *tension* setting can produce pieces that pucker or have seams that separate slightly after stitching.

Checking the tension is especially important if you're using an older machine that hasn't been professionally serviced in a while or if you're working on a hand-me-down or borrowed machine or garage sale find. Poor tension isn't much of a problem with newer machines because they're usually equipped with safeguards to keep the tension properly set.

To make sure your tension is properly set, run this little test: Machine stitch through a double layer of fabric using a light-colored all-purpose thread in the machine and a dark-colored all-purpose thread on the bobbin. Take a close look at the resulting stitches:

- ✔ **If the dark bobbin thread is pulled to the top surface:** Loosen the upper tension on the machine just slightly. Sew another test piece and look at it again. Keep sewing, examining, and loosening the top until the stitch is even on both sides.

- ✔ **If the top thread is pulled to the bottom surface:** Your bobbin is probably adjusted too tightly. Loosen the adjusting screw slightly — a quarter-turn at a time is fine. Keep stitching, examining, and loosening the bobbin until the stitch is even on both sides.

Keeping your needle sharp

Believe it or not, I've run into people who've said, "What? Change my needle? Why should I? It still sews, and I've had it in my machine for 10 years." My only response is, "Yikes!"

Changing sewing machine needles regularly is something I just can't drill into you enough! It's absolutely essential! That needle affects the machine tension, the ability to make properly formed stitches, and the wear and tear on your fabric. A dull and rounded needle leaves larger holes than necessary in your fabric and can mess up your tension by allowing thread to travel through the holes. A needle with a *burr* on it (a sharp protrusion of metal, often cause by stitching over a pin) catches the fabric's fibers, causing it to pucker. A burr may also cause your machine thread to break or produce a fuzzy bump on your thread that won't fit through the needle's eye.

I usually insert a new needle in my machine after 40 to 50 hours of sewing. Other quilters change their needles less or more frequently depending on their machines, the types of fabric they're sewing, and their own personal preferences.

Always keep a fresh pack of needles on hand because you never know when a bad needle will start to affect your sewing or when a needle may break. (For the skinny on needles, flip to Chapter 2.)

Chain piecing to save time and thread

Chain piecing is an exercise in efficiency; it allows you to zip through a lot of piecing without all the normal starts and stops, *and* it lets you save a little thread. Before you can start chain piecing, though, you need to get your pieces pulled together and ready to go. The following steps guide you through chain piecing, from beginning to end:

1. Take two fabric pieces that need to be sewn together and pin them with their right sides facing. Do this for all your fabric pieces, pairing them in twos.

2. Place your pinned pieces in a stack next to your sewing machine.

3. Begin stitching by running one pinned pair under your presser foot. When you reach the end of the piece, feed in a second pair without stopping the machine or cutting the threads. Continue feeding each pinned pair through the machine until all are stitched and you have a chain of stitched pieces connected by thread (see Figure 9-2).

Figure 9-2:
Run your pinned pieces through your machine, one after the other, making sure to remove the pins before stitching over them for safety's sake.

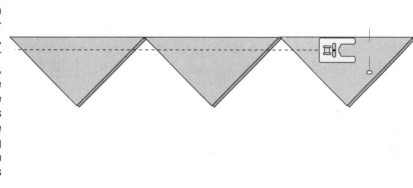

4. Cut your pieces apart at the threads in between each pair, and press them open.

Hand Piecing for the Purist

Some quilters prefer to hand piece their blocks rather than buzz through them on a sewing machine. They enjoy sticking with tradition and like the feel of the fabric flowing through their hands as they stitch. I call these fine, devoted folks "quilting purists."

As ye sew, so shall ye rip!

We're human. We make mistakes — sometimes lots of them! And that humanity is exactly why it's important to know how to use a *seam ripper* properly and always have one on hand when piecing blocks.

Notice that I said "seam ripper" and not "fabric ripper." The whole point of these handy little tools is to undo the seam on a botched stitching job — not to rip through the fabric and ruin an entire patch.

To use a seam ripper correctly, insert the tool's sharp point under the first stitch and tug to cut it. Cut the thread in the same manner every five or six stitches or until you can easily separate the two pieces of fabric. If the fabric pieces are still difficult to separate, cut the thread at closer intervals but don't forcefully separate the pieces — you risk ripping them or distorting their shapes.

Warning: Always store your seam ripper with the cover on. Proper storage not only keeps it sharp and free of moisture, but it also keeps you from getting stabbed while rummaging through your sewing supplies! If your seam ripper becomes dull or rusted, throw it out and invest in a new one.

Hand piecing is certainly a traditional and time-honored approach to patchwork quilting, but it also has the added benefit of being portable. By stashing a needle, thread, fabric pieces, and small scissors in your purse or briefcase, you can work on a project virtually anywhere.

If you commute, try piecing instead of staring out the train window. If you travel, tuck your supplies in your carry-on bag and use your flight time for stitching. Quilting beats reading the emergency evacuation guidelines over and over again (although you should certainly read them at least once) or playing tic-tac-toe on the back of an airsick bag for the hundredth time! You also can carry your supplies to your kids' baseball practices or ballet lessons. You may even find yourself making new friends who either share your interest in quilting or who would like to learn but have been too afraid to try. Become a quilting advocate!

There's very little difference between hand piecing and machine piecing; with hand piecing, you use a special template and begin and end your stitching in a particular way. Hand piecing uses a 1/4-inch seam allowance just like machine piecing. However, because you don't have the machine's presser foot as a stitching guide, you need to mark seam allowances directly onto the wrong sides of your fabric pieces to keep your seam allowances accurate.

To accurately mark your seam allowances, make or buy a *window template,* a template with a hole or window in the center for marking your seam line, for each piece. Figure 9-3 shows window templates.

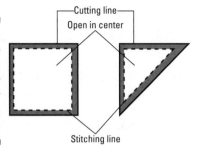

Figure 9-3:
Window
templates
with center
openings for
marking
seam lines.

Cutting line

Open in center

Stitching line

To use the template, lay it on the wrong side of the fabric you want to cut and sew, and trace around the template's outer edge with a washable pencil (see Chapter 2 for the scoop on washable pens and pencils). This first line is your *cutting line*. Next, trace around the inside edge of the template to create your *stitching line*.

To hand stitch fabric pieces together, follow these steps:

1. **Place the pieces right sides together.**

   For ease of handling, you may want to place a pin at each end of the stitching line and another at the midpoint to hold the layers together and prevent them from shifting as you stitch.

2. **Cut a length of thread no longer than your arm, and thread a hand-sewing needle with it, as shown in Figure 9-4. Knot the longer end.**

   This knot is your *waste knot* and will be cut off later.

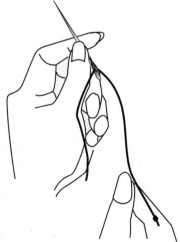

Figure 9-4:
Thread a
hand-
sewing
needle with
a single
length of
thread,
knotting the
longer end
of the
thread.

3. **To begin stitching, start your thread just inside the edge of the piece and backstitch to the edge. Then reverse your stitching direction and stitch across the entire length of the stitching line, making small, even stitches.**

   Try to space these stitches as evenly as possible — shoot for eight to ten stitches per inch.

4. **When you reach the opposite end of the stitching line, reverse the direction of your stitching again and backstitch three or four stitches.**

   Backstitching secures the thread and keeps the seam from coming undone.

5. **Cut off the thread, and carefully cut off the waste knot from your starting point.**

After you become comfortable with hand stitching, you can eliminate the waste knot. Simply backstitch a few times at the beginning, leaving a tail to trim later, and then backstitch again at the end.

Piecing Blocks with Set-in Seams

At times during the piecing process, you run into a seam that needs special attention, such as a *set-in seam*. Set-in seams result from pieces that need to be inserted into the block at an awkward angle rather than stitched as a tidy unit. You can see a set-in component in Figure 9-5; notice that stitching the shaded unit in place requires two seams (one on either angle) rather than one. (The blocks of the Pink Tulips Breakfast Set project in Chapter 18 include set-in elements.)

Figure 9-5:
The shaded piece is a set-in component.

Templates for set-in components have dots at the corners where seam allowances converge (see Figure 9-6). These dots are very important because they indicate where you need to begin and end your stitching. Be sure to transfer these dots to cut pieces of fabric before stitching the pieces to the other components.

Figure 9-6:
A set of templates for set-in components. Notice the dots that tell you where to stop and start stitching.

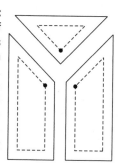

Do not go past the dots when stitching set-in pieces. If you stitch to the ends of the units, your pieces won't fit together properly; in fact, you'll end up with a pucker forming at the convergence of the seams. Sewing set-in pieces isn't rocket science — just stop at the dots and your blocks will be fine.

Set-in blocks are all different, but the stitching order is generally like the diagram shown in Figure 9-7. After you stitch along one side and end your stitching at the dot, stitch the second piece to the first from the opposite direction, also ending your stitching at the dot.

Figure 9-7:
The pieces of a block with set-in seams must come together in a particular order. First stitch two pieces together (a), add the third piece along one seam (b), and then close up the remaining seam (c).

a

b

c

Standing on a Firm Foundation

Quilters and designers are always coming up with terrific new ways to create intricate quilt blocks and stitch them accurately. *Foundation piecing* allows you to do both with one tidy printed-paper package.

Foundation piecing differs from traditional piecing methods because you actually stitch fabric directly onto paper, seam allowances and all. You typically start stitching from the center of the block outwards and watch as the block magically appears right before your eyes. It's one of my favorite techniques and easy to get hooked on!

A great benefit of working with foundation piecing is that you can make some teensy-weensy little blocks! You may even want to try using this technique to make a small wall hanging or a pieced bookmark.

What is foundation piecing?

In foundation piecing, you work with snippets of fabric that are slightly larger than you need and sew them *backward*s on a foundation of lightweight paper printed with the desired block design. Hence the "foundation" aspect of this technique — the paper is the foundation of the design (and you remove it after piecing is complete).

Patterns for foundation piecing are very simple to use. Foundation blocks are always numbered to indicate the order in which you stitch the pieces to the paper. Usually, the starting point is somewhere near the center of the block and you work outwards, adding fabric bits as you stitch to complete the design. Figure 9-8 shows a typical foundation block before piecing and a completed block. Notice that the finished block is facing the opposite direction as the pattern. That's because you stitch from the wrong side of the block rather than the front.

Foundation piecing differs from another well-loved quilt-making technique called *paper piecing* or *English paper piecing*. With paper piecing, you cut separate templates for each individual piece of a block or design. Then you wrap fabric around the paper template and sew the templates together along the folded fabric edge to make some very complex designs, such as hexagons and miniature blocks. For visual explanations of these different piecing techniques, visit www.museum.state.il.us/muslink/art/htmls/ks_tech.html.

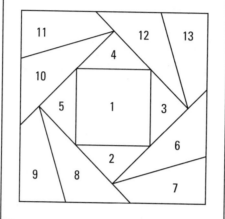
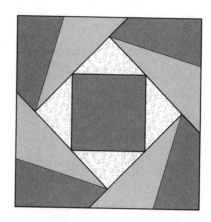

Figure 9-8:
A pattern for a foundation-pieced block and the completed block.

Putting fabric to paper

After you've chosen or designed your foundation piecing block, it's time to have some fun. Really, the stitching is the best part!

You need one printed block pattern for each quilt square you plan to make. For smaller block patterns, you can often fit several patterns on a page for printing or copying. Larger patterns may only fit one or two per page.

When copying or printing patterns for foundation piecing, use the cheapest paper you can find (cheap computer paper works best). The thinner the paper, the easier it is to stitch and see through.

The following steps explain how to start stitching a foundation pieced block. Refer to Figure 9-9 as needed.

1. **Lay out the paper pattern for one block.**

2. **Starting with the part of the pattern that's labeled number 1, cut a piece of the desired fabric slightly larger than the area you're filling.**

3. **With the right side of the fabric facing out, pin the fabric piece to the number 1 spot on the unmarked side of the paper.**

4. **Cut a piece of fabric slightly larger than area number 2, and pin it to the paper, overlapping the first piece and making sure that the right sides of the two fabrics are facing each other.**

5. **With the marked side of the paper facing up, stitch along the line on the paper where the two pieces meet.**

6. **Trim the excess fabric to within ¼ inch of the stitching line, remove the pins, and press open the newly pieced fabric**

Repeat the process until you've stitched together all the pieces of the block. The outermost pieces of fabric should extend beyond the final cutting line (the outermost edge of the pattern). To finish the block, trim away the excess fabric to the seam allowances indicated by the outermost pattern lines.

Wasn't that *fun?* I bet you'll be making more of these! (When you get comfortable with the process, consider trying the Chicken Scratch Foundation-Pieced Quilt project in Chapter 15.)

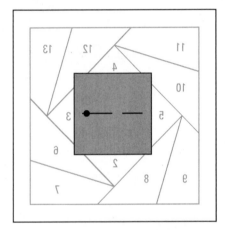

Piece one on backside of paper pattern

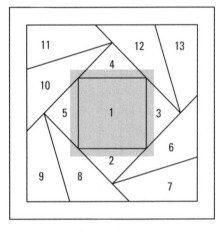

The view from the "stitching side"

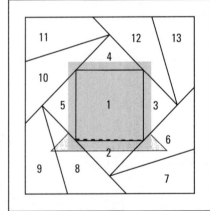

Figure 9-9: Adding pieces to the foundation pattern.

Place piece 2 against piece 1, right sides facing (from the "stitching side")
Stitch along the seam line between pieces 1 and 2

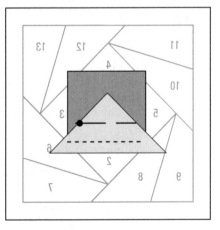

The view from the back side

Chapter 10

Do You Know the Way to Appliqué?

*T*he term *appliqué* is French (oui!) and means "to apply," which is basically what you do to appliqué a quilt: You apply bits of fabric to other fabric. Unlike patchwork, in which the pieces are cut and stitched together, appliqué calls for layering pieces one upon the other on a base or background fabric. The layers are stitched in place by hand or machine. Appliqué pieces can be any shape, giving you the freedom to use curved designs that are impossible to create with traditional patchwork methods.

In this chapter, I introduce you to the basic types of appliqué — with or without seam allowances — as well as the different methods for executing appliqué — by hand or by using a sewing machine. The methods and techniques I cover are by no means your only options; there are as many different ways of doing appliqué as there are quilters.

Appliqué: Stylistic Versatility

The versatility of appliqué enables you, the quilt maker, to consider an infinite number of design possibilities! Appliqué styles can range from traditional and folksy (see the sidebar "Spotlight on a classic American appliqué design") to contemporary or even avant-garde depending on your skills and preferences. You can also combine appliqué techniques with patchwork to create intricate blocks and use the techniques to add interest to other designs.

Spotlight on a classic American appliqué design

One of the most well-known forms of hand appliqué is the *Baltimore Album style,* which reached its greatest popularity in 19th-century Baltimore, Maryland. This style of appliqué is done in traditional shades of red and green fabric appliqués on a white background. What gives this design an album feel is the fact that each block features a different motif and is usually done by a different person. This style of appliqué has been enjoying a revival in recent years.

Consider yourself warned, however, that this style isn't really suitable for the beginning quilter because of the dozens of tiny appliqué pieces it features. Sure, it looks absolutely gorgeous, but some appliqué experience is a necessity! If you want to tackle an album-style appliqué design, practice on projects with either larger or fewer pieces and build your skills.

When creating an appliquéd quilt, you can choose from a number of different appliqué methods that vary in their levels of preparation and difficulty. I stick with the most basic methods here — such as using freezer paper to help you turn under seam allowances and fusible webbing to make everything much easier — to give you a good foundation for developing your appliqué skills.

If you're working on an appliqué project that calls for a method you're unfamiliar with, don't hesitate to substitute any of the appliqué methods in this chapter for what's listed in your project instructions. With appliqué, there are many different ways to get the job done, and there's nothing wrong with switching to an appliqué technique you enjoy or are most comfortable with.

When you feel ready to move on to projects and methods that are more difficult than what I cover in this book, turn to any of a number of books specifically devoted to appliqué to guide you through the more advanced techniques. You may even decide to take a class and discover new methods of appliqué in a hands-on setting.

Appliqué Basics for Hand and Machine

The appliqué fence is home to two birds: Hand appliqué and machine appliqué. With hand appliqué techniques, you stitch pieces of fabric, usually with turned-under seam allowances, to their background fabric by hand using a variety of stitches ranging from invisible to decorative. Machine appliqué techniques may also require the turning-under of seam allowances, but in most cases, you forgo seam allowances altogether and use satin stitch machine stitching or other decorative machine stitching to enclose the raw edges of the appliqué.

Whether you decide to go with hand or machine appliqué, the following advice applies to both:

- ✔ **First and foremost, you must select materials that are suitable for your project.** Because appliqué consists of layers of fabric — as many you like, really — you don't want to use any heavyweight fabrics. The heavier the fabrics, the harder it is to stitch through them and the heavier the final quilt is. Stick to the fabrics that are most suitable for other quilt-making techniques, such as quilter's cottons or other lighter-weight fabrics (see Chapter 2 for details). You can add a bit of specialty fabrics if you like, such as gold or silver lamé, but make sure they, too, are lightweight and can be laundered in the same manner as the other fabrics in your project.

- ✔ **Before stitching any shapes to your background fabric, mark the background fabric to make sure you place your appliqués exactly where you want them.** To mark your background fabric, place the fabric over the appliqué pattern, and trace the pattern lightly with a water-soluble pencil or tailor's chalk. These tracing lines will disappear when you wash the project later.

- ✔ **Before cutting any fabrics, figure out exactly how you're going to appliqué your pieces.** Do you want to do traditional hand appliqué with turned-under seam allowances? If so, you need to add seam allowances to appliqué patterns that don't already include them before you make your first cut. If you want to use fusible webbing and machine appliqué your pieces, you don't need to add any seam allowances.

Doing Seams: Appliqués with Seam Allowances

Using appliqués with seam allowances gives your quilt a very polished, traditional look because the seam allowances are turned under and are hidden away beneath the appliqué itself. The appliqués seem to float on the background fabric because the stitches that hold them in place are hidden as well. This type of appliqué requires more time to produce than fusible webbing appliqué (see "Look, Ma, No Seam Allowances! Fusible Machine Appliqué" later in the chapter), but the results can be breathtaking!

In this type of appliqué, the seam allowances are ¼ inch, just like every other standard seam allowance in quilting. (You may notice that some quilting books call for a mere ⅛-inch seam allowance. Don't worry about that right now; build your skills before you stitch appliqués with narrower seam allowances.) To make an appliqué with a turned-under seam allowance, trace your appliqué template onto the fabric of your choice. If the template includes seam allowances, cut out the shape along your marked line. If it doesn't have a seam allowance, cut out the shape ¼ inch from your marked line.

TIP

You can tell if your template includes seam allowances simply by looking at it (check out Figure 10-1). One solid line around the outside means no seam allowance has been accounted for. A solid outside line with a dashed inside line indicates that the seam allowance is included in the template.

Figure 10-1: The template on the left includes a ¼-inch seam allowance; the one on the right does not.

Turning under the seam allowance

After tracing and cutting out appliqué shapes, you need to turn under the seam allowance using one of the following methods:

- ✔ Turn-and-baste appliqué
- ✔ Freezer-paper appliqué
- ✔ Glue-stick appliqué

REMEMBER

No matter what method you use, when turning under a seam allowance around a curve, you need to cut slits in the seam allowance to make it lie flat. Be sure not to cut beyond ¼ inch, and make your slits approximately ¼ inch apart. For inverted points, notch out the point itself so that you can fold up either side without the added bulk. When turning under the seam allowance at a corner, turn up the point first and then turn up the seam allowances on either side of the point. Figure 10-2 illustrates the slits required around the curves and inverted point of a heart shape as well as the fold necessary to create a clean corner.

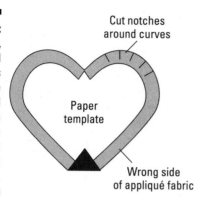

Figure 10-2:
Curves, points, and corners require special attention when you're working with seam allowances.

Cut notches around curves

Paper template

Wrong side of appliqué fabric

Turn-and-baste appliqué

Turn-and-baste appliqué is very time-consuming but gives good results. After tracing and cutting your appliqué shape with seam allowances,

1. **Clip into the appliqué's seam allowance around any curves or inverted points.**

2. **Turn the seam allowance to the wrong side of the appliqué.**

3. **Secure the seam-allowance folds by basting them in place by hand.**

    To baste the seam allowance, follow these two simple steps:

    1. Thread a needle (any kind) with a length of all-purpose thread (any color).

    2. Stitch around the appliqué shape ⅛ inch from the folded edges in a running stitch, which you can see in Figure 10-3.

After you baste the seam allowance around all the edges, the shape is ready to be appliquéd.

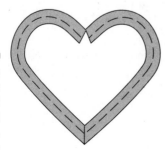

Figure 10-3:
A fully basted appliqué piece.

Freezer-paper appliqué

Freezer-paper appliqué is my favorite technique for appliqués with seam allowances, which explains why it's the method you're instructed to use for several of the projects in this book. In my humble opinion, freezer-paper appliqué, sometimes known as *English paper appliqué,* is the best method to use when preparing your pieces for machine or hand appliqué because you gather the seam allowance of your appliqué around an inside shape, giving you smooth, accurate results with very little fuss.

You can purchase freezer paper at any grocery store; it's usually located on the same aisle as aluminum foil and plastic wrap. Be sure to purchase freezer paper that has wax on one side and plain paper on the other. The wax on the freezer paper is what makes this technique work. ***Note:*** Don't confuse freezer paper with waxed paper. Freezer paper really is paper — it's heavy, white, and has a light wax coating on only one side, whereas waxed paper is transparent and heavily waxed on both sides, making it unsuitable for this technique.

To use the freezer-paper appliqué technique, follow these steps:

1. **Cut out your appliqué with seam allowances included, as you would for turn-and-baste appliqué (see the preceding section).**

2. **Trace your appliqué pattern *without* seam allowances on the wax-free side of the freezer paper, and cut out the shape.**

3. **Center the freezer paper shape on the wrong side of the fabric appliqué shape, placing the waxy coating toward the fabric (see Figure 10-4a). With an iron preheated to the cotton setting, press the freezer paper shape to the appliqué fabric.**

   You only need to press long enough to melt the wax (don't worry, you won't harm the fabric in any way).

4. **Clip the curves and points of your seam allowance as you would for turn-and-baste appliqué.**

5. **With a hand-sewing needle and thread that matches the appliqué fabric, sew a running stitch around the seam allowance, pulling the thread slightly to gather the seam allowance around the freezer paper shape (see Figure 10-4b). Knot your thread at the end so the gathering stitches don't slip.**

   Figure 10-4c shows how it should look when you've finished sewing.

6. **Press the appliqué with the freezer paper still inside.**

The shape is now ready to be appliquéd.

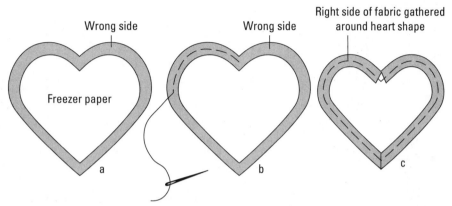

Figure 10-4:
Gathering
the seam
allowance
around a
paper
template
makes
turning
under seam
allowances
easy.

Glue-stick appliqué

Glue-stick appliqué is similar to the freezer-paper method in that it uses a form to provide shape. However, instead of freezer paper, you use plain white paper (copier paper or computer paper works great) and use a glue stick to secure the seam allowances directly to the paper.

Quilting and sewing supply stores sell glue sticks made for use on fabrics, but the glue sticks you find in any office supply store work just as well. My favorite is the UHU stick. It always gives me great results and washes out of my fabrics thoroughly. (If the end of your glue stick feels a bit dry, cut off about ¼ inch of the glue with a knife and start fresh.)

To use the glue stick appliqué technique, follow these steps:

1. **Cut out your fabric appliqué with seam allowances included. Clip the seam allowance to accommodate any curves and points.**

2. **Trace your appliqué pattern *without* seam allowances onto a sheet of plain paper, and cut out the shape.**

3. **Place a small amount of glue on the center of the back side of the paper shape, and press the paper shape to the wrong side of the appliqué fabric.**

   The glue holds the paper in place on the fabric as you fold over the seam allowance.

4. **Working in increments of ½- to 1-inch, apply a line of glue around the edge of the paper shape (see Figure 10-5) and immediately press the seam allowance onto the glue. Hold the fabric in place for a moment until it stays of its own accord.**

Figure 10-5:
Using a glue stick to secure the seam allowance saves time and sore fingertips.

5. **Continue adding glue to the edges of the paper and folding in the seam allowance until all the fabric is glued down.**

The shape is now ready to be appliquéd.

Hand stitching the appliqués

After you prepare your appliqué pieces, hand stitching is one option for attaching them to the background fabric. Simply follow these steps:

1. **Arrange your prepared appliqué pieces on the background fabric.**

2. **Pin, baste, or glue them in place to keep them from falling off or shifting as you work.**

   If your design involves layering appliqués on top of one another, work from the ground up: Secure the first layer of pieces that go directly on the background fabric, and then start applying the pieces that overlap your first layer, then your second layer, and so on (see Figure 10-6). Because they're only held in place at this point, you can remove overlapping pieces temporarily to secure or adjust the ones underneath — just be sure to put them back in the proper places.

3. **Thread a needle (either a sharp or a between; see Chapter 2 for details) with thread to match the color of the first appliqué.**

4. **Using the appliqué stitch, which leaves nearly invisible stitches, stitch the edges of the appliqué to the background fabric. Secure your stitches with a hidden knot when you're finished.**

   See the sidebar "Mastering the appliqué stitch" later in this chapter for instructions on executing the appliqué stitch.

5. **If you're using the turn-and-baste method, remove the basting stitches after you stitch around the appliqué.**

Figure 10-6:
When dealing with overlapping appliqué pieces, start with those closest to the background fabric and build your design from there.

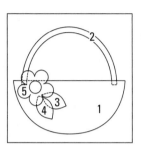

6. **If you're using the freezer-paper or glue-stick method,**

    1. Stitch around the shape, stopping within ¾ inch of your starting point.

    2. Using tweezers or your fingers, pull the paper out through the opening. The freezer paper should peel off the fabric very easily; the glued paper may need a spritz of water to soften the glue before removal.

    3. After removing the paper, finish your appliqué stitching. Secure your stitches with a hidden knot when you're finished.

If you have many appliqués overlapping one another, reduce some of the bulk before attempting to quilt it later! Flip over your piece so that you're looking at the wrong side of the background fabric, and trim away the background fabric ¼ inch from the appliqué stitching, as shown in Figure 10-7. (You can use this bulk-eliminating technique with both hand- and machine-stitched appliqués.)

Figure 10-7:
Eliminate bulk by removing some of the background fabric from underneath your appliqué pieces.

Mastering the appliqué stitch

To work the appliqué stitch,

1. **Bring your needle up from the back side of the background fabric to the top side of the appliqué, just *barely* grabbing the edge of the appliqué.**

2. **Insert your needle back into the background fabric, just off the edge of the appliqué, to make a stitch.**

   You will barely see this stitch if it's close to the edge of the appliqué (like ⅟₃₂-inch close!).

3. **Bring your needle back up to the top side of the quilt ³⁄₃₂-inch further along the edge of the appliqué.**

4. **Repeat Steps 2 and 3 around the entire appliqué shape.**

You'll notice that you have some diagonal-looking stitches on the wrong side of the block (just like in Figure 10-7, where you see the back side of an appliqué). These stitches are unavoidable and mean that you're doing the appliqué stitch exactly right!

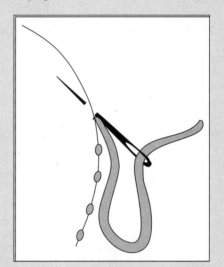

Machine stitching the appliqués

If you would rather not hand stitch your appliqués, you can turn to your trusty sewing machine. To machine appliqué the pieces in place on the background fabric, follow these steps:

1. **Arrange the pieces on the background fabric, and pin or baste them in place as you would if you were planning to hand stitch them (see the preceding section).**

   Basting is the better choice because you can sew right over the stitches. In contrast, it's easy to get your presser foot or sewing thread hung-up on pins.

2. **Cut a piece of tear-away stabilizer to fit the appliqué area, and pin it in place on the wrong side of the background fabric.**

   Stabilizer is essential to proper machine appliqué because it adds support to the fabric, preventing it from being shoved through the hole in the machine's throat plate while stitching. Be sure to use the stabilizer for all methods of machine appliqué, whether your pieces have seam allowances or not. For more about stabilizer, see the sidebar, "Stabilizer: How stable is it if you can tear it away?."

3. **Stitch around the edges of the appliqué pieces using either stitch type described in the sections that follow.**

Invisible machine appliqué

Invisible machine appliqué, also known as *blind-stitch appliqué,* mimics the look of hand appliqué in that the stitches are virtually invisible — unless you're looking awfully hard for them. However, it takes a fraction of the time to execute.

To use invisible machine appliqué,

1. **Thread the top of your machine with nylon monofilament.**

   You can find this thread at any sewing, quilting, or fabric store. Use clear monofilament for stitching over light- to medium-colored fabrics; use the smoky-colored monofilament for stitching over darker fabrics.

   Don't substitute fishing line for monofilament even though it's similar and you think it could suffice! Fishing line is much heavier than monofilment made for sewing and could damage your machine.

2. **Load your bobbin with a neutral color of thread, preferably one that matches your background fabric.**

3. **Set your machine to the blind-stitch (refer to your sewing machine owner's manual for instructions on setting a stitch).**

   You can see the blind-stitch in Figure 10-8; it consists of a length of straight stitches followed by an inward zigzag.

Stabilizer: How stable is it if you can tear it away?

A *stabilizer* is a nonwoven product made from polyester that's used to support the project as you stitch. The stabilizer holds the project above the sewing machine's feed dogs (the teeth that pull the fabric through the machine as the presser foot sews), preventing the material from being crammed through the machine's throat plate hole while you sew.

You can purchase stabilizer at any fabric store. Different types are available for different uses, but all the references in this book are for *tear-away stabilizer.* When you go stabilizer shopping, look for brands such as Tear-Away or Stitch and Tear; be careful not to confuse tear-away stabilizers with those that need to be washed out or cut away after you finish stitching the appliqué.

Figure 10-8:
The blind-
stitch.

Figure 10-8:
The blind-
stitch.

4. **Change your machine's foot to one with an "open toe" (again, refer to your manual for instructions on changing the foot).**

   An open-toe foot allows you to see where you're going much better than a standard foot, which is closed at the front.

5. **Carefully stitch around each of the appliqué shapes, with the straight stitch running only in the background fabric, just outside the edge of the appliqué piece. The zigzag stitch should pick up the appliqué, as shown in Figure 10-9.**

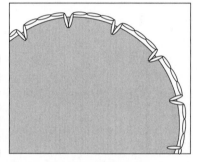

Figure 10-9:
Blind-
stitching an
appliqué in
place.

Straight-stitch appliqué

Straight-stitch appliqué, also known as *topstitch appliqué,* is exactly as it sounds: You stitch around the appliqué using the machine's most basic stitch. The only trick is that you must try to stitch as close to the edge as you're comfortable with so that the edges of your appliqués are secured and not left flapping in the breeze (see Figure 10-10).

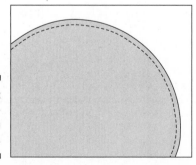

Figure 10-10:
Straight-
stitch
appliqué.

The distance between your stitching line and the edge of the appliqué piece depends on your skill level and your bravery quotient. For some folks, ⅛ inch from the edge is as good as it gets. Experienced sewers often topstitch so close to the edge that it's difficult to see if the stitches are on the appliqué at all!

Decorative machine stitches

Decorative machine stitches with a loose, open design, such as those in Figure 10-11, are best suited to appliqués with turned-under seam allowances because you have a clean edge to work with. (If you use these looser stitches on appliqués that don't have seam allowances (see the next section), you may wind up with frayed fabric edges poking through your beautiful stitching!)

Figure 10-11:
Your machine's loose, decorative stitches work best on appliqués with seam allowances.

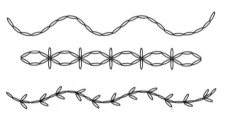

Look, Ma, No Seam Allowances! Fusible Machine Appliqué

Appliqué without seam allowances basically falls under the domain of *fusible machine appliqué.* Why? Because sewing machine stitches and fusible webbing are the best tools for keeping the edges from fraying on appliqués that don't have turned-under seam allowances. And preventing fraying is important if you expect your quilt to be used, loved, and laundered.

Another interesting product available for machine appliqué is the *pressing sheet,* which is easy to use and allows for very accurate appliqué layouts. Instead of fusing the pieces to background fabric, you fuse the pieces to the pressing sheet by laying the transparent pressing sheet over your pattern and ironing it. When all the pieces are in place, you lift the entire appliqué off the pressing sheet (they aren't permanently fused to this special sheet), place the whole appliqué onto the background fabric, and fuse it in place as one unit. Best of all, you can reuse the pressing sheet over and over again.

Buying fusible transfer webbing

For fusible machine appliqué, you need to purchase *fusible transfer webbing*. The instructions in this book call for fusible webbing that has a paper backing on one side. This webbing is made by several different manufacturers and even comes in different weights — standard, lightweight, and heavy-duty.

For machine appliqué quilting, stick to the standard weight fusible webbing. It's an all-purpose weight and is ideal for any fabrics you may be using. (The lightweight variety is meant for sheer, lightweight fabrics and has considerable flexibility. The heavy-duty weight is a bit stiff and is best suited to heavier fabrics, such as denim or canvas.)

Webbing products are normally found in the section of the store containing interfacing. Fusible webbing usually is sold by-the-yard or prepackaged in varying sizes. (I prefer to buy it by the yard.) Some fusible webbing brand names include WonderUnder, Stitch Witchery, HeatnBond, and Trans-Web. Any brand will suffice. When in doubt, ask store personnel for advice — that's what they're there for.

Don't prewash fusible webbing (unless you want to ruin it), and when storing, don't fold it! Folding can sometimes cause the webbing material to separate from the paper backing, rendering it almost useless. Instead, roll the webbing up with the instruction insert it came with and secure it with a rubber band.

Preparing for machine appliqué

When using fusible webbing for seam allowance–less machine appliqué, you need to prepare your pattern template differently than you would for hand appliqué work. Follow the instructions in this section carefully, or you'll find yourself with everything facing the wrong direction.

Because it looks very different — and very wrong — when reversed, I use the letter "Q" as an appliqué shape example throughout the figures in this section. To create an appliqué shape with fusible webbing attached, follow these instructions:

1. **Trace the appliqué pattern onto tracing paper. Mark the side with the traced shape "RS" (right side). Turn the paper over, and mark the other side "WS" (wrong side), as shown in Figure 10-12.**

   I know seeing writing on the opposite side of the paper backward is annoying, but you'll get used to it.

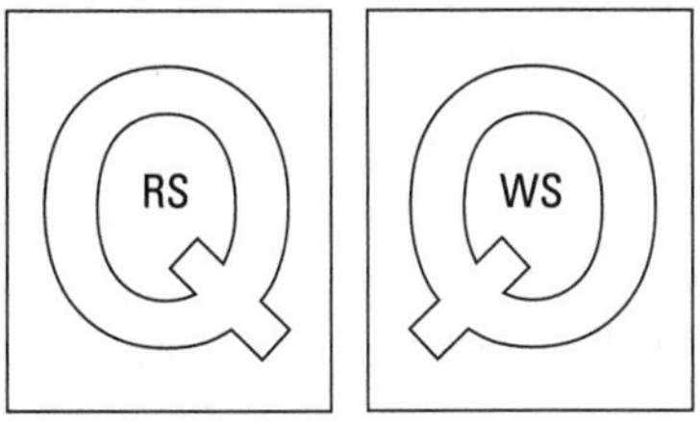

Figure 10-12:
The figure
on the left
shows the
pattern
before its
flipped, and
the figure on
the left is
the flipped
appliqué
pattern with
the shape
facing the
opposite
direction.

2. **Place the traced pattern on your work surface RS down (or WS up depending on which way you look at the world). Tape the paper down to your work surface along the top and bottom edges.**

3. **Place your fusible webbing over the pattern with the paper side up (facing you). See Figure 10-13.**

   The webbing is nearly transparent, so you can easily see the pattern through it.

Figure 10-13:
The pattern,
visible
through the
webbing, is
ready to be
traced.

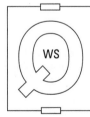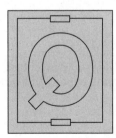

4. **With a regular pencil, trace the pattern onto the paper side of the fusible webbing.**

5. **Cut out the shape roughly, as shown in Figure 10-14.**

   At this point, cutting shapes perfectly along the lines is just a waste of time because you cut out the shapes neatly after fusing them to the fabrics.

Figure 10-14:
Neatness isn't important when you cut the shape from the webbing.

6. **Lay your appliqué fabric right side down on an ironing board or iron-safe work surface. Position the fusible webbing shape on the wrong side of the appliqué fabric, having the webbing (rough) side toward the fabric and the paper facing upward, toward you.**

7. **Use a hot iron to fuse the shape to the appliqué fabric.**

   For iron settings, refer to the manufacturer's insert that accompanies the webbing you're using.

8. **Cut out the shape neatly.**

   Don't worry; the image is supposed to be reversed.

9. **Remove the paper backing from the appliqué by peeling it away, exposing the adhesive that has been fused to the wrong side of the fabric.**

10. **Place the appliqué glue side down on the background fabric.**

    Tada! Your shape is now facing the right direction!

11. **Following the webbing manufacturer's directions, use a hot iron to fuse the appliqué to the background fabric (see Figure 10-15). Use an up-and-down pressing motion instead of sliding the iron, which could cause your appliqué to shift.**

    The hot iron melts the glue on the webbing and adheres it to the background fabric, holding the appliqué in place for you. No pins required!

Figure 10-15:
Fusing the appliqué to the background fabric.

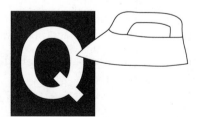

12. **Cut a piece of tear-away stabilizer the same size as the background fabric, and pin the stabilizer to the wrong side of the background fabric at the corners.**

    For information about this stabilizer, check out the sidebar "Stabilizer: How stable is it if you can tear it away?" earlier in this chapter.

With your appliqué firmly attached to the background fabric, it's ready to be finished using one of the machine-appliqué stitches described in the following section.

Stitching it all in place

After you fuse your appliqués to the background fabric (see the preceding section), it's time to take them to the machine and stitch everything in place. You have a number of different machine stitching options at this point, depending on the look you want to achieve. Do you want a sleek, smooth look? If so, satin stitch is the way to go. Prefer something a little more casual or rustic? Try zigzag appliqué (see the sidebar "Loosen up with zigzag appliqué") or blanket stitch. You can even peruse your machine's owner's manual for preprogrammed decorative stitches.

Satin stitch

Everybody loves *satin stitch!* It looks gorgeous and can be stitched in different widths depending on preference. This stitch is composed of zigzag stitches spaced very close together — so close that you're unable to see the fabric through the thread. Completely enclosing the raw edges of the appliqué under a barrier of thread make the appliqué very durable.

Satin stitching requires your machine to be in good working condition. To set your machine for satin stitching, refer to the owner's manual. Beginners should start with a stitch width of ⅛ to ¼ inch. Anything narrower can be a bit difficult to handle and requires more experience. The knob for *stitch width* controls the width of the satin stitch, and the knob for *stitch length* controls the density of the satin stitch (how closely spaced the stitches are).

Before you tackle satin stitching around your quilt appliqués, test sew a line of satin stitching on a scrap of fabric with another scrap of fabric fused to the center of it. This test allows you to make sure that your stitch width and density is just right and gives you a chance to practice your technique if necessary. To test your satin stitch settings:

1. **Load the top of the machine with a dark color thread.**

2. **Wind a lighter color thread in the bobbin.**

3. **Change your machine's presser foot to one with an open toe.**

   An open-toe foot differs from a closed-toe foot in that the front area of the foot is cut away (see Figure 10-16). Using an open-toe foot allows you to see where you're stitching much better than a closed-toe foot.

4. **Using scrap fabric, sew around your test shape.**

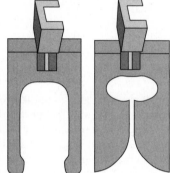

Figure 10-16:
Open-toe foot on left, closed-toe on right.

When you're done with your test, examine the satin stitching on your scrap fabric, and ask yourself the following questions:

✔ **Is the stitching nice and even? Do the stitches cover the edges of the appliqués, or are there gaps? Does the stitching need to be denser, or should it be less dense?**

If you can see the edges of the fused fabric through the line of satin stitching, the stitching should be denser, and you need to shorten the length of the stitch. If the satin stitching bunches up on itself, increase the length of the stitch.

✔ **Looking closely at the ridge of satin stitching, can you see any of the light-colored bobbin thread on the surface?**

If the bobbin thread is visible, you need to loosen the upper tension on your machine very slightly. Test sew again, and check the stitch quality for improvement. If you continue to see the bobbin thread, keep loosening the tension in small increments until no bobbin thread appears on the surface. If this adjustment doesn't work, you may need to increase the tension of the bobbin thread (see Chapter 8 for additional instructions on proper tension settings). If nothing works to eliminate visible bobbin thread on the surface of your stitching, have your machine professionally serviced.

When you're satisfied that your satin stitch is perfect, it's time to sew the appliqués in place:

1. **Replace the upper thread with whichever thread you want to be visible on your quilt top. Use a neutral thread in the bobbin.**

2. **Place your project under the open-toe presser foot, and gradually lower the needle, stopping before it enters the fabric.**

3. **As the needle approaches the fabric, note whether the needle is positioned to the left or to the right (because the satin stitch is a zigzag, the needle moves back and forth from left to right).**

   - **If the needle is to the left,** position your project so that the needle enters the appliqué fabric.

   - **If the needle is to the right,** position your fabric so that the needle enters the background fabric.

4. **Stitch around the edges of all appliqués shapes, having the left swing (zig) of the needle in the appliqué and the right swing (zag) in the background fabric.**

Many beginning quilters complain that their satin stitches are bumpy and uneven. Following a few simple instructions can help you avoid these problems. Most important is to use a bit of caution when you approach a corner or curve or when you're stitching along a point. The following list addresses these tricky areas:

✔ **To stitch inside corners,** stitch beyond the corner as far as the stitch is wide, and leave the needle in the fabric at the left-swing position, as indicated by the dot on Figure 10-17. Raise the presser foot, and turn the fabric so that you can stitch along the next side of the corner. Lower the presser foot, and continue stitching. Your stitches should overlap at the corner.

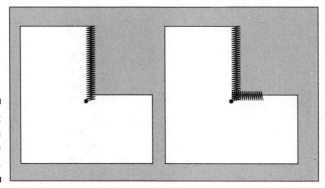

Figure 10-17:
Turning an inside corner.

✔ **To stitch outside corners,** stitch to the end of the appliqué, and leave the needle in the fabric at the right-swing position, as indicated by the dot in Figure 10-18. Raise the presser foot, and turn the fabric so you can stitch along the next side of the corner. Lower the presser foot, and continue stitching. Your stitches should overlap at the corner.

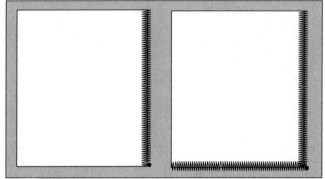

Figure 10-18:
Turning an outside corner.

✔ **To stitch around curves smoothly,** pivot the fabric as you sew. If you're stitching along an inside curve (see Figure 10-19a), leave the needle in the appliqué piece, which should be the left swing of the needle. If you're stitching along an outside curve (see Figure 10-19b), leave the needle in the background fabric, which should be the right swing of the needle. Raise the presser foot, and turn the fabric just slightly so that your stitching will follow the appliqué edge. Lower the presser foot, and continue stitching. Repeat until you've stitched along the entire curve. The number of times you need to pivot depends on the curve: A slight curve needs fewer pivots than a tight one.

Figure 10-19:
Stitching an inside curve (a) and an outside curve (b).

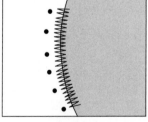 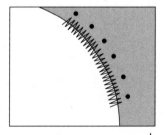

a   b

✔ **To stitch along a sharp point,** gradually decrease the width of the satin stitch as the point narrows, as shown in Figure 10-20. When you reach the point, leave the needle in the fabric, raise the presser foot, and pivot your fabric so that your stitches continue along the opposite side of the point. Increase the stitch width as you move away from the point.

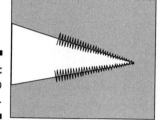

Figure 10-20:
Tapering to
a point.

When you finish satin stitching the appliqués, remove the pins holding the stabilizer in place. Tear the stabilizer from the back side of the project; it should tear away easily. Be sure to remove all the stabilizer because anything left on the back of the block could show on the front side.

Use a tweezers to pull off any small bits of stabilizer that are too tiny to grasp with your fingers.

Machine blanket stitch

The *machine blanket stitch*, also known as the *buttonhole stitch*, closely mocks the hand blanket stitch but is so much quicker! This stitch gives appliqué projects a primitive look that today's quilters love. It's composed of multiple vertical stitches followed by one horizontal stitch. The machine blanket stitch is terrific for rustic or country-style appliqués because it gives the look of a hand stitch without the hassle. (If you want to attempt the machine blanket stitch by hand, check out the sidebar "Blanket stitch on the go.")

Loosen up with zigzag appliqué

Zigzag appliqué is the lazy quilter's version of satin stitch, which I discuss in the "Satin stitch" section. I'm not afraid to admit that I like being lazy at times, so I'm fond of the zigzag appliqué stitch.

Zigzag appliqué tends to have a fun and relaxed look to it, so you can load your machine with whatever thread you choose (all-purpose, monofilament, or buttonhole-twist) in any color you want (matching or clashing with your quilt design). With your threads in place, simply stitch around the edges of the appliqué shape in a loose zigzag.

Note: Blanket stitch can be done in any color thread, but the most commonly used color is black. Therefore, my instructions in this section only refer to black thread. If you choose to use a different color, simply substitute it for the black when you read the following steps. (A real no-brainer tip, eh?)

To blanket stitch your appliqués, follow these steps:

1. **After fusing your appliqués in place and backing them with stabilizer (see "Preparing for machine appliqué" earlier in the chapter), set your machine to the blanket stitch (refer to your owner's manual), and make sure that you have an open-toe presser foot on your machine.**

2. **Load your bobbin with black all-purpose thread. For the top thread, you have two options: all-purpose thread or buttonhole twist (topstitching) thread.**

   Some quilters use the buttonhole twist because they prefer a heavier thread on the edges of their appliqués. Others use all-purpose, which is a bit lighter in appearance. (For a complete rundown of threads, see Chapter 2.)

3. **Test sew the blanket stitch on a piece of scrap fabric to make sure you get a good, solid stitch.**

   If the blanket stitch looks ragged or has skipped stitches, refer to your owner's manual and Chapter 9 for tips on adjusting your machine's tension.

4. **When your stitch looks perfect, stitch around the edges of your appliqués.**

   The straight-stitch edge of the blanket stitch should be *in the ditch,* which means right where the appliqué meets the background fabric. The long "legs" of the stitch should extend into the appliqué itself, as shown in Figure 10-21.

Figure 10-21:
The machine blanket stitch.

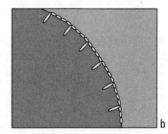

a   b

Turning corners and stitching around points can be a matter of trial and error with this method of appliqué. Try to get one of the blanket stitch "legs" situated in the corner or point, as shown in Figure 10-22. Keep in mind that the blanket stitch is supposed to be a "primitive-looking" type of appliqué, and perfection isn't necessary.

Blanket stitch on the go

After fusing appliqués in place, you may want to forgo the sewing machine and tackle the blanket stitch by hand. The blanket stitch is an easy stitch to do by hand, and because you aren't relying on a sewing machine, you can carry your work with you and make progress as you wait in doctors' offices or at soccer practices.

When blanket stitching by hand, you don't need to use stabilizer — it just gets in your way. Instead of all-purpose or buttonhole twist thread, use black pearl cotton or two strands of embroidery floss in a large-eyed needle to appliqué the pieces in place. These heavy threads give a nice rustic look to your handwork.

To execute the hand-embroidered blanket stitch, follow these instructions:

1. **Bring your needle up through the underside of the foundation fabric along the outside edge of the appliqué piece.**

2. **Insert the needle into the appliqué fabric about ⅛ inch in from the edge of the appliqué and ⅛ inch to the right, at a diagonal from your entry point in Step 1.**

3. **Bring your needle up through the underside of the foundation fabric, at the very edge of the appliqué piece, as in Step 1, but this time, stop the needle partway through and loop the thread behind the needle to catch it in the stitch. Proceed pulling the needle through the top side of the fabric.**

4. **Repeat all the way around the appliqué.**

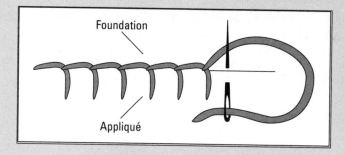

Foundation

Appliqué

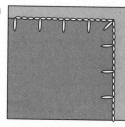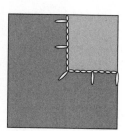

Figure 10-22: Navigating corners and points with the blanket stitch.

When you finish blanket stitching the appliqués in place, remove any pins and tear away the stabilizer.

Decorative machine stitches

Does your machine have tons of neat decorative stitches that you've never used? Here's your chance: Use them for appliqué!

Some of the denser, tighter stitches, such as those shown in Figure 10-23, can be used on fused appliqués. Simply substitute them for the satin stitch or machine blanket stitch that I cover in the preceding sections.

Figure 10-23:
Use your machine's dense, decorative stitches on appliqués made with fusible webbing.

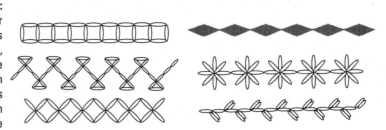

The Scrappy Pines Lap or Nap Quilt project in Chapter 17 is a great opportunity to use decorative stitches.

Don't be afraid to experiment with your machine's stitch repertoire on scraps of fabric, and let your creative juices flow!

Part IV
Ahead to the Finish: Quilting the Pieces in Place

The 5th Wave   By Rich Tennant

"I really wouldn't worry. The person performing your operation is one of the country's finest quilters."

In this part . . .

This part helps you to put the quilt top, batting, and backing together so that all three layers stay put and the quilt looks fantastic. I give you plenty of quilting design ideas to choose from, and I walk you through the steps involved in basting the fabric sandwich in place and binding the edges for a piece you can be proud of. Now's the time to see the quilt you've been picturing in your head take actual shape. Happy quilting!

Chapter 11

The Plan of Attack: Deciding How to Quilt Your Quilt

. . . .

In This Chapter

▶ Deciding on hand or machine quilting

▶ Figuring out the right quilting intervals

▶ Getting creative with stitching patterns

. . . .

*A*fter you cut and stitch the pieces of your quilt top, you're ready to quilt your quilt. "What," you say, "what have I been doing up to now? I thought I was quilting." Well, you're right . . . in a way. You've been piecing and/or appliquéing a quilt, but you don't really have a quilt until you assemble the three sandwich layers into one cozy project, and that's where the real quilting begins.

In this chapter, I guide you through all the ins and outs (a little needle-humor there) of quilting your project, including outline and echo quilting, decorative quilting designs, and how to use quilting templates to really make your project pop.

Machine versus Hand Quilting

As with piecing your quilt, you have the choice of hand stitching or machine stitching in the quilting stage. But before you decide on a method, you need to think about what your project will be used for: Will it get much use and regular washing, such as a baby's bib? Is it for looks rather than function, such as a wall hanging or a holiday vest? Also important to consider is whether you want to finish this project in a hurry or take your sweet time:

> ✔ **Machine quilting is quick — really quick.** However, it can sometimes have a less-than-heirloom look, and your skill level may not allow you to create intricate quilting designs by machine.

> ✔ **Hand quilting is slow — really slow.** But for the beginning quilter, decorative quilting patterns are best worked by hand because you have complete control. Hand quilting is much easier to pick up on than machine quilting.

I'm a machine queen. I prefer to hand quilt only when I'm working on something I consider "heirloom quality," and by that I mean a project I'm going to give to someone as a gift or a quilt I'm making to commemorate a special event. Nothing shows you care quite like something you've put extra time and effort into. Your choice of technique, however, is totally up to you.

Considering Spacing

Although both hand and machine quilting are suitable for any project, the spacing of the quilting isn't always so universal; you need to consider the batting manufacturer's recommended quilting intervals when making your decision to hand or machine quilt. The batting you choose for your project helps you determine how to quilt your quilt.

If you have the opportunity to look closely at antique quilts, you'll notice that the quilting is very closely spaced. This spacing keeps the batting's cotton fibers from migrating into corners and creating lumpy pockets.

Fiber migration is common in most battings — even those that claim it won't be a problem. In reality, any fiber batting can migrate if not quilted and laundered properly. The quilting stitches that you set are what keep the three layers of your quilt functioning together as one unit. The denser the quilting (the closer your stitches are to one another), the better the quilted item performs as a wall hanging, bedcovering, place mat, or whatever you intend.

For example, if you're making a quilted vest that you know you'll love to wear and therefore wash often, space your quilting intervals close together. The more an item is washed, the more you risk having the fibers migrate into pockets, so your close stitching intervals will help hold the batting in place.

Today, you can quilt at wider intervals than quilters past without ending up with a lumpy mess, but you still must keep the manufacturer-recommended intervals in mind when deciding how to quilt your project. Be sure to read batting packages carefully before making a selection that fits your quilting design plan (refer to Chapter 3 for the full scoop on batting).

Choosing a Stitching Pattern

When it comes to choosing quilting-stitch patterns, you have a wide range of options (and you can even invent your own!). In this section, I cover the most popular designs.

Outline quilting to enhance shapes

By far the most popular method of quilting is to enhance the shapes of the patchwork or appliqué with some type of *outline quilting* (see Figure 11-1). Outline quilting can be either:

- **In-the-ditch:** This type of quilting is characterized by stitching very near — almost on top of — the seams in a patchwork block. Its name comes from the fact that the seam areas form a sort of ditch that's very easy to follow.

  In-the-ditch quilting is a good choice for machine quilting but can be difficult to hand stitch because of the multiple layers present in a seam. When hand quilting, do your in-the-ditch stitching on the side of the seam that has the least amount of bulk.

- **Quarter-inch:** This type of quilting is characterized by stitching ¼ inch from the seam line on each piece of your quilt top. This technique is also referred to as *echo quilting* because the stitching echoes the shape of the piece, like ripples on the surface of water. I talk more about echo quilting in the "Free-style fillers" section later in this chapter.

  Quarter-inch quilting is best suited for hand quilting (and especially beginners) because it steers clear of the multiple layers in seam allowances. This type of quilting can be done on a machine but requires a bit of experience to get it right because it's a free-motion stitch, which means that the feed dogs are disengaged and you must guide the quilt by hand.

When outline quilting an appliqué piece, you can space your stitches very close to the shape of the appliqué, much like in-the-ditch quilting. You can then use the filler stitches described in the next section to fill in the outside areas of the block or continue to echo the shape of the appliqué until you fill the entire area.

Filler patterns for quilting large areas

Filler patterns are useful for quilting large areas in which you don't have a particular shape to stitch around. The quilting designs explained in this section are suitable for both hand and machine quilting and are easy to stitch. You can use these patterns on your entire quilt or just in areas where you need to fill a large amount of background. The choice is yours.

Figure 11-1:
Outline
quilting
provides a
bit of texture
without
being too
distracting
to the eye.

Cross-hatch quilting

Cross-hatch quilting, also known as *grid quilting,* is one of the most common and traditional-looking filler options. Cross-hatch quilting is quick and texturally interesting.

To prepare your quilt top for this pattern without marking it with a pen or pencil, you need to first baste the quilt layers together, either with large stitches or safety pins (see Chapter 12 for details on basting). Then follow these steps:

1. **Decide how far apart you want the lines.**

   ½- or 1-inch intervals are the norm no matter what type of batting you use

2. **Visit your local hardware, art supply, or quilting supply store to purchase a roll of masking tape the width you need (if you don't already have some on hand).**

   I'm not kidding; masking tape works beautifully and is so accurate! Plus, one roll lasts a while because you can reuse the strips. Masking tape is available in widths as narrow as ⅛ inch and ¼ inch and goes as wide as ½ inch, 1 inch, 1½ inches, and even 2 inches!

3. **Lay a strip of tape 12 inches or so in length on your basted quilt at a 45-degree angle to the sides of the quilt (see Figure 11-2).**

With your tape in place, you either hand or machine quilt along its edges, and the tape does the spacing for you. You don't need to end your stitching just because you get to the end of the tape; simply lift the tape, move it to the next spot, and continue stitching. You can peel off the masking tape and move it as many times as you need to, but when it starts to lose its stickiness, discard it and tear another strip off the roll.

Figure 11-2:
Cross-hatch
quilting
using
masking
tape as a
guide.

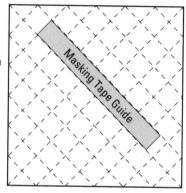 

Diamond quilting

A variation on cross-hatch quilting is *diamond quilting,* which is shown in Figure 11-3. For this quilting style, you stretch your rows so that they intersect at a different angle to create diamonds instead of squares.

Figure 11-3:
Diamond
quilting.

You can create a diamond quilting design using the masking tape method described in the preceding section. Instead of placing the tape at a 45-degree angle to the sides of the quilt, place it at a 30-degree angle.

TIP

Using masking tape to mark your quilting designs opens up a host of options besides cross-hatch and diamond quilting. You can play around with the tape layout to create other fun variations. Use the examples in Figure 11-4 for inspiration!

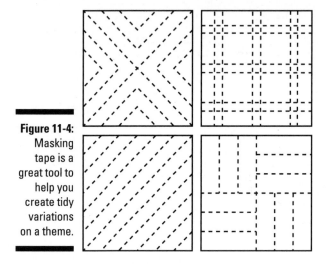

Figure 11-4: Masking tape is a great tool to help you create tidy variations on a theme.

Clamshell quilting

Clamshell quilting is an easy-to-stitch filler that requires premarking before you baste together the layers of your quilt. (See Chapter 12 for basting techniques.)

To mark your quilt top with a clamshell design, follow these steps:

1. **Using a compass, draw a circle on a piece of cardboard and cut it out.**

   Although the circle can be any size, 3 to 4 inches in diameter suits most quilt battings.

2. **Mark a line through the center of the circle across the diameter. Mark another line vertically through the radius only.**

   These lines act as guides when tracing around the template onto your fabric. By lining up the horizontal line each with the halfway mark on each circle and matching the vertical line with the converging point of two half circles, you'll be able to make very accurate clamshells in a straight line. (When in doubt, use a piece of masking tape to mark the horizontal target.)

3. **Trace the top half of the template on the fabric. Work your way across the row, then move down a row and continue tracing, staggering the placement of the template as shown in Figure 11-5a.**

   Clamshells only use half the circle, making them clams on the half shell!

Figure 11-5:
Creating a
clamshell
design using
half a circle
or an
orange peel
design using
the entire
circle.

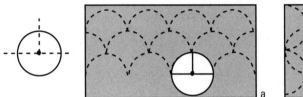
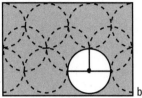

A variation on the clamshell design is called *orange peel quilting.* To create these intersecting circles (see Figure 11-5b), use the same template as for clamshell quilting, but instead of tracing around only the top half of the circle, trace around the entire circle. Stagger each row as you would for the clamshell, using the circle's markings as a guide for positioning the template halfway intersecting the circles of the previous row.

Free-style fillers

Free-style fillers are a bit more complicated than geometric cross-hatch, diamond, and clamshell fillers, but they're well worth the extra effort. Instead of following a specific grid or pattern, you cut loose and do whatever feels good! Although free-style fillers take a bit of time to master, you're beautifully rewarded for your efforts and dedication!

Two of the most popular free-style fillers are:

- **Echo quilting,** which consists of multiple lines of quilting stitches that run parallel to the edges of any shape, echoing the shape. This type of quilting is rarely premarked, so you need a bit of practice to get your lines evenly spaced in ¼-inch intervals. You can premark the lines if you wish, but it takes quite a bit of time and really isn't necessary. If the lines aren't perfectly spaced at ¼ inch, you really won't notice because the overall effect is quite casual and relaxed. (For more on echo quilting, see the section "Outline quilting to enhance shapes" earlier in this chapter.)

- **Stipple quilting,** which is characterized by a wandering line that wiggles and winds back on itself. Stipple quilting, which you can see in Figure 11-6, takes some time to master by hand, but it's a breeze to do on the machine. Because of the concentrated stitches, this style of quilting essentially flattens areas where it's used. Stipple quilting is most commonly used in appliqué blocks because this flattening effect enables the appliqués to stand out nicely, giving them a puffy look.

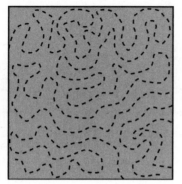

Figure 11-6:
Stipple quilting creates a strong texture.

Decorative quilting patterns and stencils

For intricate and artistic quilting options, consider using decorative quilting patterns and stencils. You can find decorative patterns in books specializing in quilting designs, and you can pick up precut stencils at quilting and fabric shops. Decorative quilting patterns and stencils are available in many designs — florals, geometrics, meandering vines, feathers, and more — in both traditional and contemporary styles.

Decorative quilting patterns and stencils come in two types: those used in blocks and those intended for borders (see Figure 11-7). Patterns and stencils are often available in matched sets so you can create a coordinated look.

Figure 11-7:
Decorative patterns and stencils intended for blocks and borders.

To mark your quilt top with a decorative quilting design from a book, you need to trace the design onto a piece of paper and then transfer the design to your fabric. To transfer a design, you may be able to trace it directly onto the fabric or you may need to use a light box or carbon paper. (For guidance on these methods, see Chapter 12.)

Quilting stencils aren't the same stencils sold for painting decorative borders on your walls; quilting stencils are specially cut templates intended for quilting. They have narrow slits cut into them so that you can trace the design onto your quilt top by running your marking pencil through the slits to mark the lines, as shown in Figure 11-8.

Figure 11-8:
Tracing a
stencil
design onto
your quilt
top.

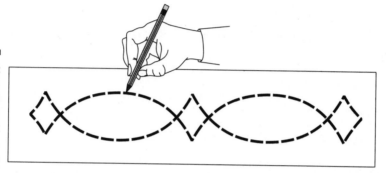

Chapter 12

Assembling the Quilt Sandwich

In This Chapter

▶ Marking your quilting design

▶ Layering your quilt

▶ Handling bed-size quilts

Good going, quilter! With a completed quilt top, you're ready to layer it with batting and backing fabric to assemble your sandwich and prepare it for quilting. A finished quilt is finally visible on the horizon!

Keep in mind that before you can assemble the sandwich, you have to answer the following questions:

▶ **How do you want to quilt your quilt?** You want a sturdy and decorative stitch pattern for your quilt top and back, but you have a lot of options. You may have already chosen a nice design such as a floral border or a geometric block design. If not, refer to Chapter 11 for inspiration and advice about settling on a design.

▶ **Are you quilting by hand or by machine?** Each option has its advantages and disadvantages. See Chapter 11 for issues to consider when making this decision, including the size of your project.

Some designs need to be marked on a quilt top before assembly, so in this chapter, I explain how to do this marking. Then I walk you through the steps of assembling the layers of the quilt and basting them together so that nothing shifts during quilting and handling.

Marking Your Quilting Stitch Designs

Transferring your quilting designs to your quilt top isn't as difficult as it sounds, and you have a number of options for getting your chosen designs onto the quilt and ready to go. For the sake of simplicity, in this section I cover the most common techniques.

If you're planning to stitch (this is the REAL *quilting!*) a decorative motif or border, always mark the quilting design on your quilt top before you assemble the quilt sandwich. After the sandwich is assembled, adding designs is a lot trickier due to the bulk of it all. And be sure that you use only a water-soluble marking pencil or chalk when marking the design. Always test your marking pencil to make certain it will wash out, regardless of color or what the package says.

I recommend marking your entire quilt top before layering the quilt sandwich. To mark your quilting stitches, you can

✔ **Trace the design.** If your fabric is light in color and the design has nice dark lines, you may be able to transfer the design directly from its source by laying the fabric on the design and tracing it.

✔ **Use a light box.** Tape the design to a light box, and then place the quilt top over the design. To hold the quilt top in place while you trace, either tape it or hold it if you can.

✔ **Use dressmakers' carbon paper.** This type of carbon paper comes in many colors to a package. To mark your quilt top, select the lightest color that shows up on your fabric. To transfer the design, pin the dressmakers' carbon facedown over your quilt. Center the design to be quilted over the carbon, and transfer it to the quilt top by tracing over the design with a regular pencil, peeking a bit along the way to make sure it transfers properly.

Before you use carbon paper to mark up your whole quilt top, test it on a scrap of fabric to be absolutely certain it will wash out of your finished quilt. Also, stay away from heat transfer paper, which becomes permanent as soon as you iron the design on the fabric!

✔ **Make a template.** If you're using a simple design such as a heart or leaf and only want to outline the shape, cut the design from lightweight cardboard or heavy paper (an old file folder works great). Place the cutout on your quilt top, and hold it in place with one hand while tracing around it with the other. Trace designs from purchased quilting templates in the same manner.

If you plan on quilting along seam lines, around the shapes in your quilt top, or in a grid pattern, marking your quilting lines isn't necessary because you can simply following the seam or shape or use masking tape as a grid line guide (check out Chapters 11 and 13 for more discussion of these designs and techniques.)

Pulling Together Top, Batt, and Back Layers

When you finish marking your quilting designs, you're ready to layer the quilt top with the batting and backing to create your quilt sandwich. Yum! After layering comes basting, which holds all the layers together while you quilt.

Assembling the quilt layers

To assemble the three layers of your quilt, follow these steps:

1. **Lay out your backing fabric on a flat work surface so that the wrong side of the fabric is facing you.**

   Your flat work surface can be a table (just be sure to protect the surface of a wooden table before you start pinning) or the floor (see the section "Taming the Bed-size Beast" later in this chapter).

2. **Center the quilt batting over the backing fabric.**

3. **Carefully center the quilt top over the batting.**

Basting the layers together

With your layers laid out neatly, it's time to *baste*. Basting is simply using some method hold the layers together. Depending on the size of your project and the method by which you plan to quilt (hand or machine), you can choose from either *thread basting* or *pin basting,* both of which I explain in this section. (When you finish basting, the sandwich is ready for you to quilt by hand or machine. In Chapter 13, I present tips to help you successfully navigate the final quilting process.)

Thread basting

Thread basting involves large, loose stitches. After your quilting is complete, you remove the basting stitches, so don't worry about what they look like. This method is best used when you plan to hand quilt your project because there are no pins to interfere with placing the item in a hoop or quilt stand. To thread baste your quilt, follow these steps:

1. **Thread a large, general-purpose sewing needle with a length of thread (any color is fine) no longer than your arm.**

2. **Put a knot in the far end of the thread.**

3. **Starting at the center of the quilt, insert the needle (either from the front or the back) at an angle through all three layers.**

4. **Pull the first stitch through somewhat, and bring the needle back through the fabric about 1 inch away from where you started.**

5. **Continue basting in this manner, making big running stitches through all three layers of the quilt top.**

6. **When you reach the edge of the quilt, clip your thread and start over at the center of the quilt.**

   Basting outwards from the center keeps the layers nice and flat and helps avoid bunching in the batting and puckering in the backing fabric or quilt top.

When you run out of thread, leave a ½-inch tail and clip it off. (You can use these tails to pull out the basting stitches later.) Then rethread your needle and continue basting.

When you reach the end of a length of thread, cut off the knot at your starting point so you don't stitch over it later. Don't worry about the basting threads working their way out of their stitches — they won't.

Your fully basted quilt should resemble Figure 12-1.

Pin basting

Pin basting uses safety pins, usually nickel-plated ones because they don't rust if they get a bit moist, to hold the quilt layers in place. This is my preferred method of basting for machine quilting because I can remove the pins before they approach the needle, leaving me with nothing that needs pulled out after quilting is finished. Pin basting is best for small- to medium-size projects because the pins add a bit of weight as you work.

As you pin baste, be sure to pin from the center outward and through all three layers of the sandwich, as you would if you were thread basting (see the preceding section). Space the pins 3 to 4 inches apart for best results — any closer together and they just get in the way.

Be sure to remove each pin before stitching over it with your machine; Jumping over pins with your machine can break the needle and put your eye out!

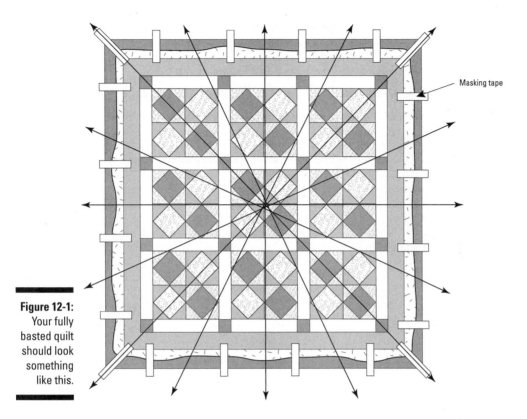

Masking tape

Figure 12-1:
Your fully
basted quilt
should look
something
like this.

Taming the Bed-size Beast

Although thread or pin basting small- to medium-size quilts is simple enough
to do on a table or other work surface, working with quilts of bed-size propor-
tions can be a challenge.

The solution? Make use of that big flat surface under your feet — whether it's
carpeted or not. Tape the beast to the floor — yet another use for the ever-
helpful masking tape tucked into your sewing basket. Kneepads aren't bad
to have on hand either, considering you'll be crawling around on the floor —
if you've got some lying around from your rollerblading phase, use them!

Make sure you have a clean floor by sweeping or vacuuming before laying out
the quilt (trust me when I say that batting is a magnet for every fuzz bunny,
bit of dirt, speck of lint, or mystery gunk on the floor). When your floor's
clean, follow these steps:

1. **Tape the backing to the floor first, with the right side of the backing fabric facing the floor and the wrong side facing you. Tape the corners to the floor first, stretching the fabric slightly to smooth any wrinkles or creases. Then tape the sides in place.**

2. **Lay the batting over the backing, and tape it in the same manner.**

3. **Center the quilt top over the batting and tape it to the floor.**

Don't be shy with the tape! Use as much as it takes to make everything smooth and secure. You don't want the sandwich coming loose when you start basting. (And unless you have a dog that loves to shed like mine, you can reuse the tape.)

After taping, your quilt sandwich should look something like Figure 12-1. Hey, it's weird, but it works. After you're finished taping, you can baste the quilt using the thread-basting method I describe in the "Basting the layers together" section earlier in this chapter. Be sure to use a large needle to make sure you get through all the layers. Although this method seems tricky, it works very well, and you *will* know when you're through those layers — trust me.

Chapter 13

Ready, Set . . . Quilt! The Ins and Outs of Quilting Your Masterpiece

My goodness, what a long way you've come! If you're reading this chapter, you're either curious about the quilting stage (nothing wrong with peeking ahead — keep peeking!), or you're actually ready for the quilting stage of the quilt-making process. If you fit into the latter category, I'm assuming that you've pieced and/or appliquéd your quilt top, selected your batting, and basted the whole shebang together. I also assume that you've selected your quilting patterns, if any (if you're stumped, see Chapter 11), and marked them on your quilt top. What a long way you've come; now you're poised and rip-roarin' ready for the quilting!

Over many years of quilt making, I've found that the actual quilting process is the most rewarding part of quilt making. Not only do I get a rush seeing everything taking shape, but the project starts to look like a real honest-to-gosh quilt. And it's almost finished!

In this chapter, I introduce you to your quilting options: hand quilting, machine quilting, and tying. I walk you through the basic steps for each technique and give you a few options for mixing things up a bit and having fun with this stage of the quilt-making process.

Introducing the Quilting Stage and Your Options

A quilt just isn't a quilt until it's quilted. Confused? The layering of quilt top, a fluffy interior, and backing and securing those layers with some manner of stitch are what truly defines a quilt.

When you get your project to the point at which it's ready to be quilted, you have a few choices to consider depending on the time you have available for quilting and the look you want the finished quilt to have. Basically, there are two ways to quilt a quilt: by hand or by machine. Each method has its variations, both functional and artistic, with pattern options from simple to sublime and everything in between. Hand quilting is the traditional method and gives a wonderful, textured look to the finished quilt, while machine quilting is a bit more orderly-looking. But both are beautiful and durable.

If you want to quilt a project on-the-go, say on vacation or while commuting, you definitely should stick to small projects and hand quilting (dragging a sewing machine around with you isn't very practical). On the other hand, if you have a large quilt that you'd like to finish quickly, machine quilting is just the ticket.

Of course, I hope you at least take a stab at quilting your own projects, but if you don't want to do the quilting yourself (some folks are solely quilt-top-divas, others are quilting aficionados), you can pay to have your quilt machine-quilted. Most quilting supply stores either offer this service or can direct you to someone who does. For a fee that's dependent on the size of the quilt and the style of quilting, skilled machine quilters quilt your project using a *long-arm quilting machine* (you can see these machines set up in most quilting stores). The machine travels along rails upon which the quilt is rolled and has a very long body, allowing large quilts to be passed through it with ease. A skilled long-arm quilter can turn out some very intricate designs, and they're usually more than happy to show off their quilt pattern repertoire if you ask.

Hooping It Up with Hand Quilting

If you choose to quilt the old-fashioned way, by hand, good for you — the ghosts of quilters past are very proud! And the meticulous hand quilters of the present honor you as well!

This section guides you through a simple process for hand quilting your project after you decide how you want to quilt your quilt (see Chapter 11) and baste everything together (see Chapter 12).

Setting things up

For hand quilting, I recommend that you place your project in a *hoop,* which is basically two circles or ovals that fit inside one another and hold your piece taut and in place as you work (see Chapter 2 for more about hoops). You can certainly quilt small projects such as pillow covers without a hoop, but if you're a beginner, you're likely to find using a hoop more comfortable until you have a bit more experience under your belt.

When working with a hoop, center a block or some other element of your quilt top face up over the inner portion of the hoop. Place the outer portion of the hoop over the quilt top–draped inner part, securing the quilt between the two circles (or ovals, depending on your hoop). Hand-tighten the wing nut on the outer hoop to keep the fabric snug and taut.

You can also place your project in a *quilting frame,* a freestanding contraption that serves the same purpose as a hoop when you're working on a large project. However, because they're expensive (and therefore somewhat cost-prohibitive) and most beginners don't have them, I don't go into detail about frames in this chapter. If you decide to invest in a quilting frame, simply follow the manufacturer's instructions for how to use your new toy.

Threading the needle 'n hiding the knot

For hand quilting, I strongly recommend you use hand quilting thread (check the label on the end of the spool to see whether the thread you have is designed for hand or machine quilting). Hand quilting thread is heavy and strong, meaning that the chance of breakage or fraying is substantially reduced.

Cut a length about 18 inches long — from your fingers to your elbow is long enough and keeps the thread from becoming tangled or weakening as you stitch — and thread a quilting needle (a size 7 or 8 *between* needle works nicely). Make a small knot in the long end of the thread.

No self-respecting quilter would ever want knots showing on the quilt's back side! So before you can start stitching, you have to hide the knot. Not only is hiding knots a tidier way to quilt, but the actual quilting stitches are made stronger because the knots aren't vulnerable to abrasion as the quilt gets used.

To hide the knot, follow these steps:

1. **Insert the needle into the quilt top 1 to 2 inches from where you plan to begin stitching.**

   Where you start your quilting stitches doesn't matter; just pick a spot that looks promising — a corner or the tip of a design element are good spots.

2. **Dig the needle slightly into the batting without piercing the backing, and pull the needle back up through the quilt top at the point where you intend to start your stitches.**

3. **Pull the thread through the quilt top, and when you get to the end of the thread where the knot is located, give the thread a little tug so that the knot pops through the quilt top and lodges in the batting, as shown in Figure 13-1.**

Figure 13-1:
Burying the
knot in the
batting.

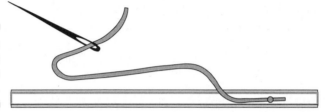

 If you tug a little too hard and pop your knot all the way through, don't worry about it. It happens to all of us. Simply insert the needle a small distance from your starting point and try again . . . just don't tug so hard! If your knot keeps sliding through the batting, add another knot to the end of the thread and try hiding it again. It may be tougher to pop through the quilt top, but the extra knot ensures that it won't budge once it's in the batting.

Hand stitching your quilt

With your quilt in the hoop, your needle threaded, and your knot hidden, turn the hoop in your lap so that the direction of the quilting runs toward you, from the upper right (around 2 o'clock, if your hoop were a clock face) to the lower left of the hoop (around 7 o'clock). *Note:* Some quilters like to stitch toward themselves and others away from themselves. Don't worry if my recommended setup doesn't work for you — just do what comes natural, and you'll be fine.

 If you're left-handed, reverse the hands and directions in the steps that follow. This warning may be completely unnecessary — you're probably used to reversing instructions anyway. After all, lefties are all highly intelligent. (This message was brought to you today by my left-handed husband and teenage daughter, who love to remind me that Albert Einstein was a lefty, and I'm a mere righty.)

Follow these instructions to hand stitch your quilt:

1. **Place your free hand (the left one, unless you're a lefty) under the hoop directly under the stitching area.**

2. **With your thimble on the middle finger of your right hand, insert the needle straight down into the quilt about ¹⁄₁₆ inch from the point where you brought the thread up through the quilt top when hiding your knot. Stop pushing the needle when it clears the backing fabric.**

You should feel the point of the needle as it pierces the quilt backing. Ouch! Sorry, but feeling the prick of the needle is the only way to know that the needle is through all the layers. If you'd rather not poke your finger to death, try placing a soft leather thimble on the "receiving" finger under the quilt. Keep the bandages and ouchie spray handy, though. After all, this *is* a learning experience.

Some quilters like to protect their tender fingertips by holding a spoon in the receiving hand under their quilt. The curved bowl of the spoon stops the needle and also assists the quilter in pushing the needle back through to the quilt top. Try it!

3. **Bring the needle back up through the quilt top by rocking the needle back.**

4. **Load two or three stitches onto the needle following Steps 2 and 3 (as shown in Figure 13-2), and then pull the needle all the way through the quilt top.**

As you become accustomed to hand quilting, you'll find that you can load more stitches on the needle at one time, speeding up the process considerably.

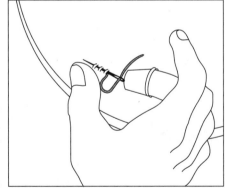

Figure 13-2:
Hand
quilting with
a hoop.

5. **After you pull the needle through, insert it again about ¹⁄₁₆ inch from where you came out of the fabric, and repeat the stitching process along your marked lines.**

6. **When you're left with about 8 inches of thread on your needle, bring the needle to the quilt top, and backstitch over your last stitch by inserting your needle into the starting point of your last stitch and up through the ending point of the last stitch, creating two stitches in the same spot.**

Bloodstains: The unwelcome embellishment

Whenever needles and fingers come together, blood may not be too far behind. The last thing you want is your pristine fabric and hard work dotted with drops. Prevention isn't always possible, however, so here are the two best options for dealing with bloodstains as soon as they occur:

✔ **Lick the spot.** Yep, you read that right, lick it. Human saliva contains certain elements that help break down proteins, so as much as you don't want to do it because it's icky, licking a blood spot is an effective way to eliminate it. It's fast and easy, and you barely miss a stitch. (And don't worry about leaving germs on the project — you'll wash it after you're done quilting anyway.)

✔ **Gently blot the spot with a cotton swab dipped in warm water.** You can even put a little bit of mild soap on the swab if you have a particularly stubborn spot. Just be sure to avoid using hot or cold water because either one will set the stain, and don't saturate the area — just blot until the swab absorbs the stain.

7. **Insert the needle into the quilt top in line with your previous stitches, travel through the batting for an inch, and come up to the surface again (it's a bit like swimming underwater). Cut the thread tail close to the quilt top.**

8. **Thread the needle with a fresh length of thread and keep going until the quilt is quilted!**

If you find that the hoop impairs your quilting, you can quilt some of the quilt area within the hoop to keep those layers in place and then remove the hoop and finish that area without it. Then use the hoop again when you start a new area. Just remember that the hoop keeps the layers from shifting, so be sure you quilt enough area to keep them in place.

Making Fast Progress with Machine Quilting

If you choose to machine quilt your project, you need to prepare your machine for the chore at hand. Each machine quilting technique requires a different type of presser foot and machine setting, so read through this section carefully.

Your thread options here are very diverse: You can use all-purpose thread in matching or contrasting colors, multi-colored or variegated thread to add a little pizzazz, or clear nylon thread so you don't have to worry about thread color at all!

Like any other quilting method, machine quilting requires your project to be basted, either with thread or with pins (I cover both methods in Chapter 12). If your quilt is pin basted, you must remove the safety pins as you approach them when quilting! Do not, under any circumstances, attempt to machine stitch over a safety pin. Not only does stitching over pins make them difficult to remove, but also it's dangerous! You can easily break your needle, sending a fragment of the needle flying, perhaps into your eye. While that's the worst thing that can happen, you can also ruin your machine's timing, and it'll never work as well again.

Preparing large-size projects

Large quilting projects, such as bed quilts, require some special handling when it comes to machine quilting.

If you're quilting a large project, such as a bed quilt, be sure you have a large surface to the rear and to the left of your machine to help you support the weight of the quilt. Large projects are very heavy and can easily pull your machine right off the table and onto the floor if you don't have things set up properly!

Prepare any quilt larger than 36 x 36 inches for quilting by rolling it as follows:

1. **Lay the basted quilt on the floor.**

2. **Roll the two sides towards the center, leaving a 12-inch swath of quilt unrolled in the middle, as shown in Figure 13-3.**

   The unrolled swath is where you begin machine quilting.

3. **Secure the rolls with safety pins or bicycle clips.**

Figure 13-3:
To make it easier to work with, roll and secure a large quilt with safety pins or bicycle clips.

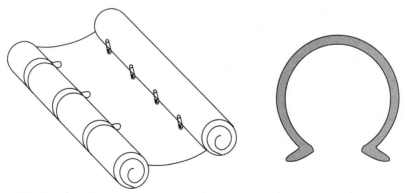

Bicycle clips are flexible metal rings with small openings; they're intended to hold your pants legs against your body while cycling so your pants don't get caught in the bicycle chain. But they're great for holding rolled up quilts in place, too! Just think of the rolled edges of the quilt as the "leg," and put the clip over this rolled leg, holding it securely in place. You can find bicycle clips at sporting goods stores and some quilting stores.

Sometimes this rolling process is too much like moving a stick around and trying to get it to bend to the shape you need. So if rolling seems too cumbersome and you can't seem to control your quilt very well this way, just bunch it up as you move it.

Starting out simply with straight-line quilting

Straight-line quilting is the easiest form of machine quilting. The results are always good, and it's quick, too! One of the easiest and fastest straight-line techniques is quilting *in-the-ditch,* which means sewing right along the seams of your patches and borders, hiding the stitches in the seam areas. If you want something more visible than in-the-ditch stitches, you can quilt ¼ inch from the ditches, framing your patches and blocks with lines of stitching.

Straight-line quilting requires an *even-feed presser foot,* which you can see compared to a regular presser foot in Figure 13-4. If your machine didn't come with an even-feed foot, take a trip to the sewing center to get one. Take your machine's manual with you so the clerk can help you find the right foot for your model.

Figure 13-4:
An even-feed foot (left) has a few more parts than a regular foot (right).

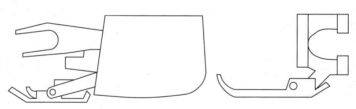

An even-feed foot produces smooth and pucker-free machine quilting stitches because it feeds the layers of the quilt through the machine evenly. Without it, the feed dogs (those teeth under the needle) only feed the bottom layer of fabric through the machine, leaving the batting and top layers vulnerable to puckering because they aren't fed through the machine at the same rate.

To commence straight-line quilting, follow these steps:

1. **Make sure the top of the machine and the bobbin are threaded properly (jump back to the "Making Fast Progress with Machine Quilting" section for instructions on what kind of thread to use). Set the stitch length on the machine at 6 to 10 stitches per inch.**

2. **Place the unrolled center area of the quilt in the machine, and slowly take one stitch.**

3. **Stop stitching after the first stitch, and with the needle up, raise the presser foot. Pull the top thread tail until the bobbin thread tail comes up through the hole in the stitch you made in Step 2.**

   You should have both tails on top of the quilt.

4. **Lower the presser foot, and take two stitches before stopping.**

5. **Put your machine in reverse, and take two stitches backward to secure the thread.**

   With the thread secured, you're ready to stitch your quilt.

6. **Continue stitching forward (without reversing) along your marked lines or in-the-ditch.**

7. **When you get to a corner and need to turn the direction of your stitching, lower the needle into the fabric, stop stitching, and raise the presser foot. Pivot the quilt so that you can continue stitching in the desired direction, and lower the presser foot again. Continue stitching.**

8. **When you reach a spot where you need to stop stitching, take two stitches backward to secure the thread, just as in Step 5, and clip the threads.**

If you don't secure the thread at the beginning and end of every line of stitching, you run the risk the stitches coming undone at these starting and stopping points. And when your stitches come out, you get an unsightly ¼ inch or so gap.

When you finish quilting the area you left unrolled initially, secure your stitches, clip the threads, and remove the project from the machine. Unroll the sides to expose an unquilted area, and continue stitching until the entire quilt is quilted.

Breaking boundaries with free-motion machine quilting

Free-motion quilting is the method used to create beautiful, fancy quilting patterns; decorative possibilities are limited only by your imagination. You can use this type of machine quilting to create graceful curved designs and floral patterns as well as popular stipple quilting designs (see Chapter 11 for more on stipple quilting.)

Mastering free-motion machine quilting requires some practice, but this section gets you started so that you can go out and gather more information on different techniques to use in your projects.

To do free-motion quilting, you need a special presser foot called a *darning* or *free-motion foot*. This type of foot has a round toe that travels just above the surface of the fabric, creating a sort of target for the needle and allowing you to see more of your stitches. In a nutshell, it's an embroidery hoop on a needle. Pretty cool.

Because you feed the quilt through the machine manually, free-motion quilting requires you to disengage your machine's *feed dogs,* the little teeth under your sewing machine foot that move fabric along as you stitch. Refer to your machine's manual to see exactly how your feed dogs work:

- ✔ On some machines, you disengage the feed dogs by turning a knob, which lowers them out of position.

- ✔ On other machines (especially older models), you don't lower the feed dogs to disengage them. Instead, you cover them with a metal or plastic plate that's in your machine's bag of tricks.

With free-motion quilting, you don't need to adjust the length of the straight-stitch on your machine at all. The speed at which you sew combined with the speed at which you move the quilt around under the needle determines the stitch length. The potential for very small or very large stitches is why practice is so important before attempting free-motion quilting on a large project.

After inserting the darning foot and disengaging the feed dogs, thread your machine and bobbin. Then follow these basic steps:

1. **Place the quilt under the presser foot with one hand positioned on either side of the quilt, 2 inches or so from the presser foot.**

2. **Slowly begin stitching, taking two or three stitches in the same spot to secure the thread.**

3. **As you stitch, move the quilt by guiding it with your hands. If you have a premarked design, move the quilt so that the needle follows your marked quilting lines or designs.**

   Keep the machine at a steady speed, and move the fabric slowly and smoothly so you don't end up with gaps or overly long stitches. Slow and steady is the key here!

If your fingers feel dry, or if you're having trouble moving the quilt under the machine because your fingers are sliding on the fabric, cover the first and index finger of each hand (four fingers in all) with rubber fingertips sold at office supply stores. Or purchase inexpensive knit gloves with rubbery dots on them designed for this very purpose at any quilting supply store.

Because free-motion machine quilting takes some time to get comfortable with, I recommend starting on small projects, such as pillows, place mats, or wall hangings, before progressing to larger projects. If you're just starting out with free-motion quilting, try *stipple quilting*, a great beginner's exercise because you don't have to worry about following a set pattern. Instead, you figure out how to maneuver the project under the darning foot and get some much-needed experience.

If you're new to free motion machine quilting, I suggest you make small quilt sandwiches with muslin and batting and use them as practice pallets. (Be sure to save them and look at them from time to time to see how far you've come!)

Taking the Tie Road

If your quilting project is a big, fluffy quilt full of high-loft batting, hand and machine quilting are out the window. The loft and bulk make stitching through the layers by hand or machine extremely difficult. Instead, you need to *tie* the quilt. Tying is a quick, simple process in which the three layers of the quilt are held together with pieces of thread. The principle is the same as using a tie tack to secure a man's necktie, keeping the two tails from flapping in the breeze. Tying works best with polyester battings that don't need to be quilted at tightly spaced intervals.

Tying isn't limited to fluffy quilts, though. It also works for securing cotton and blended batts (as long as your ties fit the intervals recommended by the batting manufacturer). If you're pressed for time and just want to get the darn thing done, or if your first attempt at making a quilt is just too ugly to bother quilting by hand or machine (you should have seen my first quilt!), tying is faster than hand or machine quilting. If you have a feeling your project will make a better car blanket or dog bed than wall hanging, tie it off and at least get some use out of it. No sense wasting all that hard work.

To tie a quilt:

1. **Thread a sharp-pointed, large-eyed needle with a 12-inch length of heavy thread. Don't knot the end.**

   For tying quilts you need heavy thread, such as pearl cotton, embroidery floss, narrow ribbon, or even worsted-weight yarn. Don't use all-purpose thread — it's just not strong enough to hold the tied layers together.

2. **Insert the needle straight down into the quilt top and through all three layers, and bring it back up in the opposite direction ⅛ inch from where it went down.**

3. **Pull the needle through the quilt so that you have about 4 inches of thread on the tail end (where your needle first went into the quilt). Tie the tail end to the threaded end in a double knot.**

4. **Trim the two tails to about 1 inch in length.**

5. **Repeat Steps 2 through 4 at consistent intervals — every 5 to 6 inches or however close the batting manufacturer recommends.**

When all your ties are finished, trim all the thread tails to the desired length — just make sure they're no shorter than ½ inch. Your efforts should resemble Figure 13-5.

Figure 13-5:
Tying is a
quick and
easy way
to secure
quilting
projects.

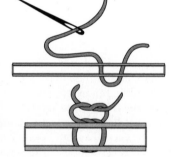

To speed up the tying process, start with a longer length of thread, follow Steps 1 through 3 above, and then, instead of cutting your thread after each stitch, continue making stitches and tying them until you're about 4 inches from the end of your thread. Tie your final knot, go back and cut the thread stretching between each of the knots, and trim the tails to 1 inch.

Chapter 14

Finishing Touches:
Bindings and More

*W*hen you finish stitching and quilting your masterpiece, you need to do something about those raw edges and the batting hanging out. Your quilt sure won't look too great left as it is!

You can choose from many ways of finishing the edges of your quilt. The most popular method is encasing the raw edges in a *binding,* either *bias* or *straight-edge,* which you can purchase or make yourself from extra fabric. Another option is to fold the excess backing fabric to the front for a *self-binding.* Or you can finish your quilt *pillow-style.*

This chapter describes each type of binding and the technique for making and using it, along with its advantages and possible disadvantages.

Calculating Your Binding Needs

To determine how much binding you need to finish off your quilting project, total the measurements of all four sides and add 12 inches. The additional 12 inches allows both for mitering the corners of the binding (which I discuss in the section "Tackling traditional bias binding" later in the chpater) and for the overlap where the binding starts and stops. (Plus, 12 inches factors in a little extra, just in case.) Table 14-1 provides a quick reference for the amount of binding needed for typical bed-size quilts.

Table 14-1	Binding Needs for Bed-Size Quilts
Type of Bed	*Amount of Binding*
Crib	5–6 yards
Twin	9 yards
Double/Full	10 yards
Queen	11 yards
King	12 yards

This table tells you the length of the binding necessary to finish off all sides of the quilt, not the amount of yardage needed to actually make that binding.

In a Bias Bind

The most common method of binding a quilt project is to apply bias binding around the edges of your quilt. *Bias* simply means that the fabric is cut diagonally across the weave of the fabric. *Traditional bias binding* and *double-fold binding* use strips of fabric cut on the bias to enclose the raw edges of the quilt.

I prefer to use a bias-cut binding on my quilts because it's more forgiving at corners and around curves, and it tends to pucker less than a binding that has been cut on-grain. The little bit of give in a bias binding also makes it easier to stitch to the quilt by offering less resistance to the feed dogs than on-grain bindings.

In this section, I tell you how to assemble bias binding strips. Then, I explain the two variations of the bias binding technique.

Creating bias strips

When making bias strips, you can either create one long strip or cut individual strips and then sew them together to get the length you need. You can use either of these methods to produce the different types of bias binding covered later in this chapter.

Making a continuous binding strip

To end up with a *continuous binding strip,* follow these steps:

1. **Cut a 44" x 44" square of fabric (with selvages removed) in half diagonally to make two large triangles (see Figure 14-1a).**

   The square is cut on-grain at this point.

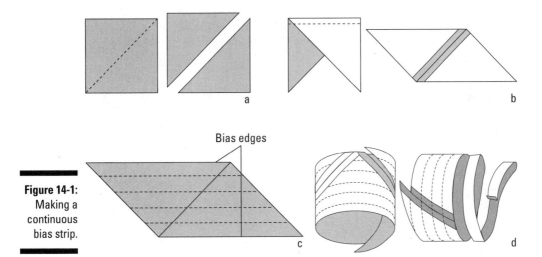

Figure 14-1:
Making a continuous bias strip.

2. **Stitch the triangles together along the short edges to make the shape shown in Figure 14-1b. Press the seam allowance open.**

   You now have a trapezoid shape with two bias edges (upper and lower).

3. **Decide how wide you need the binding to be (refer to the individual binding techniques in this chapter for help determining this measurement), and mark lines on the wrong side of the fabric using a ruler (refer to Figure 14-1c).**

4. **Stitch the short ends of the fabric together (right sides facing), offsetting the lines by one strip line to form a funny-looking tube (refer to Figure 14-1d).**

   Carefully press the seam allowance open.

5. **With scissors, cut the binding in one continuous strip, starting at the offset overhang and cutting along the marked lines.**

Taking a shortcut to making bias binding strips

The second method of creating bias strips, sewing simple strips together, is the one I use. I prefer this stitch-as-you-go method because it's a good way to use up an odd-size piece of fabric. Because I'm cutting bias strips instead of a perfect square, it doesn't matter if my choice of binding fabric has been cut into previously.

To cut bias strips using this technique, follow these easy steps:

1. **Using a ruler, mark lines on a piece of fabric on a 45-degree angle to the grain line. Space the lines the width you need for your strips (see the individual techniques in this chapter for help determining the width to mark).**

   Most see-through rulers intended for rotary cutting have 45-degree lines already marked on them, so they're especially useful for this task.

2. **Cut the strips apart using a rotary cutter (see Figure 14-2a).**

   You can use scissors if you prefer.

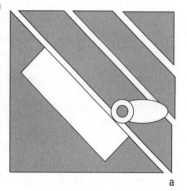
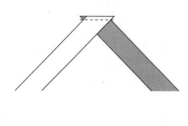

Figure 14-2: You can make bias binding by cutting strips on a diagonal (a) and then sewing them together (b).

a

b

3. **Pin together the short ends of two strips, as shown in Figure 14-2b, with the right sides together. Offset the strips so that there's a small tail at either end of the future seam.**

   Offsetting the strips slightly accommodates a ¼-inch seam allowance and produces the little tails. If you don't offset the strips as shown in Figure 14-2b, you won't have a straight smooth line along the edges of your binding.

4. **Sew the strips together where they're pinned, use scissors to trim off the little fabric tails, and press the seam allowances open.**

5. **Continue joining strips until you have enough length to bind your quilt.**

Tackling traditional bias binding

Traditional bias binding, as you would expect, is the old-fashioned way to bind a quilt. The binding is made from a wide strip of bias-cut fabric that's folded down the center lengthwise. Each lengthwise half of the strip is then folded again before being attached to the quilt, giving the top and back of the quilt each two layers of binding.

Traditional bias binding is the most durable binding method because, when you're finished stitching, you actually have two layers of fabric covering the raw edges of the quilt. Because of its durability, I recommend using traditional bias binding for bed-size quilts or anything that will undergo a lot of laundering.

To make a traditional bias binding:

1. **Using one of the methods in the "Creating bias strips" section earlier in the chapter, cut strips of fabric eight times wider than the desired width of the finished binding.**

   For example, if you prefer a binding that is ½-inch wide when finished, cut 4-inch-wide strips of bias-cut fabric (½ x 8 = 4). (See the sidebar "Getting the most binding for your buck" later in this chapter for details on how much 4-inch binding you get from various fabric cuts.)

2. **Fold in ½ inch of the beginning of the strip so that the right side of the folded fabric faces you. Then, fold the strip in half (wrong sides facing) along its entire length, as shown in Figure 14-3.**

Figure 14-3:
Fold the bias-cut fabric down the center lengthwise.

3. **Press the strip carefully along the lengthwise fold, taking care not to stretch the bias.**

4. **Place the pressed strip on the front of the quilt so that the double raw edge is even with the raw edges of the quilt top and the fold in the strip is toward the center of the quilt. Pin the strip in place.**

5. **Along one long side of the quilt, start about 4 inches from the folded end of the bias strip. Begin machine stitching the binding in place ¼ inch from the double raw edge of the binding.**

When you begin to approach a corner, slow down a bit so that you have better control, and stitch to within ¼ inch of the corner of the quilt top. (See the dot in Figure 14-4? That's where you stop stitching.) Take a back stitch or two to secure your thread before cutting it and turning the quilt to the next side.

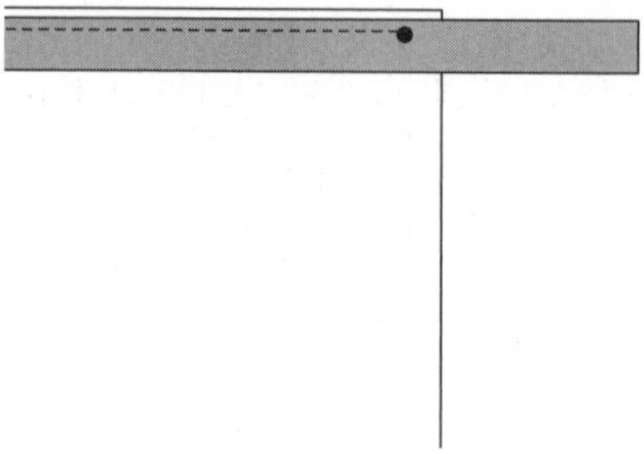

Figure 14-4:
Stop sewing about ¼ inch from the corner.

6. *Miter* **the corner by folding the bias strip upwards at the corner so that it extends the right-hand edge of the quilt (see Figure 14-5a), and then fold it down so that the newly made fold is even with the top edge of the quilt, the one you just stitched along (shown in Figure 14-5b). Holding the folded binding in place, line up the quilt in your sewing machine so that you can start stitching the strip to the next side of the quilt, around the corner.**

Figure 14-5:
Fold the binding up (a) and back down (b) to create a clean corner.

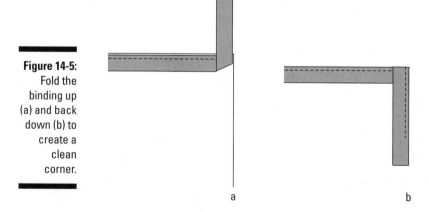

a   b

7. Continue stitching the binding to the edges as described in Step 5 and mitering the corners as described in Step 6.

8. To end your binding back where you started (what goes around comes around), trim the ending tail of the binding so that it overlaps the beginning by about 2 inches. (You left 4 inches of it unstitched, remember? If not, see Step 5.) Insert the ending tail of the binding into the folded beginning, and continue stitching through all the layers.

9. Trim away any excess backing fabric and batting (anything that extends beyond the quilt top) with scissors.

10. Fold the binding to the back side of the quilt and, using the blind-stitch, hand stitch it in place directly over the line of machine stitching on all four sides (see Figure 14-6). To create the blind-stitch:

   1. Hide your knot by inserting your needle in the backing fabric a short distance from where you want to start. Bring your needle up through the edge of the binding, and pop the knot through the backing fabric by tugging on the thread. (A firm tug is all you need; pull too hard and you'll break the thread and have to start over.)

   2. With your thread coming through the binding, insert the needle into the quilt backing directly opposite.

   3. Bring the needle up through the binding again about ⅛ inch from the first stitch in the binding. In this manner, you've traveled ⅛ inch and hidden the traveling portion of the thread in the quilt backing.

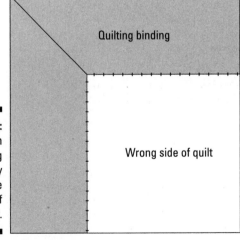

Figure 14-6: Blind-stitch the binding in place by hand on the back side of the quilt.

Quilting binding

Wrong side of quilt

Getting the most binding for your buck

The instructions I give you for making a continuous bias binding (see the section "Making a continuous binding strip") are for a 44- x 44-inch square of fabric, but you can use the same process with different size fabric squares to make less binding — it all depends on what you need for your project. Use the guide in this sidebar to help you estimate the amount of fabric needed to make the correct amount of binding for your project.

If you want binding that's 4 inches wide:

- A 44- x 44-inch square of fabric produces about 13 yards

- A 36- x 36-inch square produces 9 yards

- A 20- x 20-inch square produces only about 2.5 yards

If you want binding that's 2 inches wide:

- A 45- x 45-inch square produces 26 yards

- A 36- x 36-inch square produces 18 yards

- A 20- x 20-inch square produces 5.5 yards

Double-fold binding

The *double-fold binding* method uses a single layer of fabric on the edges of the quilt, making it more economical than traditional bias binding. This type of bias binding isn't quite as durable as traditional binding (see the preceding section), so I recommend that you use it for projects that won't be handled or washed frequently, such as wall hangings and table runners.

Double-fold binding is great for anything that has rounded corners because the natural stretch of the bias along with the single layer at the edge helps you round corners smoothly.

Pressed for time? If so, pick up double-fold bias tape in any fabric store. It comes in a variety of colors and even some prints, such as gingham. Look for packages marked "Extra-Wide Double-Fold Bias Tape." Because this premade binding is sold in packages containing 2 to 3 yards of bias tape, you're likely to need several packages.

If you're determined to make your own double-fold bias binding, follow these steps:

1. **Cut strips of fabric four times wider than the desired width of the finished binding.**

   For example, if you want a finished binding that's ½ inch wide, cut strips that are 2 inches wide (½ inch x 4 = 2). (See the sidebar "Getting the most binding for your buck" earlier in this chapter for details on how much 2-inch binding you get from various fabric cuts.)

2. Fold the strip in half lengthwise with the wrong sides together (see Figure 14-7a).

3. Press the center fold.

4. Open the strip so that the wrong side of the fabric faces up.

5. Fold each side of the strip toward the center fold so that the raw edges meet in the middle (see Figure 14-7b).

6. Press each folded side.

7. With the sides still folded in, refold the strip along the center crease, and press it to reestablish the center crease.

8. Open all the folds of the binding strip, and turn in ¼ inch at the starting end of the strip so that the right side of the folded piece faces you.

9. Place one raw edge of the binding strips along the raw edge of the quilt top (right sides facing), and machine stitch in the ditch of the binding crease nearest the edge (see Figure 14-7c), about 4 inches from the end of the length of binding, leaving a tail.

   When you begin to approach a corner, slow down a bit so that you have better control, and stitch to within ¼ inch of the corner of the quilt top. Backstitch once or twice before cutting the thread and turning the quilt.

10. *Miter* the corner by folding the bias strip upwards at the corner so that it extends the right-hand edge of the quilt, and then fold it down so that the newly made fold is even with the top edge of the quilt, the one you just stitched along. Holding the folded binding in place, line up the quilt in your sewing machine so that you can start stitching the strip to the next side of the quilt, around the corner.

11. Continue stitching the binding to the edges as described in Step 9 and mitering the corners as described in Step 10.

12. To end your binding back where you started (what goes around comes around), trim the ending tail of the binding so that it overlaps the beginning by about 2 inches. (You left 4 inches of it unstitched, remember? If not, see Step 9.) Insert the ending tail of the binding into the folded beginning, and continue stitching through all the layers.

13. Trim away any excess backing fabric and batting (anything that extends beyond the quilt top) with scissors.

14. Fold the binding to the back side of the quilt.

   The center crease should lie along the very edge of the quilt.

15. On the back side, use the blind-stitch (see the section "Tackling traditional bias binding" earlier in this chapter for blind-stitch instructions) to hand stitch the binding in place along the remaining crease, stitching directly over the machine stitching line.

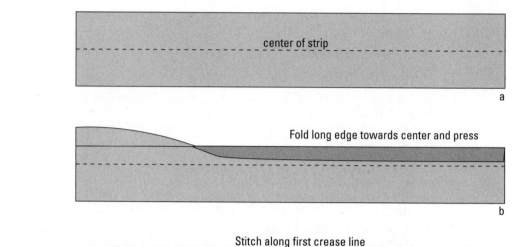

center of strip

a

Fold long edge towards center and press

b

Stitch along first crease line

Front of quilt

c

Figure 14-7:
Folding
(a, b) and
stitching (c)
a double-
fold binding.

Using What You Already Have: Self-Binding

Self-binding is a quick and easy way to bind small projects. Also known as *fold-over binding,* a self-binding is made from excess backing fabric that's trimmed to size and folded to the front side of the quilt to enclose the raw edges.

I recommend this binding only for small projects because it's a straightedge binding and therefore doesn't have the flexibility of a bias binding. In fact, self-binding tends to ripple the edges of the project slightly if used on long sides of a project. It's fine to use on place mats and wall hangings, but I don't recommend you use it on anything larger than a baby quilt.

If you want to make your project self-binding, be sure to

✔ **Cut your backing fabric at least 3 inches larger than your project on all four sides.**

For example, if you have a 30- x 30-inch project, cut your backing 36 x 36 inches.

✔ **Center your quilt top on the backing fabric carefully before basting and quilting it.**

✔ **Keep in mind that whatever you use as your backing fabric will be visible on the front of the quilt, so choose the backing accordingly.**

Follow these steps to make your project self-binding:

1. **After quilting your project, trim excess batting from the edges of the quilt so that it doesn't extend beyond the edges of the quilt top.**

   Be very careful not to cut through the backing fabric.

2. **Trim the backing fabric so that the amount that extends beyond the edge of the quilt top measures two times the desired width of the binding.**

   For example, if you want a ½-inch binding, trim the backing fabric to 1 inch (½ inch x 2 = 1) beyond the edges of the quilt top.

3. **Fold the backing fabric toward the front of the quilt just slightly less than ½ inch, and press, keeping the iron away from the batting (see Figure 14-8).**

4. **Fold the backing fabric over again ½ inch toward the front of the quilt, covering up the raw edge.**

   Don't press this fold or you may flatten the batting at the edges of your quilt.

5. **Stitch the self-binding in place on the quilt front by machine or by hand using the blind-stitch (see the section "Tackling traditional bias binding" earlier in this chapter for blind-stitch instructions).**

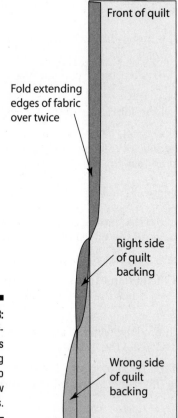

Front of quilt

Fold extending
edges of fabric
over twice

Right side
of quilt
backing

Wrong side
of quilt
backing

Figure 14-8:
A self-
binding uses
backing
fabric to
finish raw
edges.

Keeping It All Inside:
Pillow-style Finishing

Pillow-style finishing is a way of finishing a quilt project without using a binding at all. With this method, you enclose the raw edges of the quilt in the quilt itself, and you do the quilting *after* the three quilt layers are sewn together — which I guess is why some people call this method *birthing* a quilt. Go figure!

I recommend pillow-style finishing only for very small projects, such as place mats and hot pads. Anything larger can be too bulky to handle comfortably and is a pain in the neck to try and push through the sewing machine.

Hand-Quilted Starburst Pillow
and Trapunto Mini-Pillow
(Chapter 15)

Dancing Blossoms
Wall Hanging
(Chapter 15)

Traditional Basket
Wall Hanging
(Chapter 15)

Chicken Scratch
Foundation-Pieced Quilt
(Chapter 15)

Rosy Wreath Quilt
(Chapter 16)

Scrappy Bloomers Wall
Hanging or Lap Quilt
(Chapter 16)

Snow Crystals
Lap Quilt
(Chapter 16)

Winter Holly
Lap Quilt or
Wall Hanging
(Chapter 16)

Pieced Flower Pots
Wall Hanging
(Chapter 17)

Pieced Blossoms Lap Quilt
(Chapter 17)

American Appliqués Banner
(Chapter 17)

Scrappy Pines Lap
or Nap Quilt
(Chapter 17)

Appliquéd Bluebirds
Breakfast Set
(Chapter 18)

Pink Tulips
Breakfast Set
(Chapter 18)

*Blue Star Placemat
and Hot Pad Set*
(Chapter 18)

*Pastel Nine-Patch
Wall Hanging*
(Chapter 18)

For pillow-style finishing, cut your border strips ¼ to ½ inch wider than your desired finished width so that you don't end up with a project smaller than you intended. The seam allowance required by the finishing technique takes up the excess.

To finish a project pillow-style, follow these steps:

1. **Cut backing and batting pieces at least 2 inches larger than your quilt top all around.**

2. **Lay the batting out on a flat work surface. Center the quilt top over the batting right side up, and trim the batting to match the quilt top perfectly.**

   Because batting tends to stretch and relax, you'll end up trimming the batting even if you cut it to size from the start.

3. **Place a pin through the layers — the center of the piece works best — to keep them from shifting during the next steps.**

4. **Turn the whole thing over so that the batting faces you and the quilt top faces your work surface.**

5. **Place the backing fabric right side up on your work surface. Center the quilt top unit over the backing fabric, with the right sides of the backing and the quilt top together. (The batting should be facing you.)**

6. **Pin all three layers together, spacing your pins no less than 2 inches apart.**

   Use lots of pins to tame the batting.

7. **Place the piece in the sewing machine, and stitch ¼ inch to ½ inch (depending on your preference and comfort level) in from the raw edge around all four sides, leaving a 6-inch opening along one side for turning.**

   Figure 14-9 shows where you stitch, beginning and ending at the dots.

8. **Clip the points off the corners close to but not through the stitching (see Figure 14-9).**

9. **Turn the piece right side out through the opening by putting your hand through the opening, grabbing one of the far corners, and pulling it toward you. Continue pulling the fabric through the opening until the whole thing is right side out.**

10. **Hand stitch the opening closed by tucking in the raw edges and using the blind-stitch (see the section ""Tackling traditional bias binding" earlier in this chapter for blind-stitch instructions).**

11. **Using pins or thread, baste through all three layers to prepare the project for quilting (check out Chapter 12 for basting details). Then quilt it however you want to (see Chapter 10 for quilt design ideas).**

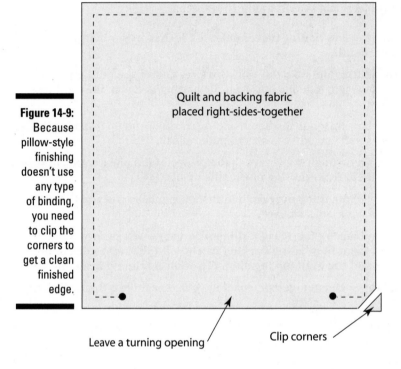

Figure 14-9:
Because pillow-style finishing doesn't use any type of binding, you need to clip the corners to get a clean finished edge.

Quilt and backing fabric placed right-sides-together

Leave a turning opening

Clip corners

Part V
Completing the Circle: Projects to Try

In this part . . .

This part is full of neat, not-too-complicated projects to get your creative juices flowing. These projects run the gamut from wall hangings to lap quilts, and I've organized them into the following categories:

✔ **Fabulous Skill Builders:** These are great beginner's projects that will help you develop the basic skills necessary to make a quilt.

✔ **Mixed-Technique Projects:** In this chapter, I show you projects that use a variety of techniques, including mixing appliqué with patchwork and adding embroidered accents.

✔ **Projects for the Machine Queen:** As a quilter, your sewing machine is your best friend. In this chapter, I give you project ideas that put your machine to good use.

✔ **Small-Scale Projects:** Not all quilts have to be for the bed or wall! In this chapter, I give you some ideas for using your quilting skills to make smaller projects such as kitchen accessories and mini-quilts.

Now choose a project and start slicing and dicing that fabric you've been itching to cut into!

Chapter 15

Fabulous Skill Builders

· ·

In This Chapter

▶ Honing your hand quilting on pillow projects

▶ Appliquéing floral designs the traditional and modern ways

▶ Playing around with foundation piecing and whimsical designs

· ·

*T*here's more to quilting that just cutting out a few squares of fabric and sewing them together. Quilting is also an art form, and like any great form of art, the more skills you develop, the better you become as an artist. The projects in this chapter use techniques that are a little more advanced and, as such, can help take you from beginner to intermediate quilter.

Hand-Quilted Starburst Pillow

Are you ready to try hand quilting? Great! Here's a quick, fun project to get you started. The small size (14 inches square) makes it more than manageable for the beginner. This pillow makes a great take-along project, too: Just whip it out of your bag whenever you find a few precious moments of spare time.

Stashing your materials

The following list covers the fabrics and notions you need to create this pillow:

✔ 10½- x 10½-inch square of off-white tone-on-tone fabric

✔ ⅓ yard of yellow print fabric

✔ 15- x 15-inch piece of off-white tone-on-tone fabric

✔ 15- x 15-inch piece of low-loft cotton or polyester batting

✔ 15- x 15-inch piece of coordinating print fabric

✔ 2 yards of purchased piping in navy blue

✔ All-purpose thread in off-white

✔ Hand quilting thread in navy blue

✔ A *between* needle (a short, sharp needle made especially for quilting or other detailed handwork; see Chapter 2)

✔ Stuffing or a 14-inch pillow form (see the sidebar "A word about pillow forms")

Preparing the pillow top for quilting

In the following steps, I explain how to transfer the quilting design onto the pillow top and prepare the top for quilting:

1. **Fold the 10½-inch off-white square into quarters and press it. Unfold the square, and lay it flat.**

   The resulting creases help you center your quilting pattern.

2. **Using the creases as a guide, transfer the quilting pattern at the end of this project section to the center of the square by tracing or using dressmaker's carbon and a sharp pencil (see Figure 15-1).**

A word about pillow forms

The pillow forms sold in fabric and craft supply stores these days come in standardized sizes — 12-, 14-, 16-, 20-, and 24-inch. In addition to different sizes, pillow forms also come in different weights; some are meant for soft, squishy pillows, and others are firmer to give you a well-stuffed look.

In an effort to have a nice, plump pillow and avoid sad, empty corners, some folks purchase a pillow form that's an inch or two larger than the cover. This approach is never a good idea because stuffing a 24-inch insert into a 20-inch pillow covering invites disasters such as split seams and a lumpy filling.

With quilted pillow covering projects, you automatically add thickness and support to the top of the pillow, so the corners shouldn't cave in if you use the right materials. I would never recommend that anyone buy an oversized pillow form. Something stuffed that firmly isn't a pillow — it's a mini-mattress! Yikes!

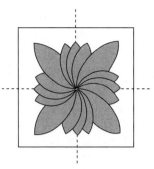

Figure 15-1:
Center the starburst design on the pillow top fabric.

3. From the yellow print fabric, cut two 2½- x 10½-inch strips for the upper and lower borders, and cut two 2½- x 14½-inch strips of the same fabric for the side borders.

4. Using the all-purpose thread and a ¼-inch seam allowance, machine stitch the upper and lower borders to the marked off-white square (see Figure 15-2). Press the seam allowances toward the borders.

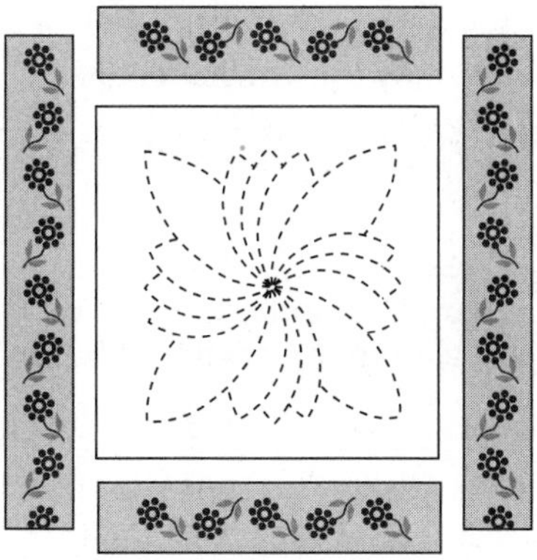

Figure 15-2:
The center of the pillow gets a simple print border.

5. Repeat Step 4 with the side borders.

6. Layer the pillow top with the batting and the off-white solid lining fabric, and thread baste the layers together to prepare them for quilting (see Figure 15-3).

Figure 15-3:
The top of the pillow actually consists of three layers: the pillow top, batting, and lining.

Quilting the pillow top

The following steps tell you how to quilt the starburst pattern onto the pillow top. Refer to Chapter 13 if you need more information about the quilting process:

1. **Thread a between needle with a length of quilting thread about as long as the distance from your elbow to your fingertips.**

2. **Starting wherever you feel like on the quilting pattern, bury the knot in the batting, and begin quilting.**

    Take small, evenly spaced stitches.

3. **Outline the off-white center square by hand quilting ¼ inch away from either side of the seam line connecting the center with the borders, as shown in Figure 15-4.**

Figure 15-4:
Straight stitches alongside the border seams define the borders and frame the center of the pillow top.

Assembling the pillow

After you quilt the pillow top, you're ready to finish the project. The following steps explain how to assemble the pillow so you that can put your quilting skills on display:

1. **Thread your sewing machine with off-white all-purpose thread. Machine stitch about ⅛ inch away from the raw edges of the pillow top.**

2. **Trim away the excess lining fabric and batting that extend beyond the edges of the pillow top.**

3. **Machine stitch the piping around the edges of the pillow top by aligning the raw (not rounded) edge of the piping along the raw edge of the pillow top. Begin stitching at the center of one side, leaving a 2-inch tail of piping hanging free.**

4. **When you approach a corner, stop stitching ¼ inch from the corner, and clip into the seam allowance of the piping *close to, but not through,* the stuffed area of the piping.**

   Clipping the seam allowance eliminates the bulk that would have resulted at the corners if you had tried to turn them without stopping and clipping. Clipping results in nice, pointed corners.

5. **Turn the corner, and resume stitching the piping. When you arrive back at your starting point, overlap the remaining piping and the tail you left at the starting point, and stitch across them. Trim the excess tails of the piping so that they're only about ½ inch long (see Figure 15-5).**

   The layers of fabric and batting are a bit bulky, so you need to stitch slowly to avoid breaking your needle.

Figure 15-5:
The two tails of piping should overlap at your starting and ending point.

6. **Place the completed pillow top against the 15- x 15-inch piece of coordinating backing fabric, right sides together. Pin the two pieces together to keep them from shifting during assembly.**

7. **Stitch the pillow top to the backing along the same line of stitches you used to attach the piping, leaving a 10-inch opening along the bottom edge for turning (see Figure 15-6).**

8. **Clip the corners close to the stitching line, *but not through it,* to eliminate bulk at the corners (refer to Figure 15-6).**

Figure 15-6:
Without an
opening,
you can't
get the
pillow form
or stuffing
inside the
cover. And
clipping the
corners
ensures a
cleaner
point.

9. **Turn the pillow top right side out by pulling it through the opening.**

10. **Insert the pillow form or stuff the cover until it's as firm as you like.**

11. **Tuck in the seam allowances of the opening, and hand stitch the opening closed using the whip stitch.**

   To work the whip stitch,

   1. Knot the end of a single length of thread.

   2. Insert the needle on the underside of the quilt, bringing it up to the right side on one side of the slit.

   3. Cross to the other side of the slit and take a stitch, whipping back and forth between the left- and right-hand sides of the slit until it's closed.

No need to worry about laundering this pillow — it's really easy! Simply pop the whole thing into the washer on a delicate setting, and then let it air dry. You don't need to remove the cover because the polyester stuffing in the pillow form is completely machine washable. If you have any fiber migration (like if the filling seems to gather in one corner of the pillow), bounce the pillow on your knee a few times to redistribute the fluff.

Half-Size Starburst Quilting Pattern

Enlarge 200 percent for a full-size pattern.

Trapunto Mini-Pillow

Trapunto is a fancy style of hand quilting in which areas are stuffed for added loft. Certain parts of the quilt's design are puffier than others because you carefully insert extra materials into those areas to make them stand out.

Although it's a bit more time-consuming than standard hand quilting, Trapunto is very easy to do, and the results are gorgeous! This old Italian technique traditionally has been used to add interesting highlights to white-on-white bridal quilts and other *whole-cloth quilts* (quilts that don't have any appliqué or piecing).

The following sections tell you how to create a beautiful Trapunto Mini-Pillow with a flower petal design. The finished size of the pillow is only 7 x 7 inches, so it's a great project to ease you into the Trapunto technique.

Stashing your materials

The following list describes the fabrics and notions you need to make the Trapunto Mini-Pillow:

- ✔ One 5½- x 5½-inch piece of off-white tone-on-tone fabric
- ✔ ¼ yard of yellow print fabric (a fat quarter works nicely here)
- ✔ One 8- x 8-inch piece of off-white tone-on-tone fabric
- ✔ One 8- x 8-inch piece of coordinating print fabric
- ✔ All-purpose thread in off-white
- ✔ Hand-quilting thread in off-white
- ✔ A between needle
- ✔ 1 yard of purchased piping in navy blue
- ✔ One 20-ounce bag of polyester stuffing (fiberfill) for stuffing the pillow (pillow forms are not available in this small size)
- ✔ Rug-weight yarn in off-white (available at any fabric shop)
- ✔ A large-eyed needle

Preparing the pillow top

Follow these steps to get the pillow top assembled and ready to be quilted:

1. **Fold the 5½-inch square of off-white fabric into quarters, and press it. Unfold the square, and lay it flat.**

2. **Using the crease lines as a guide, transfer the flower petal quilting pattern at the end of this project section to the center of the square by tracing or using dressmakers' carbon and a sharp pencil (see Figure 15-7).**

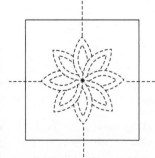

Figure 15-7:
Center the quilting design on the pillow top.

WARNING!

Pressing the quilt top fabric at this point may set the markings permanently, so don't chance it. There's no need to press the fabric anyway because handling will cause the creases to fall out.

3. **From the yellow print fabric, cut two 1½- x 5½-inch strips for the upper and lower borders, and cut two 1½- x ½-inch strips for side borders.**

4. **Using the all-purpose thread and a ¼-inch seam allowance, machine stitch the upper and lower borders to the square (see Figure 15-8). Press the seam allowances toward the borders.**

5. **Repeat Step 4 with the two side borders.**

Figure 15-8: Add border strips to the upper and lower edges of the center and then to the sides.

6. **Layer the pillow top with the batting and the 8- x 8-inch solid off-white piece, which acts as the backing for the quilted portion of the pillow. Thread baste the three layers together in preparation for quilting (see Figure 15-9).**

Figure 15-9: The quilted pillow top consists of three layers: top, batting, and lining.

Quilting the pillow top

Before anything else, the pillow top needs to be quilted. Follow these steps:

1. **Thread a between needle with a length of quilting thread about as long as the distance from your elbow to your fingertips.**

2. **Starting wherever you feel like on the quilting design, bury the knot in the batting, and begin quilting, following the petal pattern you marked on the center square.**

   For best results, take small, evenly spaced stitches. For full coverage of hand quilting, check out Chapter 12.

3. **Outline the off-white center square by hand quilting ¼ inch away from either side of the seam line connecting the center with the borders, as shown in Figure 15-10.**

Figure 15-10:
Hand quilting two squares adds definition to the center and borders.

4. **Stipple quilt the entire off-white area surrounding the flower petal design by taking small, meandering stitches (see Figure 15-11).**

   Refer to Chapter 11 for information on stipple quilting. This stipple quilting helps "raise" the main quilting motif by squishing down the areas surrounding it.

Figure 15-11:
The meandering pattern of stipple quilting makes the center design pop.

Adding dimension to the pillow top

These steps tell you how to give your pillow top the Trapunto look:

1. **Thread a large-eyed needle with a doubled length of rug yarn.**

2. **Turn the pillow top over so that the wrong side (the lining) is facing you.**

3. **Starting at the center end of a petal channel (which resulted from quilting the design in the center of the pillow top), insert the needle between the batting and the lining fabric, as shown in Figure 15-12. Don't go through the front layer!**

   When doing Trapunto, you need to keep the yarn between the batting and the lining because otherwise you can see the yarn through the top layer of fabric. Also, instead of creating a smoothly filled channel, inserting the yarn below the wrong layer makes the channel bumpy.

4. **Pull the needle out of the fabric at the tip of the petal (see Figure 15-12a), and pull the yarn until only ½ inch is still peeking out at the starting point.**

5. **Insert the needle into the hole you just came out of (see Figure 15-12b), and run it through the channel to the other end of the petal, pulling the needle out when you reach the end.**

6. **Trim the yarn close to the hole and at your starting point, as shown in Figure 15-12c.**

   Fill each petal's channel individually. The yarn doesn't need to be knotted because your quilting keeps it in the channels.

Figure 15-12:
In the Trapunto technique, you run yarn into part of a channel (a), change direction (b), and trim the ends (c) before starting on the next channel.

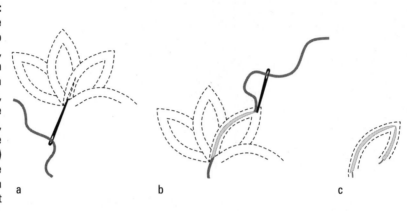

a   b   c

7. **Repeat Steps 3 through 6 in the channels of all eight petals.**

8. **With a small pair of scissors, carefully cut a small slit in the lining fabric at the center of each petal, but don't cut through the batting or the quilted layer.**

   The slit need only be ½-inch long at the most, as shown in Figure 15-13a.

9. **Using the large-eyed needle or some other sharp object, push a small amount of stuffing (about the size of a pea) into the slit. Repeat with small bits of stuffing until you fill the petal.**

10. **Carefully whip stitch the slit closed using off-white all-purpose thread in a hand-sewing needle (see Figure 15-13b).**

    To work the whip stitch,

    1. Knot the end of a single length of thread.

    2. Insert the needle on the underside of the quilt, bringing it up to the right side on one side of the slit.

    3. Cross to the other side of slit and take a stitch, whipping back and forth between the left- and right-hand sides of the slit until it's closed.

11. **After you stuff all the petals, machine stitch around the pillow top, about ⅛ inch from the raw edges.**

12. **Trim away the excess lining fabric and batting that extends beyond the edges of the pillow top.**

Figure 15-13:
To fill the center portion of each petal, you cut a slit in the lining (a) in which to insert stuffing and then whip stitch the opening closed (b).

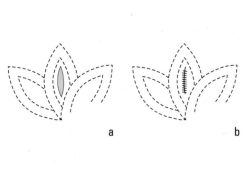

a   b

Assembling the pillow

Follow these steps to assemble the pillow:

1. **Using the all-purpose thread, begin machine stitching the piping around the pillow top at the center of one edge, leaving a 2-inch tail of piping hanging free.**

2. **When you approach a corner, stop stitching ¼ inch away from the corner.**

3. **Clip into the seam allowance of the piping *close to but not through* the stuffed area of the piping.**

   Clipping eliminates the bulk that would otherwise leave you with rounded, icky corners rather than nice, pointed ones.

4. **Rotate the pillow top around the corner, and resume stitching the piping to the next edge.**

   Repeat Steps 2 and 3 at each corner.

5. **When you return to your starting point, overlap the remaining piping with the tail you left at the starting point, and stitch across the overlapped tails to completely stitch the piping in place. Trim the excess piping to ½ inch, as shown in Figure 15-14.**

   The fabric and piping thicknesses will be a bit bulky. Stitch slowly so that you don't break your needle.

Figure 15-14:
Piping
finishes off
the top layer
of this pillow
covering.

6. **Place the completed pillow top against the 8- x 8-inch piece of coordinating backing fabric, right sides together. Pin the two pieces together to keep them from shifting during assembly.**

7. **Machine stitch the pillow top to the backing, following the stitching line you made when attaching the piping. Leave a 4-inch opening along the bottom edge for turning (see Figure 15-15).**

8. **Clip the corners close to the stitching line (but not through it) to eliminate bulk at the corners (see Figure 15-15).**

Figure 15-15:
Clip the
corners
close to the
stitching to
eliminate
bulk.

9. **Turn the pillow top right side out by pulling it through the opening.**

10. **Stuff the pillow pocket firmly with polyester stuffing.**

11. **Tuck in the seam allowances of the opening, and hand stitch the opening closed using the whip stitch.**

Full-Size Trapunto Pattern

Dancing Blossoms Wall Hanging

Hand appliqué paired with embroidery makes a dainty team, and this project is no exception. Three shades of pink fabrics make up each delicate blossom, which is enhanced by narrow embroidered stems and leaf details. The light, springtime feel of this project and its finished size (around 21 x 21 inches) make it a great wall decoration for your home.

Don't like pink? You can easily adapt the colors to your own preference by selecting three shades of your favorite color of roses — or make each square a different color. Variety is the spice of life!

Stashing your materials

The following list covers the fabrics and notions you need to make the Dancing Blossoms Wall Hanging:

- ✔ ⅓ yard of off-white solid fabric
- ✔ One fat quarter of light pink print fabric
- ✔ One fat quarter of medium pink print fabric
- ✔ One fat quarter of deep pink print fabric
- ✔ One fat quarter of pink print fabric
- ✔ One fat quarter of light green print fabric
- ✔ Assorted scraps of green print fabric totaling ⅛ yard
- ✔ One 24- x 24-inch piece of coordinating fabric
- ✔ One 24- x 24-inch piece of low- or traditional-loft quilt batting
- ✔ All-purpose threads in off-white and coordinating shades of pink and green
- ✔ Six-strand cotton embroidery floss in medium green
- ✔ 3 yards of off-white quilt binding

All seam allowances in this project are the standard ¼ inch and are included in the given measurements and directions.

Cutting the pieces

The blocks, border strips, cornerstones, and center triangles are cut first.

1. Cut the pieces listed in Table 15-1.

Table 15-1	Cutting Instructions for Quilt Top		
Piece	*Fabric*	*Measurement*	*Quantity*
Appliqué block foundation	Off-white solid	5½" x 5½"	5
Corner triangle	Pink print	5⅞" x 5⅞"	2
Side triangle	Pink print	8½" x 8½"	1
Inner border	Light green	1½" x 14½"	4

Piece	Fabric	Measurement	Quantity
Inner border cornerstone and leaves	Green scraps	½" x 1½"	4
Outer border	Light pink	2½" x 16½"	4
Outer border cornerstone	Deep pink	2½" x 2½"	4

2. **Cut the two 5⅞-inch squares of pink print in half diagonally to make two triangles from each square — four triangles in all.**

   These are the corner triangles.

3. **Cut the ½-inch square of pink print into quarters diagonally to make four triangles.**

   These are the side triangles.

Creating the appliquéd blocks

The appliquéd blocks are the focal point of this wall hanging. Follow these steps to create them:

1. **Using the templates at the end of this project section, trace the following appliqué shapes onto the wrong sides of the coordinating fabrics:**

   - Trace four bud shapes onto each of the pink print fabrics — light, medium, and dark. (The flower calls for three identical teardrop shapes to make the blossom.)
   - Trace 12 leaves onto the various green fabric scraps.

2. **Cut out each appliqué shape, adding a ¼-inch seam allowance to all sides. Turn under and baste the seam allowances (see Chapter 10 for instructions on the turn-and-baste method of appliqué).**

3. **Using the templates at the end of this project section and a water-soluble pencil, trace one blossom spray onto each of the four off-white blocks and one center leaf spray onto the remaining off-white block.**

4. **Arrange one set of appliqués (three bud pieces, two large leaves, and two tiny leaves) on an off-white square (see Figure 15-16), and pin the pieces in place.**

5. **Starting with the bottommost bud, stitch the appliqués to the base block using coordinating threads and an appliqué stitch.**

   For more on the appliqué stitch, turn to Chapter 10.

6. **Thread a hand sewing needle with two strands of the green six-strand floss. Embroider the stem lines and leaf details that you drew on the block in Step 3 using a *stem stitch* (also known as an *outline stitch*; see Figure 15-17).**

   To make a stem stitch, you insert the needle on one side of a line (drawn or imaginary) and bring the needle back to the fabric surface on the other side of the line. With each stitch, you advance along your desired path, so that the line is "wrapped" with diagonal stitches.

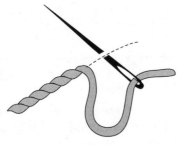

7. **Arrange the center leaf appliqués on the remaining off-white block, pin them, and stitch them in place with the appliqué stitch.**

Assembling the quilt center

Follow these steps to create the center of this quilt:

1. **Thread your sewing machine with off-white all-purpose thread.**

2. **Using Figure 15-18 as a guide, stitch two side triangles to one blossom block to make the upper-left row. Repeat with the two remaining side triangles and one other blossom block to make the bottom-right row.**

   In this quilt, your rows are built diagonally (also known as "set on point").

3. **Stitch two blossom blocks to either side of the center leaf block. Then stitch a corner triangle to each blossom block, as shown in Figure 15-18.**

   These five pieces make up the center row.

4. **Stitch the three rows created in Steps 2 and 3 together, alternating them as shown in Figure 15-18.**

5. **Stitch the two remaining corner triangles to the upper-left and lower-right blossom blocks (the long side of the triangles should be closest to the leaves in the blossom blocks).**

Figure 15-18: Orient the blossom blocks so that they create a sort of circle around the center leaf block, and assemble the rows of this project on the diagonal.

Adding the borders

This section walks you through the steps of adding borders to your quilt center:

1. **Stitch inner border strips to the right and left sides of the quilt center. Press the seam allowances toward the green strips.**

2. **Stitch inner border cornerstones to the short ends of the two remaining inner border strips, as shown in Figure 15-19.**

3. **Stitch the strips made in Step 2 to the upper and lower edges of the quilt center. Press the seam allowances toward the border strips.**

4. **Stitch outer border strips to the right and left sides of the quilt center.**

5. **Stitch outer border cornerstones to the short ends of the two remaining outer border strips.**

6. **Stitch the strips made in Step 5 to the upper and lower edges of the quilt center to complete the quilt top (see Figure 15-19).**

Figure 15-19: Inner and outer border strips as well as cornerstones in accent fabrics add interest and tie all the fabrics and colors in the quilt together.

Quilting your quilt

To finish your quilt:

1. **Lay the quilt top facedown on your work surface. On top, lay the batting and then backing fabric, right side up.**

2. **Thread or pin baste the layers together to prepare the project for quilting (for a basting how-to, flip to Chapter 12).**

3. **Hand or machine quilt as desired.**

   For design ideas, turn to Chapter 11. The quilt pictured in the color section features hand quilting stitched ¼ inch from the seam lines and a decorative pattern in the large pink borders made by using a commercial quilting template.

4. **After you complete the quilting, machine stitch very close to the raw edges of the quilt top, and trim away the excess batting and backing that extends beyond the edges of the quilt top.**

5. **Bind the edges of the quilt with the off-white binding.**

   For a refresher on how to apply premade binding or make your own, check out Chapter 14.

Blossom Spray Pattern

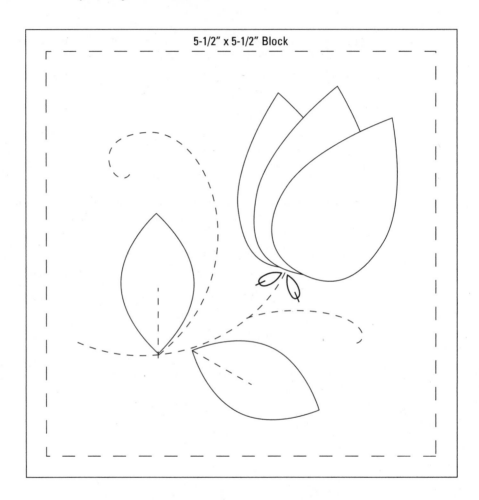

5-1/2" x 5-1/2" Block

Center Leaf Spray Pattern

Traditional Basket Wall Hanging

This little wall hanging has a very traditional design style but is constructed with a modern twist: The appliqué style mimics time-consuming hand appliqué, but you actually use machine stitching and clear nylon monofilament. (If you prefer to stitch the pieces in place by hand, refer to Chapter 10 for tips.)

This project looks best when made with random fabric scraps, but you can easily change the colors to suit your own tastes or décor. And because it's a quick project to stitch up, you may want to consider making one for a friend!

The finished size of this wall hanging is approximately 24 x 24 inches.

Stashing your materials

Because this is a scrap-basket project, I list the following required fabrics according to their measurements rather than yardage. If you can't find the right sized piece in your own scrap basket, I suggest raiding a friend's stash.

- One 14½- x 14½-inch piece of light tan print fabric
- Two 11- x 11-inch pieces of dark blue print fabric
- Four 2½- x 20-inch strips of red-checkered fabric
- Four 2½- x 2½-inch pieces of deep yellow print fabric
- One 12- x 12-inch piece of medium brown print fabric
- Two 3- x 5-inch pieces each of light green, medium green, and dark green print or solid fabrics
- Four 5- x 7-inch pieces of print fabric in assorted colors
- Four 3- x 4-inch pieces of print fabric in assorted colors
- One 26- x 26-inch piece of coordinating fabric
- 3 yards of navy blue quilt binding
- One 26- x 26-inch piece of low-loft batting
- All-purpose thread in assorted colors
- Clear nylon monofilament thread
- Wax-coated freezer paper

Creating appliqué shapes

Follow these steps to create the appliqué shapes featured in this project:

1. **Using the appliqué shapes provided at the end of this project section, trace six leaves, four flowers, four flower centers, and a basket onto the unwaxed side of the freezer paper.**

   For the basket, join the basket handle to the basket base and then trace it (not including the little tidbit hidden by the basket base). Reverse the pattern and trace the other half of the basket so that you have the full pattern (see Figure 15-20).

2. **Cut out the freezer paper shapes with scissors.**

   Be sure to use the scissors reserved for paper or other uses — don't use your fabric-cutting scissors.

Figure 15-20:
Because
the basket
template
only gives
you half the
final shape,
you have to
reverse the
template
and trace
the other
half for a
complete
basket.

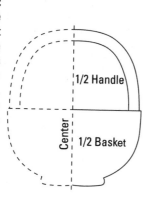

1/2 Handle

Center

1/2 Basket

3. **Start pressing with the waxed (shiny) side pressed to the wrong sides of the fabrics (see Chapter 8 for more on pressing).**

   • **Press the paper leaf shapes to the wrong sides of the light, medium, and dark green fabrics.**

   • **Press the paper flowers to the wrong sides of the 5- x 7-inch assorted print fabrics.**

   • **Press the paper flower centers to the wrong sides of the 3- x 4-inch assorted print fabrics.**

   • **Press the complete paper basket to the wrong side of the medium brown print fabric.**

To accommodate the turned under seam allowances you need when appliquéing, be sure to leave at least ½ inch between the pieces.

4. **Using fabric scissors, cut out each shape ¼ inch to ½ inch from the edges of the freezer paper.**

If you're uncomfortable with eyeballing this distance, feel free to draw a line around each shape ¼ inch to ½ inch from the edges of the paper.

5. **To prepare the leaf, flower, and flower-center pieces for appliquéing, fold the seam allowances to the wrong sides of the appliqué and secure them in place with pins.**

To accommodate the curves of your paper shape, notch the seam allowance of the fabric so that you can fold it over the paper in sections. Clipping small notches in the fabric gives you a smoother curve in the fabric edges.

6. **Starting with one appliqué, thread a hand-sewing needle with matching all-purpose thread, and carefully stitch through the seam allowance using a running stitch (see Figure 15-21). Pull the thread gently to gather the seam allowance around the paper shape.**

   The running stitch should go through the seam-allowance fabric only — not through the paper.

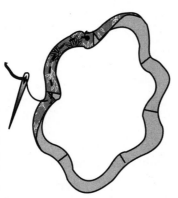

Figure 15-21: With the freezer-paper appliqué technique, you gather seam allowances around a freezer paper shape.

7. **Repeat Step 6 with the remaining appliqué shapes.**

8. **Mist the shapes with a spray bottle containing water, and press them until they're dry.**

9. **Carefully peel the freezer paper from the appliqués, leaving the running stitches intact.**

   Refer to Chapter 10 for full coverage of the freezer-paper appliqué technique.

Appliquéing the shapes

Follow these steps to appliqué the shapes onto your quilt top:

1. **Arrange the fabric appliqué shapes on the light tan print square, as shown in Figure 15-22.**

   Feel free to alter the arrangement to suit yourself.

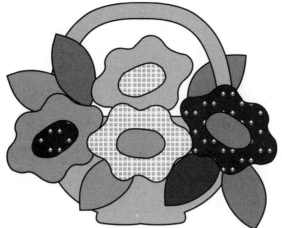

Figure 15-22:
Arrange the flowers and leaves so that they appear to spill out of the basket.

2. **Pin or thread baste the bottommost layer of pieces in place on the tan foundation to prepare them for machine appliqué.**

3. **Load light tan all-purpose thread in your sewing machine's bobbin case, and load clear nylon thread in the top of the machine. Set your machine for the blind-stitch.**

4. **On a scrap of fabric, test sew a length of blind-stitch to make sure the settings are right.**

   If you notice that the bobbin thread is being pulled to the top of the fabric, loosen the tension of the upper thread slightly until the problem is corrected.

5. **Machine appliqué the pieces to the tan foundation fabric, adjusting the fabric as necessary so that the straight-stitch portion of the stitch is off the edge of the appliqué and the zigzag portion barely catches the appliqué (see Figure 15-23).**

   Remember that you want to hide the stitches close up against the edge of the appliqué. With hidden stitches in clear nylon thread, everyone will think that you hand appliquéd the project, and you'll be a quilting hero.

6. **Repeat Steps 2 and 5 with each layer of appliqué pieces. After appliquéing all your shapes in place, remove your pins or basting stitches.**

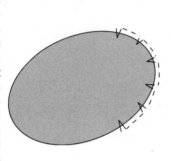

Figure 15-23:
The blind-
stitch is a
less-obvious
appliqué
stitch that
gives
machine
appliquéd
pieces a
hand
appliqué
look.

Assembling the quilt top

Follow these steps to assemble your quilt top:

1. **Cut each of the two 11- x 11-inch dark blue print squares in half on the diagonal. Fold each triangle in half, and press the fabric to mark the center of the long bias edge.**

   You should end up with four large, folded triangles.

2. **Fold the tan appliquéd square in half, and pinch the creases at the edges. Unfold the square, fold it in half the other way, and pinch the other two creases.**

   Pinching the creases temporarily marks the center point of each side of the square.

3. **Align the center of one side of the tan center square with the center crease of a blue triangle from Step 1. Using a neutral shade of thread, machine stitch the blue triangle to the side of the tan square.**

4. **Repeat Step 3 with the other three blue triangles; then press all the seam allowances towards the blue fabric.**

   Your triangles may look a little rough or downright crooked, but that's okay. Because this may be the first time you've ever attempted this type of medallion, I've padded the triangle measurements slightly to ensure you end up with an accurate square. You'll have a medallion larger than you actually need and will trim down the excess at the sides in the next step.

5. **Trim the blue triangles with a rotary cutter and ruler so that they extend just ¼ inch from the corner points of the tan square, as shown in Figure 15-24.**

   Stay squared by using your quilting ruler to make certain the sides are at right angles to each other.

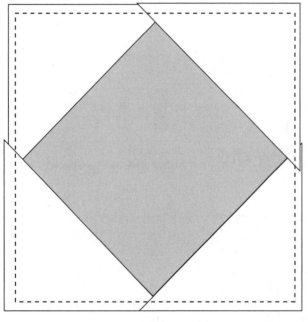

Figure 15-24: Trimming the triangles leaves enough of a seam allowance that the center square ends in nice, pointed corners.

6. **Measure the width of the entire quilt center, and trim the red-checkered border strips to match your measurement.**

7. **Stitch red-checkered strips to the left- and right-hand sides of the quilt center.**

8. **Stitch the 2½-inch deep-yellow print squares to the short ends of the two remaining red-checkered border strips, and press the seam allowances toward the darker fabric.**

9. **Stitch the strips from Step 8 to the top and bottom edges of the quilt center. Press the seam allowances toward the border strips.**

Quilting and finishing the project

Follow these steps to complete your Traditional Basket Wall Hanging:

1. **Transfer your quilting design to the quilt top.**

   At the end of this project section, you can find a full-size quilting pattern that works really well in each of the blue triangles (see Figure 15-25). But feel free to use any pattern you like or come up with a freehand design to fill the empty space.

2. **Lay the quilt top facedown on your work surface. On top, lay the batting and backing fabric, right side up.**

3. **Thread or pin baste the layers together to prepare the project for quilting (for a basting how-to, flip to Chapter 12).**

4. **Hand or machine quilt as desired.**

5. **Machine stitch close to the raw edges of the quilt top in straight stitch; then trim away the excess batting and backing that extends beyond the edges of the quilt top.**

Figure 15-25:
Before you assemble the quilt sandwich, mark your desired quilting pattern on the quilt top. The design in this illustration is provided at the end of this project section.

6. **Bind the quilt with the navy blue binding to complete the project.**

   For a refresher on how to apply premade binding or make your own, check out Chapter 14.

Half-Size Quilting Pattern and Full-Size Appliqué Templates

Enlarge the quilting pattern by 200 percent for a full-sized pattern.

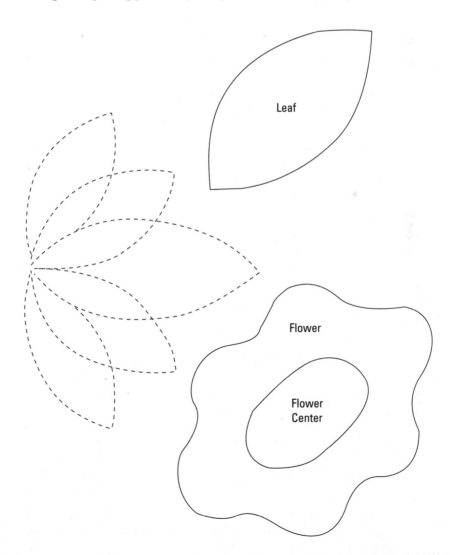

Leaf

Flower

Flower
Center

Half-Size Basket Template

Enlarge this basket by 200 percent for a full-sized pattern.

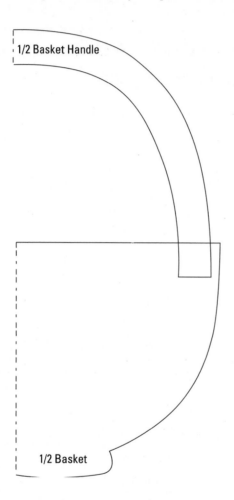

1/2 Basket Handle

1/2 Basket

Chicken Scratch Foundation-Pieced Quilt

Foundation piecing is a blast! I love the accuracy of this technique and the ease with which you can construct small blocks — all without distortion. Seeing as how the finished size of this quilt is only 20 x 25 inches, the blocks are certainly small enough to make foundation piecing the way to go!

Another great thing about this quilt is that, with the exception of the borders and backing, the whole thing's made from scraps. So dig deep into your fabric stash (you know you have one) — the more varied the fabrics, the better!

Stashing your materials

This list tells you what fabrics and notions you need to make the Chicken Scratch Foundation-Pieced Quilt:

✔ Assorted scraps of fabric in varying colors totaling about ⅓ yard

✔ Assorted scraps of off-white and tan fabrics totaling about ¼ yard

✔ ¼ yard of off-white print fabric

✔ ¼ yard of medium brown print fabric

✔ One 24- x 29-inch piece of coordinating fabric for the backing

✔ One 24- x 29-inch piece of low- or traditional-loft quilt batting

✔ All-purpose thread in off-white

✔ 3 yards of brown quilt binding

All seam allowances in this project are the standard ¼ inch and are included in the given measurements or directions.

Cutting the pieces

Cut the strips for the borders and sashing according to Table 15-2.

Table 15-2	Cutting Instructions for Border and Sashing Strips		
Piece	*Fabric*	*Measurement*	*Quantity*
Vertical sashing	Off-white yardage	1½" x 4½"	16
Horizontal sashing	Off-white yardage	1½" x 16½"	5
Border, sides	Medium brown yardage	2" x 21½"	2
Border, upper and lower	Medium brown yardage	2" x 20½"	2

Creating the foundation-pieced blocks

If you're new to foundation piecing, turn to Chapter 9 and read through my explanation of the process. This piecing technique can sound a little confusing to newcomers, but it's really fun and surprisingly simple once you get the hang of it. Follow these steps to create the pieced blocks in this quilt:

1. **Make 12 photocopies of the foundation pattern that appears at the end of this project section. (You should be able to fit two pattern blocks per sheet.) Cut out each block along the outermost solid line.**

2. **Starting at the center (piece 1) of one block, pin a tan or off-white scrap, right side up, to the back side of the paper.**

   The scrap should be slightly larger than the lines that delineate piece 1.

3. **With the paper side up, machine stitch the scrap to the paper, following the piece 1 outline on the paper.**

4. **Repeat Steps 2 and 3 with the remaining pieces in the pattern, adding any color scraps to each piece position in numbered order in any color desired.**

   As you add pieces to the foundation, pin them together them right sides facing, sew them together, and then press the seams open before adding another piece, right sides facing.

5. **Repeat Steps 2 through 4 with the remaining paper block patterns until you have 12 foundation-pieced blocks.**

6. **Trim the blocks down to their finished size (4½ inches square) along the dashed line on the paper pattern. Carefully remove the paper from the block, and press each block.**

Creating the quilt center

To create the center portion of the Chicken Scratch quilt:

1. **Stitch three blocks alternately with four vertical sashing strips to make a row (see Figure 15-26). Press seam allowances toward the sashing strips.**

   Repeat with the remaining blocks and vertical sashing strips. Make two rows in which the blocks lean to the left and two rows in which the blocks lean to the right.

Figure 15-26: In the first row, three pieced blocks are angled to the left and separated by sashing strips.

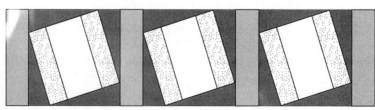

2. **Stitch the four rows alternately with the horizontal sashing strips to make the center area (see Figure 15-27).**

   Alternate the rows so that the slant of the blocks switches from one row to the next.

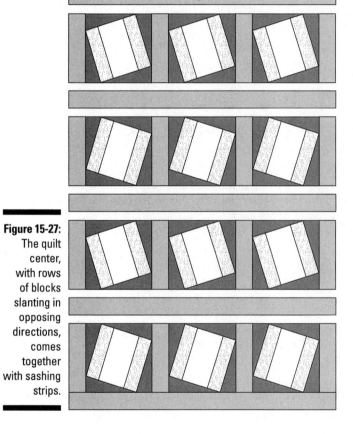

Figure 15-27: The quilt center, with rows of blocks slanting in opposing directions, comes together with sashing strips.

3. **Stitch the side border strips to either side of the quilt center, as shown in Figure 15-28. Trim any excess border fabric that extends beyond the upper and lower edges of the quilt center.**

4. **Stitch the upper and lower border strips to the upper and lower edges of the quilt center, as shown in Figure 15-28. Trim any excess border fabric that extends beyond the edge of the side borders.**

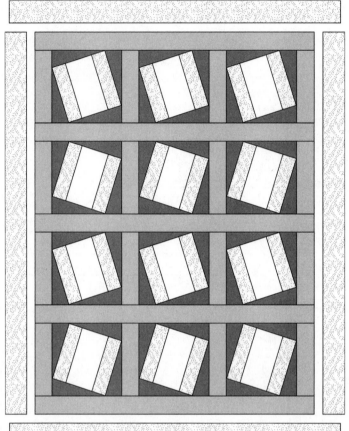

Figure 15-28:
Add border
strips to the
sides and
then the
upper and
lower edges
of the quilt
center to
finish it off.

Quilting your quilt

To finish your quilt:

1. **Lay the quilt top facedown on your work surface. On top, place the batting and backing fabric, right side up.**

2. **Thread or pin baste the layers together to prepare the project for quilting (for a basting how-to, flip to Chapter 12).**

3. **Hand or machine quilt as desired.**

   For design ideas, turn to Chapter 11. The quilt pictured in the color section features machine quilting in-the-ditch along all seam lines with clear nylon monofilament.

4. **When you complete the quilting, machine stitch very close to the raw edges of the quilt top, and trim away the excess batting and backing that extends beyond the edges of the quilt top.**

5. **Bind the edges of the quilt with the brown binding.**

   For a refresher on how to apply premade binding or make your own, check out Chapter 14.

Chicken Scratch Foundation Block Pattern

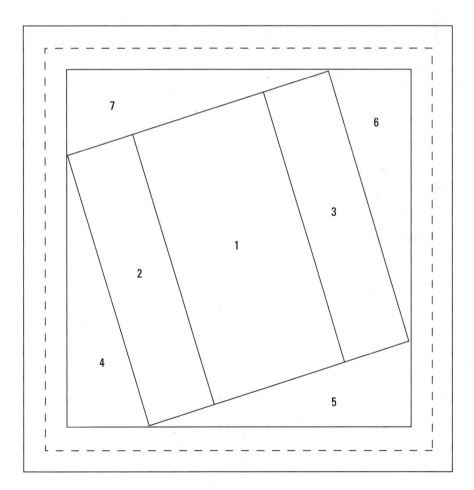

Full-size Foundation Block Pattern

Chapter 16

Mixed-Technique Projects

*M*y favorite things to design are mixed-technique quilts. I love mixing piecing with hand or machine appliqué or hand or machine embroidery. Mixing techniques gives projects a lot of character and makes them a lot more fun (this tidbit coming from an author with a short attention span!).

In this chapter, I provide you with the instructions for several projects that mix different hand and machine techniques.

Rosy Wreath Quilt

This fun and easy quilt combines strip-piecing, hand appliqué, and hand embroidery, but don't let the combination of techniques scare you! For example, the strip-piecing is a breeze and is a great way to get comfortable with your rotary cutter.

The relatively small size of this quilt — 39 x 39 inches — means it's great as a lap quilt, wall hanging, or even a child's favorite blanket! Plus, this project works up quickly and with little effort. After assembling the rose block units, prepare the leaf shapes and take the project along on your commute or vacation — the hand appliqué work is portable and easy to stitch on the run.

Stashing your materials

The following list covers the fabrics and notions you need to make the Rosy Wreath Quilt:

✔ ¾ yard of white solid fabric

✔ ⅓ yard of dark pink print fabric

✔ ⅓ yard of medium pink print fabric

- ✓ ½ yard of green print fabric
- ✓ ⅓ yard of golden yellow print fabric
- ✓ One 45- x 45-inch piece of coordinating fabric
- ✓ One 45- x 45-inch piece of low- or traditional-loft quilt batting
- ✓ ½ yard of 12-inch-wide, wax-coated freezer paper
- ✓ All-purpose thread in white and green
- ✓ Six-strand cotton embroidery floss in green
- ✓ 5 yards of pink quilt binding

All seam allowances for this project are the standard ¼ inch and are included in the given measurements or directions.

Cutting out the pieces

For best results, use a rotary cutter and ruler to cut the pieces covered in this section. Not only do you get more accurate cutting edges and more uniform pieces, but you also save a tremendous amount of time!

Referring to the details provided in Table 16-1, cut the pieces needed to construct the quilt top.

Table 16-1	Cutting Instructions for Quilt Top		
Piece	*Fabric*	*Measurement*	*Quantity*
Flower petal 1	Dark pink	2½" x 44"	2
Flower petal 2	Medium pink	2½" x 44"	2
Foundation	White	1½" x 44"	4
Vertical sashing	White	1½" x 15½"	6
Horizontal sashing	White	1½" x 33½"	3
Plain block and leaf foundation block	White	5½" x 5½"	20
Flower center	Golden yellow	1½" x 1½"	16
Inner border, upper and lower	Golden yellow	1½" x 33½"	2
Inner border, sides	Golden yellow	1½" x 35½"	2
Outer border, upper and lower	Green	2½" x 35½"	2
Outer border, sides	Green	2½" x 39½"	2

Creating the flower squares

The finished size of each flower block is 15 x 15 inches. Follow these steps to create the flower squares:

1. **Stitch one white foundation strip to the long side of one medium pink petal strip, having their right sides together. Repeat with a second white strip and the other medium pink strip. Do the same with the remaining two white strips and the two dark pink petal strips. Press all seam allowances toward the pink fabric.**

   You end up with two two-strip units of white and medium pink and two two-strip units of white and dark pink.

2. **Cut 16 2½-inch pieces from each two-strip unit that you assembled in Step 1 (see Figure 16-1).**

   These two-tone pieces are the petal units. You should have 32 units of each color (medium and dark pink), each measuring 2½ x 3½ inches.

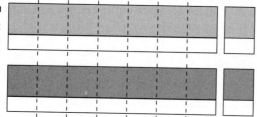

Figure 16-1: Chop up your two-tone strips into flower petal pieces.

3. **Stitch one yellow flower center to one of the dark pink petal units by placing right sides together and stitching only halfway across the yellow center square, as shown in Figure 16-2a. Press the yellow square outwards to prepare it for the next petal, as shown in Figure 16-2b.**

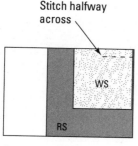
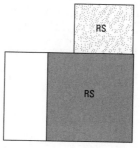

Figure 16-2: Join a flower center to a petal unit (a), and press open (b).

Stitch halfway across

RS

WS

RS

RS

a

b

4. **Stitch a medium pink petal piece to the resulting unit from Step 3, as shown in Figure 16-3a, stitching down the entire length. Press the petal unit outwards (see Figure 16-3b).**

5. **Stitch the third petal (dark pink) to the unit as shown in Figure 16-3c. Press the new petal outwards.**

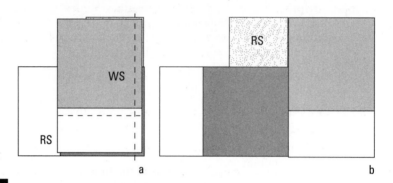

a   b

Figure 16-3:
Join two petal pieces together (a), press the new piece open (b), and add a third petal (c).

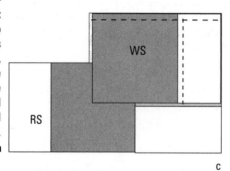

c

6. **Stitch the fourth and final petal (medium pink) to the unit by following these steps:**

1. Join the final petal to the third petal by stitching down the entire length of the piece (see Figure 16-4a). Press the petal outwards (see Figure 16-4b). The only unstitched area now runs along the top of the first petal where it meets the fourth petal through to the center square that you stitched halfway across in Step 3.

2. Fold the resulting unit in half horizontally (the top portion coming down towards you), right sides facing.

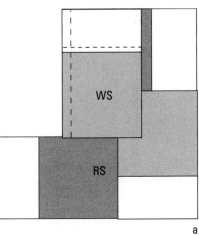 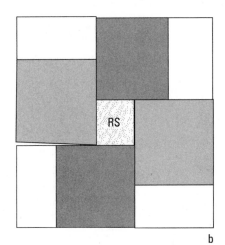

Figure 16-4:
Sew the fourth petal to the three-petal unit (a) and press open to reveal one unstitched seam (b).

a   b

3. Stitch across the open portions of the first and fourth petals, starting your stitching at the center square's halfway point (where you began your stitching in Step 3). Figure 16-5a shows how to fold the petal square and where to put your last stitches. You can see the completed flower square in Figure 16-5b.

7. Make 15 additional flower squares.

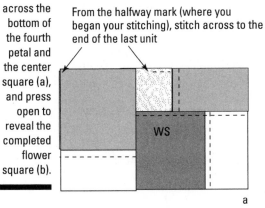 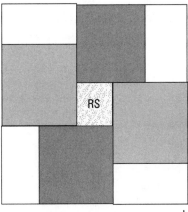

Figure 16-5:
Stitch across the bottom of the fourth petal and the center square (a), and press open to reveal the completed flower square (b).

From the halfway mark (where you began your stitching), stitch across to the end of the last unit

a   b

Creating the leaf squares

Like the flower blocks, the finished size of the leaf squares is 15 x 15 inches. To create the leaf squares, follow these steps:

1. **On 16 of the white leaf foundation blocks you cut according to Table 16-1, sketch the leaf shape and stem using the full-size pattern at the end of this project section.**

   Use a water-soluble pencil or chalk, and trace very lightly.

2. **Use the pattern at the end of this project to create two leaf templates out of cardboard or plastic template sheeting; one template should be the size of the dotted line, and the other template should be the size of the solid line, which accounts for a seam allowance.**

3. **Using the solid-line template, trace 16 leaves onto the wrong side of the remaining green print fabric. Cut out the leaves along the marked lines.**

4. **On the paper side (not the shiny side) of your freezer paper, trace the dotted-line template to create 16 leaf shapes. Cut out the paper leaves along the marked lines.**

5. **Iron one paper leaf shape, shiny (wax) side down, onto the wrong side of each fabric leaf shape (as shown in Figure 16-6a).**

   When ironed, the wax coating sticks the paper to the fabric easily.

6. **Fold the seam allowance (¼ inch) over the paper on all the leaves, and baste it by hand with a running stitch (see Figure 16-6b). Stitch only through the seam allowance and not through the paper or the right side of the leaves.**

7. **Gently pull your sewing thread to gather the seam allowance around the paper shapes, so the seam allowance stays on the underside (wrong side) of the leaves (see Figure 16-6c).**

   Press the leaves using a starch spray so that the folded edges hold a nice crease.

Figure 16-6:
Iron the paper to the fabric (a), and then baste the seam allowance around the paper leaf (b and c).

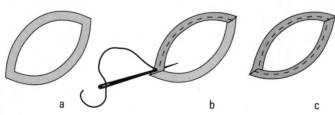

a   b   c

8. **Carefully remove the freezer paper from the center of the leaves.**

   Be gentle so as not to mess up the folded edges of the leaf shapes.

9. **Using the lines you drew in Step 1 as a placement guide, pin a leaf to each square.**

   If you don't want to fiddle with pins, you may want to use a water-soluble fabric glue such as Glue Baste to hold your leaves in place on the foundation block. One or two dots of glue on each leaf is plenty.

10. **Hand appliqué the leaves to the squares using matching thread and the blind-stitch. To execute the blind-stitch,**

    1. Start from the back side of the foundation fabric, and bring your needle up through the folded edge of the appliqué.

    2. Insert the needle into the foundation fabric right next to the spot where the thread came through the appliqué.

    3. Slide the needle forward about ⅛ inch along the appliqué edge and bring it back to the top of the piece, catching the edge of the appliqué as you did in Step 1. In this manner, you've traveled ⅛ inch and hidden the traveling portion of the thread on the wrong side of the foundation block. Continue around the appliqué shape.

11. **Cut a length of green six-strand embroidery floss (about as long as the distance from your elbow to your fingertip). Divide the floss into two lengths of three strands each, and thread a large-eyed needle with one three-strand piece of floss. Set the other piece aside for when the first runs out.**

12. **Use a stem-stitch (shown in Figure 16-7) to hand-embroider the stem line and tendril designs:**

    1. Bring the needle through the quilt top fabric at the starting point of your stem, and then insert the needle ⅛ inch or so from the starting point, following the desired stem line.

    2. Bring the needle up again through the fabric, halfway between the spot where your thread came up originally and the spot where your needle went back down.

    3. Repeat along the stem and tendril markings.

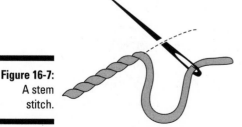

Figure 16-7:
A stem
stitch.

Assembling the quilt top

After you work through the two preceding sections, you're left with 16 petal blocks and 16 leaf blocks. Now it's time to stitch these pieces together — along with a few others — to create the quilt top. To assemble the top, follow these steps:

1. **Stitch one flower square to either side of a plain white square, as shown in Figure 16-8a. Orient the flower squares so that the medium pink petals touch the white center square. Press the seam allowances toward the white squares.**

   Do the same to the other three white squares, creating four units consisting of two flower squares with a white square in between.

a

b

Figure 16-8:
Stitch the
pieced
blocks to the
center block
(a) and to
leaf blocks
(b) to make
rows (c).

c

2. **Stitch one leaf square to either side of one flower square, orienting the leaf blocks so that the leaf on the left points up and the leaf on the right points to the right, as shown in Figure 16-8b.**

   Do the same to the remaining flower squares, creating eight units consisting of two leaf squares with a flower square in between.

3. **Stitch one double-flower row alternately with two single-flower rows, as shown in Figure 16-8c, to complete a wreath block.**

   Make four of these blocks.

4. **To create a block row, alternate three vertical sashing strips with two wreath blocks, as shown in Figure 16-9. Stitch everything together.**

   Do the same with the other two wreath blocks, giving you two wreath block rows.

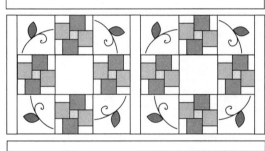

Figure 16-9: Stitch together wreath blocks and sashing strips to assemble the center of the quilt top.

5. **To complete the quilt center, alternate the two wreath block rows with the three horizontal sashing strips, as shown in Figure 16-9. Stitch everything together, and trim any excess sashing.**

6. **Stitch the golden yellow inner border strips to the quilt center, starting with the upper and lower borders before attaching the side borders (see Figure 16-10). Trim any excess. Press the seam allowances towards the border fabrics.**

7. **Repeat with the green outer border strips (upper and lower strips before sides) to complete the quilt top (see Figure 16-10).**

Figure 16-10:
Attach inner
and outer
border strips
to finish off
the quilt top.

Quilting and finishing your quilt

To finish your quilt:

1. **Lay the quilt top facedown on your work surface. Lay the batting on top of it, followed by the backing fabric, right side up.**

2. **Thread or pin baste the layers together to prepare it for quilting.**

   For a basting how-to, flip to Chapter 12.

3. **Hand or machine quilt as desired.**

   For design ideas, turn to Chapter 11. On the quilt pictured in the color section of this book, I stitched ½ inch from all seams and used free-motion stipple quilting with clear nylon monofilament inside the blocks.

4. **After you complete the quilting, stitch very close to the raw edges of the quilt top, and trim away the batting and backing that extends beyond the edges of the quilt top.**

5. **Bind the edges with the quilt binding to complete.**

   For a refresher on how to apply premade binding or make your own, check out Chapter 14.

Stem Diagram and Leaf Template

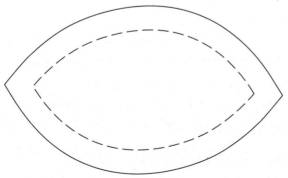

Scrappy Bloomers Wall Hanging or Lap Quilt

This section tells you everything you need to know to create my fun and colorful Scrappy Bloomers quilt. Machine blanket stitch appliqué makes this project quick to construct, although if you prefer a portable project, you can certain do the blanket stitch appliqué portion of the project by hand. The quilt's finished size — 35 x 42 inches — makes it versatile; you can display it as a decorative wall hanging or use it as a cozy lap quilt.

One of the best things about this project is that it's the perfect way to use up all those scrap-basket fabrics you've been collecting that are just too pretty to throw away. The maximum size of scrap material you need is a mere 5 inches square, so pull out all those little bits and pieces!

To make your Scrappy Bloomers quilt even more interesting, swap scraps with your friends or purchase a bunch of fat quarters to get a wide range of different fabrics.

Don't forget to prewash all fabrics before beginning this (or any) project. For prewashing instructions, jump back to Chapter 3.

Stashing your materials

You need the following materials to create this quilt:

- ¾ yard of off-white fabric
- ½ yard of multi-colored floral print fabric
- ⅓ yard of blue floral print fabric
- ⅓ yard of medium green fabric
- ¼ yard of solid tan fabric
- Twenty 5- x 5-inch (minimum) pieces of assorted medium-toned fabrics
- 2 yards of 16- to 18-inch-wide paper-backed fusible webbing
- Twenty 6- x 6-inch pieces of tear-away stabilizer
- All-purpose thread in a neutral color, such as off-white
- Buttonhole-twist or topstitching thread in dark brown
- 5 yards of off-white quilt binding, either premade or homemade according to the instructions in Chapter 11
- One 37- x-44-inch piece of low-loft batting
- One 37- x 44-inch piece of coordinating fabric

All seam allowances in this project are the standard ¼ inch and are included in all the given measurements. The appliqués don't require seam allowances.

Preparing the appliqué pieces

The first step in creating the Scrappy Bloomers quilt is preparing the flower appliqué shapes. The following steps explain this process:

1. **Using the full-size appliqué patterns at the end of this project section and a #2 pencil, trace 20 flowers, 20 centers, and 20 sets of leaves (that's 40 individual leaves) onto the paper side of the fusible webbing.**

   Because these flower pieces will be machine appliquéd onto foundation blocks rather than pieced together, you don't need to add seam allowances when tracing the shapes.

2. **Roughly cut out the fusible webbing pieces.**

3. **Using a hot iron, fuse the fusible webbing pieces to the wrong sides of their respective fabrics.**

   For iron settings, refer to the insert that accompanied your brand of fusible webbing, and fuse the leaf shapes to the green fabric, the flower center shapes to the tan fabric, and the flower shapes to the assorted scraps of fabric.

4. **Cut out the webbing-backed fabric shapes, carefully following the shape lines drawn on the fusible webbing in Step 1.**

Appliquéing the quilt blocks

After you prepare your flower shapes, you're ready to appliqué them to the foundation quilt blocks. The following steps tell you how:

1. **Referring to Table 16-2, cut out the pieces needed to put together the quilt top.**

   The letters in Table 16-2 correspond to the labeled pieces in Figures 16-12 and 16-13. For this section, you only need the foundation blocks. Set aside all the sashing and border pieces for now.

Table 16-2	Cutting Instructions for Quilt Top		
Piece	*Fabric*	*Measurement*	*Quantity*
Foundation block	Off-white	6½″ x 6½″	20
Vertical sashing (A)	Multi-colored floral	1½″ x 6½″	25
Horizontal sashing (B)	Multi-colored floral	1½″ x 29½″	6

2. **Lay out one 6½-inch off-white block. On the foundation block, arrange one flower, one flower center, and one set of leaves as shown in Figure 16-11.**

3. **Remove the paper backing from the appliqué shapes, and reset them in their spots. Use a hot iron to fuse the appliqués to the block. Repeat with the remaining appliqués and blocks.**

4. **On each block, use a washable pencil or tailor's chalk to draw a stem connecting the flower to the leaves (see Figure 16-11).**

   You can draw the stem freehand or use a ruler.

Figure 16-11:
Arrange
your
appliqués
in a flower
design, fuse
them, and
draw a stem.

A complete set of appliques,
ready for fusing.

5. **Place a piece of stabilizer against the wrong side of each block. Use straight pins to pin it in place at the corners.**

6. **Load brown buttonhole-twist thread in the upper part of your sewing machine; wind a bobbin with neutral all-purpose thread, and insert it in the machine's bobbin case.**

   The top (buttonhole-twist) thread is the one that appears around each appliqué as the top-stitching thread.

7. **Test your machine's blanket stitch by stitching on a scrap of fabric.**

   If the bobbin thread comes through the fabric and onto the top surface of the scrap fabric, loosen the tension of the upper thread slightly (refer to your machine's owner's manual for help making adjustments). Check out Chapter 10 for more on getting the machine blanket stitch just right.

8. **Machine appliqué each piece on each block using your machine's blanket stitch.**

   The machine blanket stitch adds a decorative accent to your appliqué pieces.

9. **Without changing the thread in your machine, stitch along each block's stem line with a straight stitch.**

10. **Remove the pins holding the stabilizer in place, and tear the stabilizer away from the back of the appliquéd blocks.**

Assembling the quilt top

To assemble the quilt top, collect your appliquéd quilt blocks and the sashing strips you cut in the preceding section. Follow these steps to assemble the quilt top:

1. **Stitch five vertical sashing strips (A) alternately with four appliquéd blocks to make a horizontal row, as shown in Figure 16-12. Press the seam allowances toward the sashing strips. Repeat to make five rows.**

Figure 16-12:
Five sashing
strips and
four blocks
make up
one row.

A strip

2. **Stitch the five rows alternately with the horizontal sashing strips (B) to make the quilt center (see Figure 16-13). Press the seam allowances toward the sashing strips.**

3. **Measure the quilt top from top to bottom edge, placing your measuring tape down the center of the quilt as opposed to the sides. From the blue floral fabric, cut two 1½-inch-wide strips that are as long as your measurement.**

4. **Stitch the strips from Step 3 to either side of the quilt center (see Figure 16-13). Press the seam allowances toward the border fabric, and trim the ends even with the quilt top.**

5. **Measure the quilt top from left to right edge, with the measuring tape running across the center of the quilt. From the blue floral fabric, cut two 1½-inch-wide strips that are as long as your measurement.**

6. **Stitch the strips from Step 5 to the top and bottom edges of the quilt center. Press the seam allowances toward the border fabric, and trim the ends even with the outer edges of the vertical borders from Step 4.**

7. **Repeat Steps 3 through 6 with the multi-colored floral fabric, cutting each strip 2½ inches wide.**

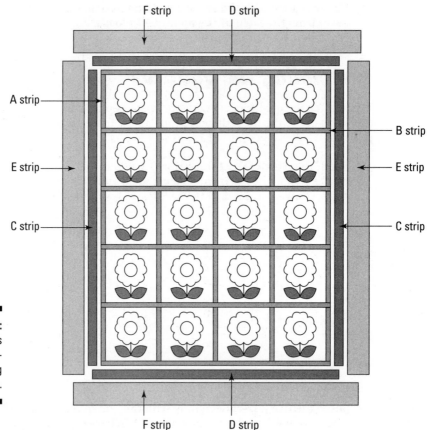

Figure 16-13:
Divide rows
with horizon-
tal sashing
strips.

Quilting and finishing the project

The following steps explain how to quilt and finish your Scrappy Bloomers quilt:

1. **Lay the quilt top facedown on your work surface. On top, place the batting followed by the backing fabric (right side up).**

2. **Thread or pin baste the layers together for quilting.**

   Check out Chapter 12 for basting instructions.

3. **Hand or machine quilt as desired.**

   For design ideas, turn to Chapter 11. On the quilt pictured in the color section of this book, I quilted in-the-ditch around each block and sashing strip with thread that matched the blocks.

4. **Machine stitch around the entire quilt, about ¼ to ⅛ inch away from the raw edges, and trim away any excess batting or backing fabric that extends beyond the edges of the quilt top.**

5. **Bind the quilt with the off-white binding to finish the project.**

   If you need help attaching binding, check out Chapter 14.

Scrappy Bloomers Template

Snow Crystals Lap Quilt

Speedy rotary-cutter techniques (covered in Chapter 8) and machine blanket stitch appliqué (covered in Chapter 10) make this quilt quicker to assemble than it appears. And because it's not very large (46 x 46 inches), the process goes even quicker!

If you don't care much for the look of blanket stitch, try satin stitch appliqué instead. For other appliqué stitching ideas, refer to Chapter 10. Just keep in mind that for speed, blanket stitch beats satin stitch.

Stashing your materials

You need the following materials to complete your Snow Crystals project:

- 2¾ yards of blue print or solid fabric
- 1¼ yards of white solid fabric
- ¾ yard of golden yellow print or solid fabric
- 1½ yards of 16- to 18-inch-wide paper-backed fusible webbing
- Nine 10- x 10-inch squares of tear-away stabilizer
- One 50- x 50-inch square of low-loft batting
- One 50- x 50-inch square of coordinating fabric
- All-purpose thread in blue, white, and golden yellow
- Buttonhole-twist thread in golden yellow
- 5½ yards of white bias binding

Preparing the appliqué pieces

The first step in creating the Snow Crystals Lap Quilt is preparing the snowflake appliqué shapes. The following steps explain this process:

1. **Using the pattern provided at the end of this project section and a #2 pencil, trace nine snowflake shapes on the paper side of the fusible webbing.**

   Because you fuse these shapes onto foundation blocks and use machine appliqué, the snowflakes don't require seam allowances.

2. **Roughly cut out the fusible webbing pieces.**

3. **Using a hot iron, fuse the fusible webbing pieces to the wrong side of the white fabric, spacing them ¼ inch apart.**

   For the appropriate iron setting, refer to the insert that accompanied your brand of fusible webbing.

4. **Cut out the webbing-backed snowflake shapes, carefully following the lines drawn on the webbing in Step 1.**

Appliquéing the snowflakes

To create the striking snowflake blocks that make up the quilt top, follow these steps:

1. **Referring to Table 16-3, cut out all the pieces needed for the project.**

   Avoid the need to piece any borders together by cutting the pieces in the order they're listed in the table. To be sure that you have enough fabric for this project, cut out all the pieces across the width of the fabric (from selvage to selvage). For instance, for the C strips, cut three 21/2- x 44-inch strips of fabric, and then recut each 44-inch strip into 10½-inch lengths (you'll get four C strips for each strip of fabric that you cut this way).

Table 16-3	Cutting Instructions for Quilt Top		
Piece	*Fabric*	*Measurement*	*Quantity*
Foundation block	Blue	10½" x 10½"	9
Outer border (A)	Blue	2½" x 42½"	4
Horizontal sashing (B)	Blue	2½" x 38½"	4
Vertical sashing (C)	Blue	2½" x 10½"	12
Sawtooth border(D-1)	Blue	14" x 29"	1
Sawtooth border (D-2)	White	14" x 29"	1
Snowflake border (E)	Golden yellow	1" x 11"	36
Accent square (F)	Golden yellow	2½" x 2½"	12

2. **Remove the paper backings from the snowflakes made in the preceding section, and fuse one snowflake to the center of each 10½-inch blue block.**

3. **Pin a piece of tear-away stabilizer to the back side of each snowflake block to prepare it for machine appliqué. Position the pins so that they won't interfere with your stitching — about ½ inch from the appliqués is a good distance.**

    The tear-away stabilizer keeps the block from being shoved down into the machine's throat plate and jammed by the actions of the needle and feed dogs — growl!

4. **Load the top of the machine with golden yellow buttonhole-twist thread. Use blue or white all-purpose thread in the bobbin case.**

5. **Using a scrap of fabric, test your machine's blanket stitch (see Figure 16-14) by sewing a bit and making setting adjustments.**

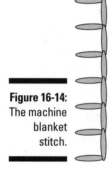

Figure 16-14:
The machine
blanket
stitch.

You want to be certain that your machine is making a well-formed blanket stitch before you begin your machine appliqué — it's better to test now than to rip out the threads later! If you notice that the bobbin thread is being pulled through the fabric onto the top surface, slightly loosen the tension for the upper thread. If you find yourself encountering difficulty, refer to Chapter 10 and consult your machine's owner's manual.

6. **When you're comfortable with the blanket stitch, machine appliqué the snowflakes to the blocks by blanket stitching along the outer edges of the snowflake shape. Remove the stabilizer when you finish.**

Assembling the quilt top

Follow these steps to assemble the top of your quilt:

1. **Fold each of the snowflake border strips (E) in half lengthwise, wrong sides facing, and press them (see Figure 16-15).**

Figure 16-15:
Fold the yellow border strips.

2. **Place one pressed E strip along one edge of the front side of a snowflake appliqué block, aligning the double raw edges of the strip with the raw edge of the block. Using matching all-purpose thread, stitch the strip in place using slightly less than a ¼-inch seam allowance, and then trim the excess strip at either end, as shown in Figure 16-16. Repeat on the opposite side of the block, and then add strips in the same manner to the two remaining sides of the block.**

   Note: Although Figure 16-16 shows a block minus the snowflake appliqué to cut the clutter, you're stitching these yellow border strips to the front side of your snowflake blocks.

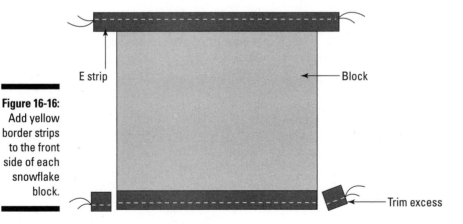

E strip
Block

Figure 16-16:
Add yellow border strips to the front side of each snowflake block.

Trim excess

3. Repeat Step 2 for each of the nine snowflake blocks.

4. **Stitch three bordered snowflake blocks alternately with four vertical sashing strips (C) to make one row, as shown in Figure 16-17. Press the seam allowances toward the sashing strips, and trim any excess from the strips.**

   Repeat with the other blocks and strips to make three rows.

Figure 16-17: Alternate snowflake blocks with sashing strips to make rows.

5. **Stitch the three rows alternately with four blue horizontal sashing strips (B) to make the quilt center (see Figure 16-18). Press the seam allowances toward the sashing, trim any excess, and set the quilt top aside.**

6. **On the wrong side of the white 14 x 29-inch rectangle (D-2), mark a grid pattern of 36 2⅞-inch squares. Mark a diagonal line through each square, as shown in Figure 16-19.**

7. **Place the marked white piece and the unmarked blue rectangle (D-1) together with right sides facing, and pin them together to keep them from shifting during sewing.**

   One pin placed in the center of every few triangles is plenty.

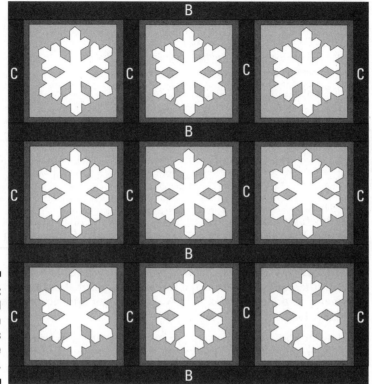

Figure 16-18:
Horizontal
strips finish
off this
part of the
quilt top.

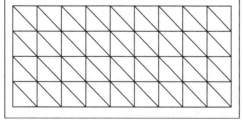

Figure 16-19:
The quilt's
decorative
border
begins
with a
marked grid
divided into
triangles.

8. **Stitch ¼ inch away from each side of the marked diagonal lines, as shown in Figure 16-20.**

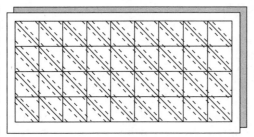

9. **Following your marked grid lines, cut out the individual squares (see Figure 16-21a), and then cut each square in half along its (unstitched) diagonal line, as shown in Figure 16-21b.**

10. **Open all the triangles to reveal two-color squares (see Figure 16-21c). The stitch or two at the tip of the triangle point should pop right off when you open the triangles. Press the seam allowances toward the blue fabric.**

I refer to these two-color squares as *half-square units* because they're made from half of a square. (Some books call them *half-triangles*.) You should end up with a total of 72 half-square units.

a   b   c

11. **Stitch nine half-square units together to form a strip. As you can see in Figure 16-22, all the units should be facing the same direction (with the blue triangle in the bottom-left corner). Press all seam allowances toward the blue fabric.**

Make four of these nine-unit strips.

Figure 16-22:
One saw-
tooth strip
made from
nine units all
leaning to
the left.

12. **Stitch nine more half-square units together, arranging them to face the opposite direction as the ones made in Step 11. As you can see in Figure 16-23, the blue triangle should be in the bottom right-corner.**

   Make four of these nine-unit strips.

Figure 16-23:
One saw-
tooth strip
made from
nine units all
leaning to
the right.

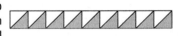

13. **Stitch one strip from Step 11 and one strip from Step 12 to opposite sides of a golden-yellow square (F), as shown in Figure 16-24. Press the seam allowances toward the golden yellow square.**

   Make four of these strips.

Figure 16-24:
Left and
right saw-
tooth strips
stitched to
either side
of a golden
yellow
square.

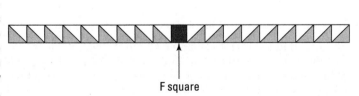

F square

14. Stitch one strip from Step 13 to the top edge of the quilt center and one strip to the bottom edge, and press the seam allowances toward the quilt center.

15. Stitch golden-yellow squares (F) to either end of the two strips remaining from Step 13, as shown in Figure 16-25, and press the seam allowances toward the golden yellow square. Stitch these two strips to the remaining two sides of the quilt center.

Figure 16-25:
Golden
yellow
squares
attached to
both ends of
the saw-
tooth strip.   F square

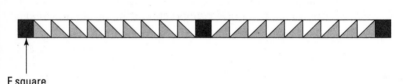

16. Stitch one blue outer border strip (A) to the top edge of the quilt center and one strip to the bottom edge.

17. Stitch a golden-yellow square (F) to each end of the remaining two outer border strips (A), and stitch these strips to the remaining two sides of the quilt center. Press all seam allowances toward the blue borders.

Quilting and finishing the project

Follow these steps to complete your quilt:

1. Lay the quilt top facedown on your work surface. On top, place the batting followed by the backing fabric (right side up).

2. Thread or pin baste the layers together to prepare it for quilting.

   Check out Chapter 12 for basting instructions.

3. Hand or machine quilt as desired.

   For design ideas, turn to Chapter 11. On the sample quilt that appears in the color insert, I stitched around the snowflakes using free-motion stippling, quilted the borders with a decorative pattern, stitched ¼ inch from the sawtooth border seams, and channel-quilted the outermost border, all with clear nylon monofilament.

4. Machine straight stitch close to the raw edges of the quilt top (about ¼ inch from the edge), and trim away the batting and backing fabric that extends from beyond the edges of the quilt top.

5. **Bind the quilt with the white bias binding to complete.**

   For a refresher on how to apply premade binding or make your own, check out Chapter 14.

Snowflake Template

Enlarge this design 200 percent for a full-sized pattern.

Winter Holly Lap Quilt or Wall Hanging

Feeling festive? Here's an easy-yet-elegant project to make for the winter holidays. Pieced holly leaves are combined with big appliquéd bows in bright red, and the blocks are accented with big red buttons to add a festive touch. The 36- x 36-inch finished size of this project makes it perfect for draping over a chair or sofa, and because it's square in shape, it also makes a lovely table centerpiece.

Use an assortment of green fat quarters to give your quilt a charming, old-fashioned look. You can even use this pattern to create a *charm quilt* by trading green fabric pieces with your friends and using a different green for each leaf. Or if you prefer more of an engineered look, select only two green fabrics — a light and a dark — and use one on the left side and one on the right side of each holly leaf. Whatever your choice, this quilt's a stunner!

Stashing your materials

You need the following materials for the Winter Holly project:

- 1 yard of cream fabric
- At least six different fat quarters of green print fabrics (the more variety the better!)
- ½ yard of red print fabric
- 1 yard of paper-backed fusible webbing
- One 40- x 40-inch piece of coordinating fabric
- One 40- x 40-inch piece of traditional or lightweight batting
- All-purpose threads in cream, green, and red
- 4½ yards of dark green quilt binding
- One ⅞-inch red button
- Four ¾-inch red buttons

Cutting out the pieces

Follow these steps to cut out all the pieces you need for this project:

1. **Using the patterns at the end of this project section, create templates for the full-size leaf and bow patterns.**

For a template-making how-to, flip to Chapter 5.

2. **Cut the border strips, sashing strips, and block pieces according to the measurements in Table 16-4, and then set them aside.**

   The letters in Table 16-4 correspond to labeled pieces in the steps for this project.

Table 16-4	Cutting Instructions for Quilt Top		
Piece	*Fabric*	*Measurement*	*Quantity*
Outer border, upper and lower (A)	Cream	2½" x 36½"	2
Outer border, sides (B)	Cream	2½" x 32½"	2
Accent border, upper and lower (C)	Red	1½" x 32½"	2
Accent border, sides (D)	Red	1½" x 30½"	2
Inner border, upper and lower (E)	Cream	2½" x 30½"	2
Inner border, sides (F)	Cream	2½" x 26½"	2
Horizontal sashing (G)	Cream	1½" x 26½"	2
Vertical sashing (H)	Cream	1½" x 8½"	6
Piece (I)	Cream	4½" x 8½"	4
Piece (J)	Cream	4½" x 4½"	4
Square	Cream	2⅞" x 2⅞"	24

3. **Cut the 24 cream squares in half diagonally to make 48 triangles, as shown in Figure 16-26.**

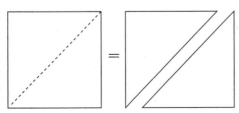

Figure 16-26: Divide each cream square into two equal-sized triangles.

4. **Use the leaf template to cut a total of 48 pieces from your green fabrics.**

To speed up this step, cut your green fabrics into 2-inch-wide strips of any length. Stack the strips as shown in Figure 16-27, and cut through all the layers at once using your rotary cutter and see-through ruler. (Place your template under the see-through ruler to give you the right shape.)

Figure 16-27:
Cutting multiple leaf units from strips

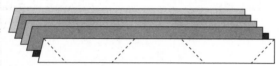

5. **Using your template and a #2 pencil, trace four bow shapes onto the paper side of the fusible webbing.**

6. **Lay out the red fabric remaining after you cut the border strips called for in Table 16-4. Fuse the four bow shapes to the wrong side of this fabric, and then cut them out neatly with your fabric-only scissors.**

Creating holly blocks

The Winter Holly quilt is made up of holly blocks with a finished size of 8½ x 8½ inches. Follow these steps to assemble the blocks:

1. **Assemble a leaf section by stitching one cream triangle to the shorter side of a green leaf piece (see Figure 16-28) with cream thread.**

Create 48 of these leaf sections.

Figure 16-28:
These two pieces make up half a leaf.

2. **Stitch two leaf sections together, green pieces together, to form a leaf square (see Figure 16-29).**

Create 24 leaf squares. It doesn't matter which green fabrics you stitch together to form the leaf squares. The squares can be as scrappy or as orderly as you like.

Figure 16-29:
The holly leaf takes shape.

3. **Assemble the three blocks shown in Figure 16-30 (for the sake of convenience, I call them Blocks 1, 2, and 3):**

   • **Block 1:** Make Block 1 by stitching four leaf squares together so that the green leaves form an X shape. Block 1 is the center block of the quilt, so you only need to make one.

   • **Block 2:** Make Block 2 by stitching two leaf squares together and then stitching the two-leaf unit to one cream I piece. Block 2 goes in the center of each side, so you need four of these blocks.

   • **Block 3:** Make Block 3 by stitching two leaf squares together and then stitching one leaf square to one cream J piece. Stitch the two-leaf unit to the one-leaf unit to make a block. Block 3 goes in each corner of the quilt top, so you need four of these blocks.

Figure 16-30:
Different arrange-ments of leaf squares create the blocks needed for this quilt: the center block (1), the center side blocks (2), and the corner blocks (3).

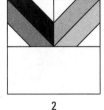
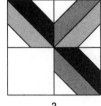

1   2   3

Assembling the quilt top

Follow these steps to create the top of this quilt:

1. **Stitch two vertical sashing strips (H) to either side of one Block 2. Then stitch a Block 3 to the opposite side of each sashing strip, arranging the Block 3s so that they're mirror images of one another, as shown in Figure 16-31. Press all seam allowances toward the sashing.**

   Make two of these rows.

Block 2

Figure 16-31:
This block arrangement is used for both the top and bottom rows of the quilt top.

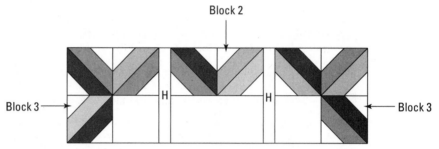

Block 3 →   ← Block 3

2. **Stitch two vertical sashing strips (H) to either side of one Block 1. Then stitch a Block 2 to the opposite site of each sashing strip, arranging the Block 2s so that they're mirror images of one another, as shown in Figure 16-32. Press all seam allowances toward the sashing.**

Block 1

Figure 16-32:
This block arrangement is the middle row of the quilt top.

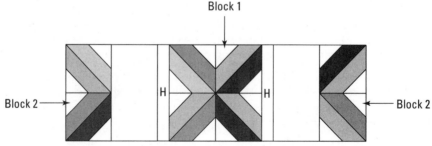

Block 2 →   ← Block 2

3. **Stitch the three holly block rows together with two horizontal sashing strips (G) between them, as shown in Figure 16-33.**

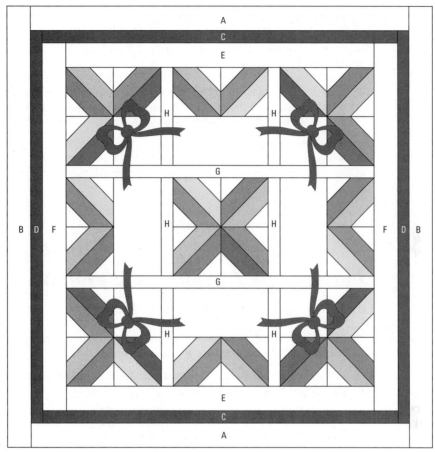

Figure 16-33:
Holly blocks, sashing, and multiple borders all come together.

4. **Stitch the cream inner border strips to the quilt top, first stitching the E strips to the upper and lower edges and then the F strips to the sides. Press the seam allowances toward the borders.**

5. **Stitch the red accent border strips to the borders attached in Step 4, first stitching the C strips to the upper and lower edges and then the D strips to the sides. Press the seam allowances toward the red borders.**

6. **Stitch the cream outer border strips to the red borders from Step 5, first stitching the A strips to the top and bottom edges and then the B strips to the sides. Press the seam allowances toward the red borders.**

Appliquéing the bows

Red bows add festive decoration to this quilt design. Follow these steps to appliqué the bows on your quilt top:

1. **Remove the paper backing from the bow shapes (created in the section "Cutting out the pieces" earlier in this project section), and fuse one bow to each corner block of your quilt.**

   As shown in Figure 16-33, the loops of the bow should overlap some sashing and two of the leaf blocks slightly, with the bow's ends dangling toward the center holly block. (See Chapter 10 for more on using fusible webbing.)

2. **Machine appliqué the bows in place using red all-purpose thread and a medium-width machine satin stitch.**

Quilting and finishing the project

Follow these steps to finish your project:

1. **Lay the quilt top facedown on your work surface. On top, place the batting and backing fabric (right side up).**

2. **Thread or pin baste the layers of the quilt sandwich together to prepare your project for quilting.**

   Check out Chapter 12 for basting instructions.

3. **Hand or machine quilt as desired.**

   I machine quilted the sample in this book's color insert in a large, meandering stipple pattern, but you're free to choose another approach. You may want to do some echo quilting around the shapes or go with a straight line grid pattern. For more ideas, turn to Chapter 11.

4. **Machine straight stitch ⅛ inch from the raw edges of the quilt top, and trim away the excess batting and backing fabric that extends beyond the edges of the quilt top.**

5. **Bind the quilt with the green binding.**

   For a refresher on how to apply premade binding or make your own, check out Chapter 14.

6. **Hand stitch the large red button to the center holly block with red thread. Stitch the smaller buttons to the center-side squares in the same manner — they're the holly berries!**

Leaf Template and Half-Size Appliqué Pattern

Enlarge the bow pattern 200 percent for a full-size pattern. (The leaf template is ready to use.)

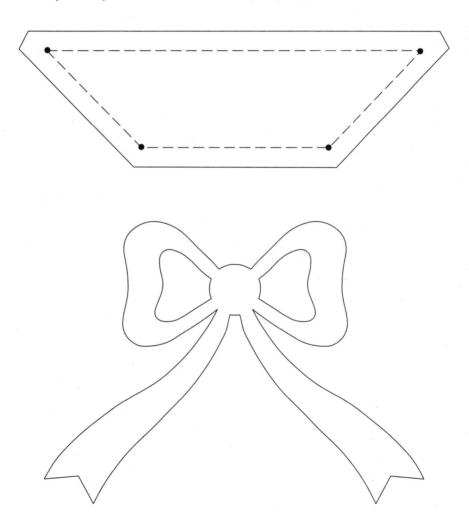

Chapter 17

Projects for the Machine Queen

· ·

In This Chapter
▶ Piecing together floral motifs
▶ Appliquéing the patriotic way
▶ Putting fabric scraps to good use

· ·

*O*ur ancestors may have spent hours and hours hand piecing quilts, but quilt makers today have the wonderful option of using a sewing machine. It's one of the best things ever invented, in my opinion!

Using the sewing machine to create quilts saves you time, allows for very accurate piecing methods, and is a lot of fun, especially when you start playing around with decorative stitches. In this chapter, I show you ways of using your machine to its best advantage by giving you projects that involve speed-piecing and decorative stitching techniques.

Get to know your machine well. It's sure to become your new best quilting friend.

Pieced Flower Pots Wall Hanging

Not all quilt blocks are square! This just-too-easy pieced flower pot quilt is a beginner's dream. It looks involved, but it's actually very simple to construct because it's made of only strips and squares — no triangles with bias edges to worry about. Also, because this wall hanging is relatively small (the finished size is only 25 x 33 inches), you shouldn't feel overwhelmed by the time commitment necessary to turn out a great result.

To speed up the cutting process, use your rotary cutter, and when stitching, be sure to keep your ¼-inch seam allowance accurate.

Stashing your materials

You need the following materials to complete the Pieced Flower Pots Wall Hanging:

- ✔ 1 yard of green print fabric
- ✔ ½ yard of tan print fabric
- ✔ ⅓ yard of blue print fabric
- ✔ ⅓ yard of yellow print fabric
- ✔ ¼ yard of peach print fabric
- ✔ ½ yard of rust print fabric
- ✔ One 28- x 36-inch piece of coordinating fabric
- ✔ One 28- x 36-inch piece of low-loft cotton or polyester quilt batting
- ✔ 4 yards of quilt binding in a coordinating color
- ✔ All-purpose thread in a neutral color such as off-white

Cutting the pieces

As you can see in the color insert photo, this quilt consists of a lot of pieces. So before you can do anything else, you have to cut. Follow the cutting instructions in Table 17-1 to produce all the pieces you need for assembly.

Some pieces are labeled with letters that correspond to figures in the assembly section; for now, you don't need to pay attention to those labels.

Table 17-1		Cutting Instructions for Quilt Top	
Piece	*Fabric*	*Measurement*	*Quantity*
Background strip (A)	Tan	1½" x 4½"	8
Background rectangle (B)	Tan	2½" x 3½"	8
Background strip (C)	Tan	1½" x 2½"	28
Flower and border strip (C)	Blue	1½" x 2½"	26 (use 8 for borders and 18 for blocks)
Flower strip (C)	Yellow	1½" x 2½"	18
Background square (D)	Tan	1½" x 1½"	52
Leaf square (D)	Green	1½" x 1½"	36

Piece	Fabric	Measurement	Quantity
Flower square (D)	Yellow	1½" x 1½"	12
Flower square (D)	Blue	1½" x 1½"	12
Background square (E)	Tan	2½" x 2½"	8
Background strip (F)	Tan	1½" x 3½"	12
Flower pot strip (F)	Peach	1½" x 3½"	4
Flower pot strip (G)	Peach	2½" x 5½"	4
Flower pot strip (H)	Rust	1½" x 7½"	4
Cornerstone	Yellow	2½" x 2½"	4
Vertical sashing	Rust	1½" x 13½"	6
Horizontal sashing	Rust	1½" x 21½"	3
Border, upper and lower	Green	2½" x 19½"	2
Border, sides	Green	2½" x 27½"	2

Assembling the pieced blocks

To assemble the four blocks of this quilt (each of which has a finished size of 9 x 13 inches), you make two blocks in each _colorway_, or color arrangement. One colorway consists of a block with two yellow flowers and one blue flower (Block 1), and the second colorway is the opposite — a block with two blue flowers and one yellow (Block 2). This quilt has two blocks of each colorway.

All seam allowances are ¼ inch and are included in the given measurements. Press all the seam allowances toward the darker color.

Follow these steps to assemble your flower blocks:

1. **To make row 1 (the top row) of Block 1, stitch together one blue D square to two tan A strips, as shown in Figure 17-1. Repeat with the second colorway for Block 2, using the yellow D square. Make two strips of each colorway.**

2. **To make row 2 of Block 1, stitch together two tan B pieces, two blue C strips, and one yellow C strip in the order shown in Figure 17-2a. Reverse the blue and yellow colorway for Block 2, as shown in Figure 17-2b. Make two of each strip.**

Figure 17-1:
The top row of the block contains the tip of a flower.

A $+$ D $+$ A

Feel like you're getting the hang of it now?

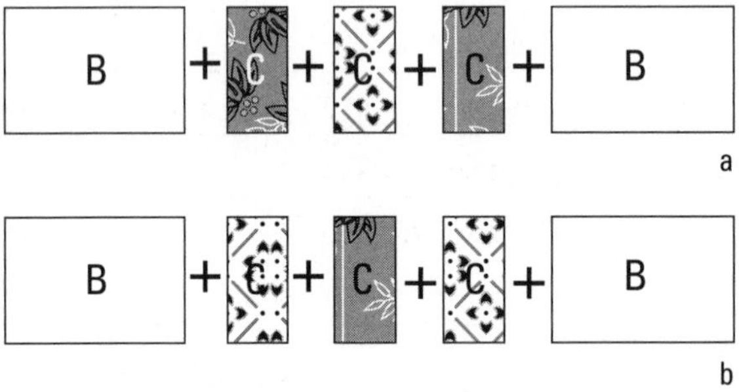

Figure 17-2:
The center portions of one blue flower (a) and one yellow flower (b).

B $+$ C $+$ C $+$ C $+$ B

a

B $+$ C $+$ C $+$ C $+$ B

b

3. **For row 3 of Block 1, stitch together two tan C strips, two yellow D squares, two tan D squares, and one blue D square in the order shown in Figure 17-3 (the blue D square should be in the center). Make two of this row, and then reverse the blue and yellow colorway and make two more rows for Block 2.**

Figure 17-3:
This row contains the tips of three different flowers.

C $+$ D $+$ D $+$ D $+$ D $+$ D $+$ C

4. **For row 4 of Block 1, stitch together the following C strips in the order shown in Figure 17-4a: three tan, four yellow, and two blue. Make two rows like this, and then reverse the blue and yellow colorway (see Figure 17-4b) and make two more rows for Block 2.**

Figure 17-4:
This row contains the center portions of two flowers for Block 1 (a) and Block 2 (b).

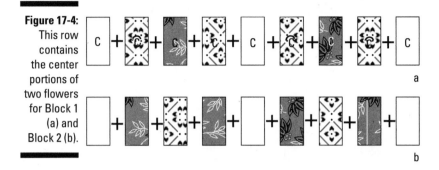

5. **For row 5 of Block 1, stitch together the following D squares in the order shown in Figure 17-5a (each colored square alternates with a tan one): three green, four tan, and two yellow. Make two rows like this, and then change out the yellow squares in the pattern for blue ones (see Figure 17-5b) and make two more rows for Block 2.**

Figure 17-5:
This row contains the first leaf pieces in Block 1 (a) and Block 2 (b).

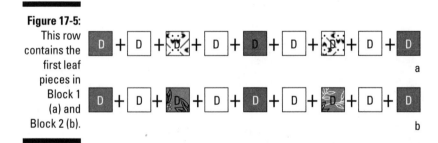

6. **To make row 6 of all four blocks, alternate five tan D squares with four green D squares (see Figure 17-6). Make four of this strip.**

Figure 17-6:
Alternate leaf squares with background squares.

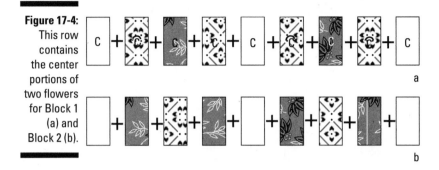

7. To make row 7 of all four blocks, stitch together two tan C strips, two green D squares, and one tan F strip as shown in Figure 17-7. Make four of this strip.

Figure 17-7:
This row
containing
two leaf
squares is
the same
in all four
blocks.

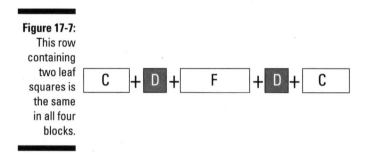

8. To make row 8 of all four blocks, alternate two tan D squares with one rust H strip, as shown in Figure 17-8. Make four of this strip.

Figure 17-8:
The pot rim
consists of
three pieces.

9. To make row 9 of all four blocks, alternate two tan E squares with one peach G strip, as shown in Figure 17-9. Make four of this strip.

Figure 17-9:
This strip
forms the
body of the
flower pot.

10. To make row 10 of all four blocks, alternate two tan F strips with one peach F strip, as shown in the Figure 17-10. Make four of this strip.

11. To assemble Block 1, stitch together rows 1 through 10 of the first colorway, as shown in Figure 17-11a. Make two of this block. Repeat with the second colorway to assemble Block 2, as shown in Figure 17-11b.

Figure 17-10:
This strip forms the base of the flower pot.

You now have four flowerpot blocks — two of Block 1 (with a blue flower at the top) and two of Block 2 (with a yellow flower at the top).

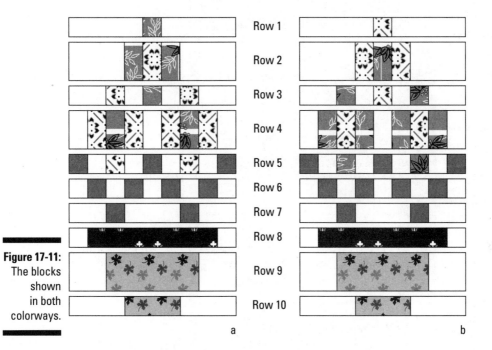

Row 1
Row 2
Row 3
Row 4
Row 5
Row 6
Row 7
Row 8
Row 9
Row 10

Figure 17-11:
The blocks shown in both colorways.

a   b

Assembling the quilt top

Follow these steps to arrange your quilt blocks and finish assembly of the quilt top:

1. **Stitch three vertical sashing strips alternately with one Block 1 and one Block 2 to make a row. Repeat with the three remaining vertical sashing strips and the remaining two blocks, reversing the placement of the blocks, as shown in Figure 17-12.**

2. Stitch the two block rows alternately with the three horizontal sashing strips to make the quilt center. Press the seam allowances toward the sashing strips.

3. Stitch one blue C strip to either end of each green border strip.

4. Stitch the side border strips to either side of the quilt center.

5. Stitch one yellow cornerstone square to either end of the upper and lower border strips. Stitch these strips to the top and bottom edges of the quilt center to complete the quilt top. See Figure 17-12.

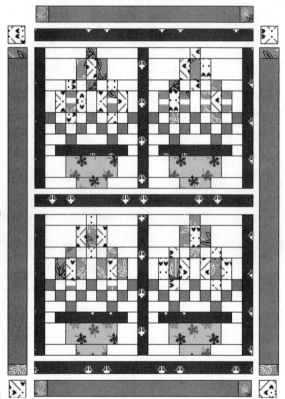

Figure 17-12: Blocks, sashing, borders, and cornerstones come together to form the Pieced Flower Pots quilt top.

Quilting and completing the project

Follow these steps to finish your project:

1. **Lay the quilt top facedown on your work surface. On top, lay the batting and backing fabric (right side up).**

2. **Thread or pin baste the layers together to prepare it for quilting (for a basting how-to, flip to Chapter 12).**

3. **Hand or machine quilt as desired.**

   For design ideas, turn to Chapter 11. The quilt that appears in the color insert features stipple quilting in the background space, echo quilting in the flower pots, and straight-line designs.

4. **Machine stitch close to the outside edges of the quilt top, and trim away the excess batting and backing fabric that extends beyond the edges of the quilt top.**

5. **Finish the quilt by stitching the quilt binding around the edges.**

   For a refresher on how to apply premade binding or make your own, check out Chapter 14.

Pieced Blossoms Lap Quilt

The interesting thing about the Pieced Blossoms project is that it has a "controlled" scrappy look to it. It has a lot of fabric variety to catch the eye, but everything comes together in a neat and orderly pattern. You can stitch this quilt in a multitude of bright, cheery spring pastels or perhaps choose some spunky primary tones for a real splash of color. For best results, I suggest using a multitude of different pink fabrics — the more the better!

This quilt utilizes template-free rotary cutting techniques (see Chapter 8), which means you can complete the project quickly and effortlessly. (The finished size of this quilt — 36 x 51 inches — makes it easy-to-manage as well.) Although you trim and discard small bits of fabric, this quilt is not at all wasteful, and you'll love the speed-piecing techniques. No need to trace tedious pattern pieces with this one!

This is a great project on which to use *fat quarters* (those precut 18- x 22-inch nuggets of lovely fabric available in fabric and quilting stores) from your fabric stash (don't deny it — I know you have a fabric stash!). The yardage requirements listed in the next section are approximate due to the fact that you may want to add to or scale down the number of pinks in the project according to your own preferences.

Stashing your materials

You need the following materials for the Pieced Blossoms Lap Quilt:

- ✔ ¾ yard of off-white solid fabric
- ✔ ½ yard of multicolored print or floral fabric
- ✔ ¼ yard each of six to eight different shades of pink print fabric (fat quarters are okay)
- ✔ ¼ yard each of six to eight different shades of green print fabric (fat quarters are okay)
- ✔ Scraps of assorted yellow prints (as many as you would like)
- ✔ ⅓ yard of yellow print fabric
- ✔ One 40- x 55-inch piece of coordinating fabric
- ✔ One 40- x-55-inch piece of quilt batting, any loft except high-loft
- ✔ All-purpose threads in off-white, pink, green, and yellow
- ✔ 6 yards of green quilt binding

All seam allowances are ¼ inch and are included in all given measurements and directions.

Cutting the pieces

For best results, use a rotary cutter and ruler to cut the pieces. Not only will you get more accurate cutting edges, but you'll also save a tremendous amount of time!

1. **Referring to Table 17-2, cut the strips for the borders and sashing, and then set them aside.**

Table 17-2	Cutting Instructions for Border and Sashing Strips		
Piece	*Fabric*	*Measurement*	*Quantity*
Outer border, sides (A)	Multicolored print	3½" x 45½"	2
Outer border, upper and lower (B)	Multicolored print	3½" x 36½"	2
Inner border, sides (C)	Yellow	1½" x 43½"	2
Inner border, upper and lower (D)	Yellow	1½" x 28½"	2

Piece	Fabric	Measurement	Quantity
Vertical sashing (E)	Off-white	1½" x 13½"	12
Horizontal sashing (F)	Off-white	1½" x 28½"	4

2. **Referring to Table 17-3, cut the pieces for the blocks.**

Each block requires two different shades of pink and green, so you need to plan out your fabric design for each block before you cut. In Figure 17-13, I broke down one block into individual units (all labeled to match the table) so you can get a better visual idea of the pieces you need for each block.

Note: In the "Piece" column of Table 17-3, I've labeled the two different pink fabrics in each block pink 1 and pink 2. For one block, cut two pieces for pink 1 from one pink fabric, and cut two pieces for pink 2 from a second pink fabric. Each block can feature different pink 1 and 2 fabrics, or you can reuse pink fabrics in multiple blocks (as long as pink 1 and 2 remain different from one another).

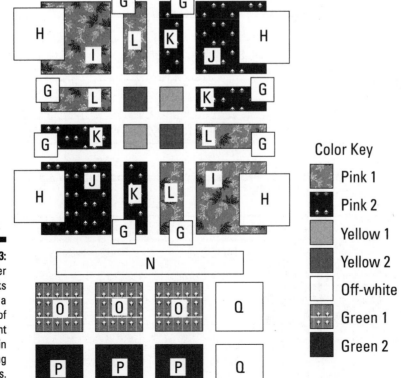

Figure 17-13: Each flower block breaks down into a number of different pieces in varying fabrics.

Color Key

- Pink 1
- Pink 2
- Yellow 1
- Yellow 2
- Off-white
- Green 1
- Green 2

Table 17-3	Cutting Instructions for Flower Blocks		
Piece	*Fabric*	*Measurement*	*Quantity*
Small background square, flower (G)	Off-white	1½" x 1½"	72
Large background square, flower (H)	Off-white	2½" x 2½"	36
Flower petal 1 (I) —	Pink	3½" x 3½"	18 (2 pieces of the same color per block)
Flower petal 2 (J)	Pink	3½" x 3½"	18 (2 pieces of the same color per block)
Flower petal strip 1 (K)	Pink (same as I pieces)	1½" x 3½"	36 (4 pieces of two different colors per block)
Flower petal strip 2 (L)	Pink (same as J pieces)	1½" x 3½"	36 (4 pieces of two different colors per block)
Flower center (M)	Yellow print	1½" x 1½"	72 (4 pieces of two different colors per block)
Background strip (N)	Off-white	1½" x 8½"	9
Leaf 1 (O)	Green	2⅞" x 2⅞"	27 (3 pieces of the same color per block)
Leaf 2 (P)	Green	2⅞" x 2⅞"	27 (3 pieces of the same color per block)
Leaf background (Q)	Off-white	2⅞" x 2⅞"	18

3. **Cut all the O, P, and Q squares in half diagonally to make triangles (see Figure 17-14).**

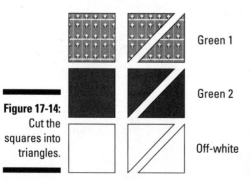

Figure 17-14:
Cut the squares into triangles.

Green 1

Green 2

Off-white

Creating the petal blocks

With all the block pieces cut, it's time to stitch them together into flower blocks. The finished size of each block is 8 x 13 inches.

Throughout the assembly stage, always press seam allowances toward the darker fabric unless the instructions say otherwise.

1. **On the wrong side of each off-white G and H square, mark a diagonal line, as shown in Figure 17-15.**

Figure 17-15:
Mark (but don't cut) the background squares for the flower portion of the block.

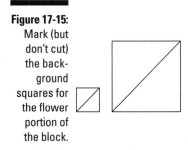

Do not cut this line! It's actually a stitching line.

2. **Place a marked H piece on one corner of each pink I piece, right sides facing (see Figure 17-16).**

3. **Stitch along the diagonal line of each H piece. Trim the excess from the corners, ¼ inch from the stitching lines as shown in Figure 17-16, and press the corners open to make square petal units.**

You should end up with 18 of these petal units.

Figure 17-16:
Two pieces make up each flower petal.

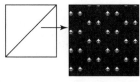

4. **Repeat Steps 2 and 3 using the pink J pieces and the remaining H pieces.**

   You should end up with 18 of these petal units.

5. **Stitch one off-white G piece to one pink K piece, stitching along the marked line on the wrong side of the G piece (see Figure 17-17a). Trim the corner excess ¼ inch from the stitching line, and discard. Press the unit open.**

   Make 18 of these right-facing petal strips. (By *right-facing,* I mean that the pink fabric runs from top to bottom on the right-hand side of the strip.)

6. **With the remaining G and K pieces, repeat Step 5 with a slight variation: The diagonal stitching line should run from the upper-left to lower-right corners, as shown in Figure 17-17b.**

   Make 18 of these left-facing petal strips. (By *left-facing,* I mean that the pink fabric runs from top to bottom on the left-hand side of the strip.)

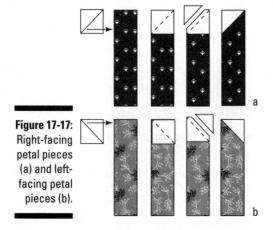

Figure 17-17: Right-facing petal pieces (a) and left-facing petal pieces (b).

7. **Repeat Steps 5 and 6 with the pink L strips and the remaining G squares.**

   As Figure 17-18 shows, you should end up with 18 left-facing petal strip units for both pink 1 and pink 2, and 18 right-facing petal strip units for both pink 1 and pink 2 (that's 36 left and 36 right).

Figure 17-18:
These strips serve as the inside edges of each flower petal.

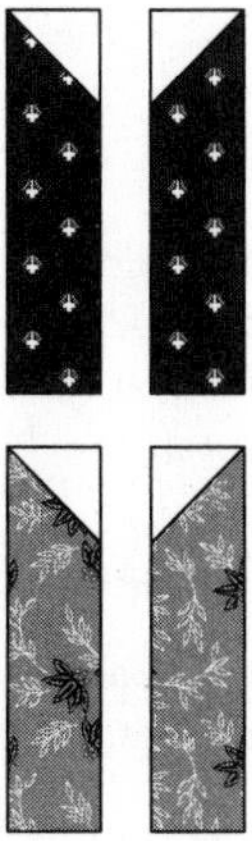

8. **Stitch a yellow M square to the bottom edge of every right-facing petal strip (see Figure 17-19). Press open.**

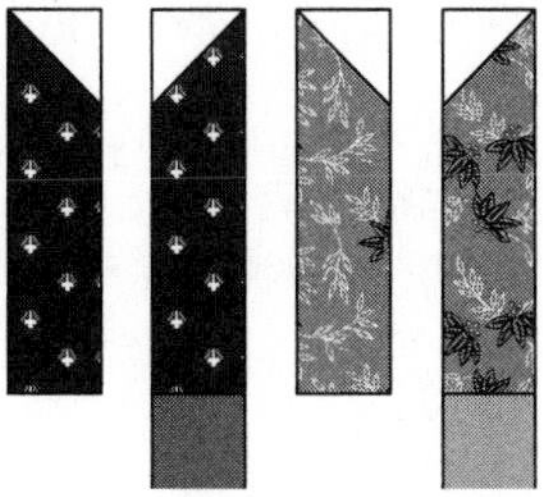

Figure 17-19:
The yellow squares attached to the right-facing petal strips.

9. **As shown in Figure 17-20, stitch a left-facing petal strip to each petal unit that you made in Steps 2 through 4. Then stitch a strip from Step 8 to the piece you've just created.**

Be sure to stitch petal strips from pink 1 to the petal units from pink 1 and vice versa, so that each petal block contains only one pink fabric.

The petal blocks in Figure 17-20 may look like they're put together differently, but they're actually just the same block rotated a ¼ turn. So you can assemble all the petal blocks in the same manner and then adjust their layout to get the right look.

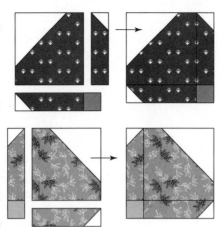

Figure 17-20:
Each petal block consists of one petal unit and two petal strips. You rotate each block to get the desired layout.

Joining petals to make flower blocks

Each flower block in the Pieced Blossoms project contains four petal blocks. This section covers instructions for flower block assembly, including the leaf portion of each block.

1. **Stitch two petal blocks of each fabric together to form a flower block, as shown in Figure 17-21, and press the seams. Make nine of these flowers.**

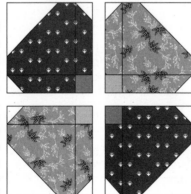

Figure 17-21:
Arrange and sew four petal blocks together, with the yellow squares converging in the center.

2. **Referring to Figure 17-22, stitch four green O triangles to four green P triangles to form leaf tips.**

Figure 17-22:
Use two
different
green print
fabrics for
the leaf
bodies.

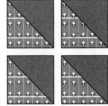

3. Stitch two green O triangles to two off-white Q triangles to form a leaf edges, as shown in Figure 17-23a. Repeat with two green P triangles and two off-white Q triangles, as shown in Figure 17-23b.

Figure 17-23:
Make the
flat edges of
the leaves
by sewing
off-white
triangles to
two different
green
triangles
(a and b).

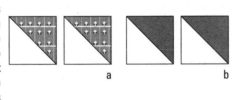

a   b

4. Following the layout shown in Figure 17-24, stitch together the eight leaf sections made in Steps 2 and 3.

Figure 17-24:
Arrange the
leaf sections
so that the
two shades
of green
alternate.

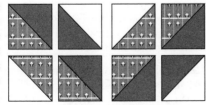

5. Create a leaf unit by stitching an off-white N strip to the top edge of the leaf piece made in Step 4 (see Figure 17-25).

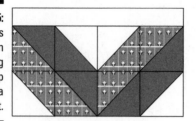

Figure 17-25: The leaves plus a plain strip along the top make up a leaf unit.

6. **Repeat Steps 2 through 5 to create nine leaf units.**

7. **Stitch the nine completed leaf units to the nine completed flower blocks (see Figure 17-26) to make the nine full flower blocks that form the quilt top.**

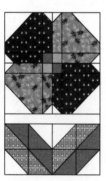

Figure 17-26: Each full flower block consists of a flower block top and a leaf unit bottom.

Assembling the quilt top

With nine full flower blocks ready and waiting, all that's left to do is add sashing and border strips to make the full quilt top.

1. **Stitch three full flower blocks alternately with four vertical sashing strips (E) (see Figure 17-27). Press seam allowances toward the sashing strips. Make three of these flower block rows.**

2. **Stitch three block rows alternately with four horizontal sashing strips (F) to make the quilt center, shown in Figure 17-28.**

3. **Stitch the inner side borders (C) to the sides of the quilt center. Stitch the remaining inner border strips (D) to the top and bottom of the quilt center.**

4. **Repeat Step 3 with the outer borders (A and B).**

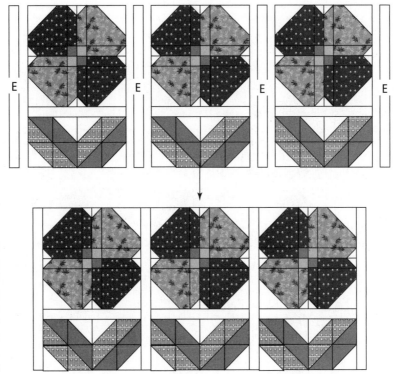

Figure 17-27:
Vertical sashing strips divide the flower blocks in each row.

Quilting and finishing your quilt

To finish your quilt:

1. **Lay the quilt top facedown on your work surface. On top, place the batting and backing (right side up).**

2. **Thread or pin baste the layers together to prepare it for quilting (for a basting how-to, flip to Chapter 12).**

3. **Hand or machine quilt as desired.**

   For design ideas, turn to Chapter 11. The quilt that appears in the color insert features in-the-ditch quilting in the full flower blocks and stipple quilting in the background space, which gives the quilt a nice texture.

4. **Machine stitch close to the raw edges of the quilt top. Trim away any batting and backing that extends beyond the edges of the quilt top.**

5. **Bind the quilt with the green quilt binding to complete the project.**

   For a refresher on how to apply premade binding or make your own, check out Chapter 14.

Row 1

Row 2

Row 3

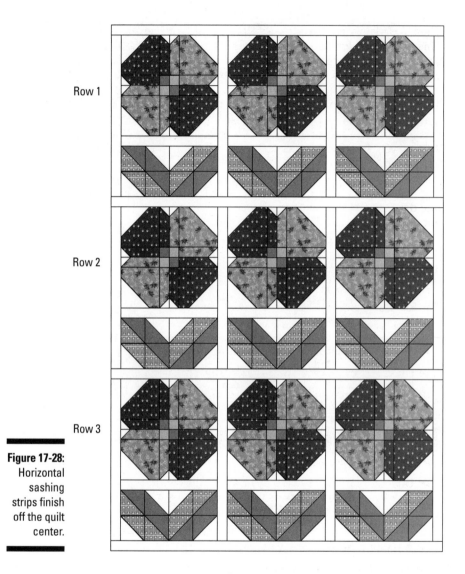

Figure 17-28:
Horizontal
sashing
strips finish
off the quilt
center.

Americana Appliqués Banner

This project utilizes strip quilting and rotary cutting (see Chapter 8) and is a fabulous skill-builder if you're new to either technique. *Strip quilting* is a huge timesaver for quilters! Instead of cutting out individual squares of fabric and stitching them together, you cut strips of fabric to the proper width and then sew them together along their long sides to make a multi-colored strip.

Then you simply cut the strip into the proper-sized units — no muss, no fuss! This technique also allows for greater accuracy and is a fabulous way to make checkered strips or other sections of a quilt made from multiple small squares or stripes.

Another fun thing about this project is that except for the backing fabric, it's made entirely from *fat quarters,* those delightful 18- x 22-inch cuts of yardage that abound in all sorts of colors and patterns at any quilting or fabric store. This project gives you a good excuse to stock up on fat quarters in red, off-white, and blue!

The finished size of this project is 20 x 20 inches, making it the perfect patriotic decoration for your home. Bring it out for the Fourth of July, or leave it out year-round and admire your handiwork.

Stashing your materials

The following list covers the fabrics and special notions you need to make the Americana Appliqués Banner:

- ✔ One fat quarter of light blue print fabric
- ✔ One fat quarter of off-white print fabric (off-white 1)
- ✔ One fat quarter of a different off-white print fabric (off-white 2)
- ✔ One fat quarter of medium blue print fabric
- ✔ One fat quarter of red print fabric (red 1)
- ✔ One fat quarter of a different red print fabric (red 2)
- ✔ One fat quarter of golden tan print fabric
- ✔ One 24- x 24-inch piece of coordinating fabric
- ✔ One 24- x 24-inch piece of low-loft quilt batting
- ✔ ¼ yard paper-backed fusible webbing
- ✔ Five natural-colored buttons, ½-inch in size
- ✔ All-purpose thread in off-white
- ✔ 2½ yards of off-white quilt binding

All seam allowances are the standard ¼ inch and are included in the given measurements and directions.

Cutting out the pieces

Follow the cutting instructions in Table 17-4 to produce all the pieces you need to assemble the Americana Appliqués quilt top.

Rotary cutting is definitely the way to go with this project. It saves you lots of time and energy and ensures that you get accurate, straight cuts — especially in the striped areas.

Table 17-4	Cutting Instructions for Quilt Top		
Piece	*Fabric*	*Measurement*	*Quantity*
Border stripe	Red 1	2½" x 18"	3
Border stripe	Off-white1	2½" x 18"	3
Inner stripe	Medium blue	2½" x 18"	1
Inner stripe	Off-white 2	2½" x 18"	1
Star square	Light blue	4½" x 4½"	5
Corner triangle	Red 2	5½" x 10½"	1
Corner triangle	Light blue	5½" x 10½"	1

Creating the quilt center

Follow these steps to create both the outer accent stripes and the center of the quilt design:

1. **Stitch the red 1 and off-white 1 border strips together alternately along their long sides to form a striped rectangle of fabric. Press the seam allowances toward the red fabric.**

2. **Using your rotary cutter, ruler, and mat, cut four 4½-inch-wide stripe units from the rectangle, as shown in Figure 17-29.**

3. **Using the template provided at the end of this project, trace five star shapes onto the paper side of the fusible webbing. Cut the shapes out roughly.**

4. **Using a hot iron (and following the instructions that came with the webbing), fuse the webbing stars to the wrong side of the golden tan fabric. Cut them out neatly.**

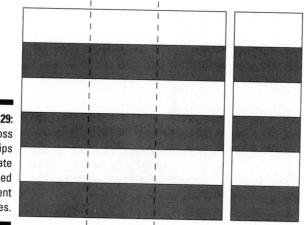

Figure 17-29:
Cut across
joined strips
to create
striped
accent
pieces.

5. **Arrange one star on each of the five light blue squares. Peel the paper backing from the shapes, and fuse the stars to the squares with a hot iron.**

6. **Using the all-purpose thread and a medium-width machine satin stitch, appliqué the stars to the squares.**

For a review of appliqué techniques, turn to Chapter 10. For a different look, you may want to try a raw-edge appliqué, which allows the edges of the shape to fray slightly. Simply stitch around the appliqués ⅛ to ¼ inch from the edges by hand with a running stitch or by machine with a straight stitch. This fast and easy appliqué technique gives this project a down-home look.

7. **Pin the light blue and red 2 5½ x 10½-inch rectangles together, right sides facing. Using your ruler and a water-soluble pencil, mark two 4⅞-inch squares on the light blue piece. Draw a diagonal line through each square.**

8. **Stitch ¼ inch from either side of the marked diagonal line, as shown in Figure 17-30.**

9. **Cut out the squares along the marked lines, and cut along the diagonal marked lines to produce four double triangles. Open each double triangle to reveal a two-tone square (see Figure 17-30). Press the seams toward the red fabric.**

10. **Stitch the medium blue and off-white 2 inner stripes together along their long sides. Cut the resulting strip into four inner-stripe units measuring 4½ inches wide (see Figure 17-31).**

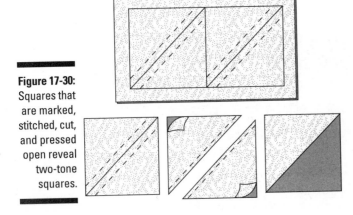

Figure 17-30:
Squares that
are marked,
stitched, cut,
and pressed
open reveal
two-tone
squares.

Figure 17-31:
Stitching
strips
together
and then
cutting them
into squares
is a fast,
easy way to
get uniform
two-color
squares.

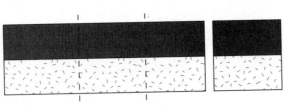

11. **Stitch two-tone squares from Step 9 to either side of two inner-stripe unit as shown in the top and bottom strips of Figure 17-32.**

    The two-tone squares should be oriented so that the light blue triangles are in the outer corners of the strip, and the inner-stripe unit should be oriented with the off-white portion on top. Make two of these strips.

12. **Stitch inner-stripe units to two opposing sides of one star block (see the center strip in Figure 17-32).**

    The inner-stripe units should be oriented so that the stripe runs vertically, with the blue portions touching the star block.

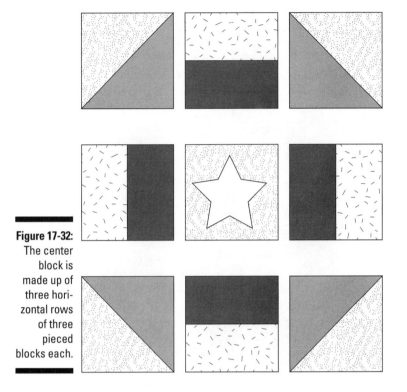

Figure 17-32: The center block is made up of three horizontal rows of three pieced blocks each.

13. **Stitch the three strips made in Steps 11 and 12 together alternately to make the center block (see the center portion of Figure 17-33).**

    The strip with the star in it should be in the middle, bordered above and below by the two other strips. The outer strips should be oriented so that the star block is surrounded by blue pieces.

14. **Stitch two border stripe units made in Steps 1 and 2 to the left and right edges of the center block made in Step 13 (see Figure 17-33).**

    Orient the border stripes as follows: The stripe on the left should have a red piece at the top and an off-white piece at the bottom, and the stripe on the right should be the reverse.

15. **Stitch one star square to each end of the remaining two border stripe units made in Steps 1 and 2.**

16. **Referring to Figure 17-33 for orientation, stitch the star/stripe borders to the upper and lower edges of the quilt center.**

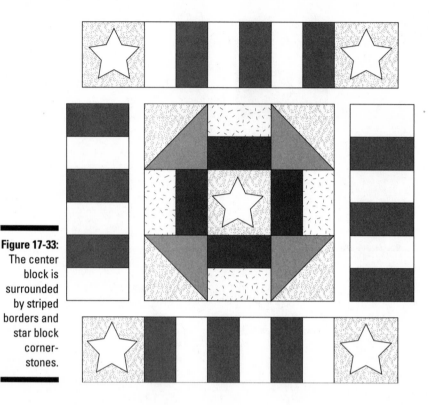

Figure 17-33:
The center
block is
surrounded
by striped
borders and
star block
corner-
stones.

Quilting your quilt

Follow these steps to finish your Americana Appliqués Banner quilt:

1. **Lay the quilt top face down on your work surface. On top, place the batting and backing fabric (right side up).**

2. **Thread or pin baste the layers together to prepare the project for quilting (for a basting how-to, flip to Chapter 12).**

3. **Hand or machine quilt as desired.**

   For design ideas, turn to Chapter 11. The quilt that appears in the color insert features machine quilting in off-white thread to add contrast to the dark fabrics. I quilted ¼ inch from all the seam allowances.

4. **Machine stitch very close to the raw edges of the quilt top, and trim away the excess batting and backing that extends beyond the edges of the quilt top.**

5. **Bind the edges of the quilt by attaching the off-white quilt binding.**

   For a refresher on how to apply premade binding or make your own, check out Chapter 14.

6. **Stitch one button to the center of each star to complete the project.**

Americana Star Template

Scrappy Pines Lap or Nap Quilt

I love scrap basket projects! They have such a warm and inviting look to them. And when you use the scrappy approach on a perfect nap-sized quilt (such as this one, which has a finished size of 50 x 79 inches), you've got a snuggly combination. Pull lots of different green and brown fabrics from your stash to make this Scrappy Pines quilt. If you find yourself low on a particular color, trade fabrics with a friend or stock up on an assortment of fat quarters while they're on sale at your favorite fabric store.

A unique feature of this quilt is that it allows you to play with some of your sewing machine's decorative or utility stitches. If you haven't played around with these stitches yet, refer to your owner's manual for instructions on setting up the machine for decorative stitching. Of course, you can substitute satin stitch appliqué for the decorative stitching, if desired, but feel free to experiment with your machine's stitch repertoire!

Stashing your materials

This list covers the fabrics and notions you need to make the Scrappy Pines Lap or Nap Quilt:

- ✔ Twenty 6½- x 10½-inch rectangles of assorted tan fabrics (tan 1)
- ✔ Twenty 5- x 8-inch pieces of assorted green fabrics (green 1)
- ✔ Twenty 1- x 2-inch pieces of assorted brown fabrics
- ✔ ½ yard of tan fabric (tan 2)
- ✔ ⅓ yard of rust print fabric
- ✔ 2 yards of green print fabric (green 2)
- ✔ 2 yards of 18-inch-wide paper-backed fusible webbing
- ✔ Twenty 5- x 9-inch pieces of tear-away stabilizer
- ✔ All-purpose thread in green, brown, and tan
- ✔ One 55- x 85-inch piece of coordinating fabric
- ✔ One 55- x 85-inch piece of low- to medium-loft quilt batting
- ✔ 8 yards of rust-colored quilt binding

The seam allowances for this quilt are ¼ inch and are included in the given measurements and instructions.

Cutting out the pieces

For best results, use a rotary cutter and ruler to cut the pieces listed in Table 17-5. Not only will you get more accurate cutting edges, but you'll also save a tremendous amount of time!

Table 17-5	Cutting Instructions for Quilt Top		
Piece	*Fabric*	*Measurement*	*Quantity*
Block border, sides	Rust	1" x 10½"	40
Block border, upper and lower	Rust	1" x 7½"	40
Horizontal sashing	Tan 2	½" x 38½"	6
Vertical sashing	Tan 2	2½" x 11½"	25
Border, sides	Green 2	6½" x 67½"	2
Border, upper and lower	Green 2	6½" x 50½"	2

Appliquéing the tree blocks

The finished size of each tree block is 6 x 10 inches. Because the trees are appliqué pieces, you don't have to be concerned with seam allowances in the following steps.

1. **Using the template provided at the end of this project, trace 20 tree tops (minus the trunks) on the paper side of the fusible webbing. Cut out the shapes roughly. Repeat with the trunks.**

2. **Using a hot iron, fuse the tree tops to the wrong sides of the assorted green fabrics. Cut out the shapes neatly.**

3. **Repeat Step 2 with the trunk shapes and the assorted brown fabrics.**

4. **Remove the paper backings from the appliqués, and center one tree and one trunk on each of the 20 assorted tan rectangles.**

   Tuck the top edge of the trunk just under the tree bottom to conceal the raw edge.

5. **Use a hot iron to fuse the tree and trunk pieces in place on the blocks.**

   Refer to the insert that accompanied your fusible webbing for iron settings.

6. **Pin a piece of tear-away stabilizer to the wrong side of each tree block.**

   Place the pins at the corners to keep them away from the stitching areas.

7. **Using brown all-purpose thread, machine appliqué the trunks in place on all blocks using a variety of decorative or utility stitches. Change the thread to green, and repeat with the trees.**

8. **Remove the pins, and tear away the paper stabilizer from the blocks.**

Assembling the quilt top

After you cut and appliqué all the tree blocks, you need to stitch the blocks together and assemble the quilt top:

1. **Stitch two side block border strips to each tree block. Press the seam allowances toward the rust strips.**

2. **Stitch two upper and lower block borders to each tree blocks, and press the seam allowances toward the rust strips.**

3. **Stitch five vertical sashing strips alternately with four appliquéd blocks to make a row, as shown in Figure 17-34. Make five of these rows.**

4. **Stitch five tree block rows alternately with six horizontal sashing strips to make the quilt center (see Figure 17-35).**

Figure 17-34:
Each row
consists of
four tree
blocks
divided by
sashing
strips.

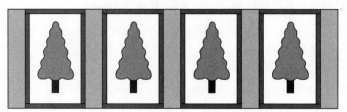

5. Stitch the green side borders to the sides of the quilt center (see Figure 17-36), and press the seam allowances toward the green fabric.

6. Stitch the green upper and lower borders to the top and bottom edges of the quilt center (see Figure 17-36), and press the seam allowances toward the green fabric.

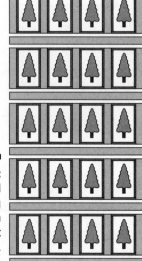

Figure 17-35:
Horizontal
sashing
strips finish
the quilt
center.

Quilting and finishing your quilt

To finish your quilt:

1. Lay the quilt top facedown on your work surface. On top, place the batting and backing fabric (right side up).

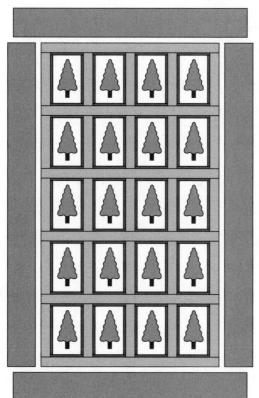

Figure 17-36:
Wide bor-
ders give
the quilt top
a crisp, fin-
ished look.

2. **Thread or pin baste the layers together to keep them from shifting during quilting (for a basting how-to, flip to Chapter 12),**

3. **Hand or machine quilt as desired.**

   For design ideas, turn to Chapter 11. The quilt that appears in the color insert features in-the-ditch quilting in clear nylon monofilament along all seam lines. I also stitched around the trees close to the edges, but echo quilting would be really nice around the trees as well. The border was quilted using a purchased quilting template with a wavy pattern.

4. **Machine stitch close to the raw edges of the quilt top, and trim away the excess batting and backing fabric that extends beyond the edges of the quilt top.**

5. **Bind the quilt with the rust-colored quilt binding to complete it.**

   For a refresher on how to apply premade binding or make your own, check out Chapter 14.

Pine Tree Template

Chapter 18

Small-Scale Projects

· ·

In This Chapter

▶ Cooking up breakfast sets

▶ Machine-piecing a versatile small quilt

▶ Creating a cute small-scale wall hanging

· ·

*N*ot all quilted projects have to be big enough to cover your bed. You can use quilting techniques to create useful objects to be enjoyed every day in other areas of the home as well. In this chapter, I give you some small-scale projects that you can make for the kitchen or to display in another room of your home.

These small projects use many of the same techniques as large-scale projects, including precision machine piecing or appliqué techniques; the only real difference is that here they're used on smaller items. Because of their size, these can be great take-along projects while traveling or commuting, too!

Appliquéd Bluebirds Breakfast Set

This plump little bluebird adds cheer to four different projects. Three are absolute no-brainers because they use premade items! All the projects in this breakfast set prove that you can appliqué on many different objects. And the bluebird's rounded curves give you ample practice on mastering machine satin stitch appliqué. Have fun!

Stashing your materials

To create the appliquéd bluebird pillow, place mat, napkin, and kitchen towel (that is, all four projects), you need the following materials:

- ✔ ¾ yard of off-white print fabric
- ✔ ¼ yard of dark blue print fabric
- ✔ ¼ yard of medium blue print fabric

- ⅛ yard of light blue solid fabric
- Scraps of golden yellow print or solid fabric
- One 15- x 15-inch square of off-white solid fabric
- 2 yards of premade blue piping
- All-purpose thread in medium blue and golden yellow
- Rayon or all-purpose thread in three shades of blue that match the blue fabrics
- One 15- x 15-inch square of low-loft quilt batting
- 1 yard of 18-inch-wide paper-backed fusible webbing
- 1 yard of 18-inch-wide tear-away stabilizer
- One off-white kitchen towel, prewashed
- One off-white cotton place mat with matching napkin
- One 14-inch pillow form (or enough stuffing for a 14-inch pillow)
- Two ¾-inch dark blue buttons
- Three ½-inch dark blue buttons

Making the pillow

The finished size of the appliquéd bluebird pillow is 14 x 14 inches. Follow these steps to make the pillow:

All seam allowances on the pillow assembly are ¼ inch and are included in the measurements and instructions.

1. **Referring to Table 18-1, cut the border, center, and backing pieces from the fabrics indicated.**

   The letters following the pieces in the table correspond to the labels in Figures 18-1 and 18-3.

Table 18-1	Cutting Instructions for Pillow Top and Backing		
Piece	*Fabric*	*Measurement*	*Quantity*
Backing	Off-white	15" x 15"	1
Center (A)	Off-white	7½" x 8½"	1
Outer border, sides (E)	Off-white	2½" x 10½"	2

Piece	Fabric	Measurement	Quantity
Outer border, upper and lower (F)	Off-white	2½" x 14½"	2
Platform (B)	Yellow	1½" x 8½"	1
Inner border, sides (C)	Dark blue	1½" x 8½"	2
Inner border, upper and lower (D)	Dark blue	1½" x 10½"	2

2. **Stitch the yellow strip (B) to one short side of the rectangular piece (A) to make a square, as shown in Figure 18-1.**

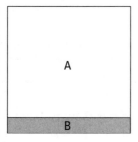

Figure 18-1:
Connect the center of the pillow top to the platform on which the bluebird stands.

3. **Double the size of the appliqué pattern provided at the end of this project section, and trace the four pieces of the large bluebird (head, beak, wing, and body) on the paper side of your fusible webbing.**

4. **Roughly cut out all the shapes.**

   You will cut them neatly after fusing them onto the fabrics.

5. **Fuse the webbing shapes to the wrong sides of their corresponding fabrics:**

   - Beak: Golden yellow fabric
   - Head: Light blue fabric
   - Wing: Medium blue fabric
   - Lower body: Dark blue fabric

   For details on fusible webbing and fusing shapes to fabric, see Chapter 10.

6. **Cut out all the fused shapes neatly following the pattern lines on the fusible webbing.**

7. **Using Figure 18-2 as a guide, use a washable pencil to lightly draw the bird and its legs onto the square you created in Step 2.**

   Sketching the bird in this manner gives you a reference point for where to place your fabric pieces.

Figure 18-2:
The posi-
tioning of
the bird on
the center
block.

8. **Remove the paper backings from the four fabric bird parts, and arrange them on the square using your markings as a guide.**

   Overlap the pieces slightly so that none of the off-white background fabric shows between the pieces (see Figure 18-6).

9. **Fuse the pieces in place by pressing them with an iron preheated to the cotton setting (or about halfway between medium and high heat).**

10. **Cut a piece of stabilizer just slightly larger than the bird, and pin it to the back (wrong) side of the square so that it covers the shape of the bird.**

11. **Machine appliqué the four pieces using a satin stitch and threads that match the pieces.**

    The width of the satin stitch should be about ⅛ inch. For more on the satin stitch, check out Chapter 10.

12. **Using the same width of satin stitch, stitch along the leg markings to machine embroider the legs.**

13. **When you finish with the satin stitch and all the pieces are appliquéd, remove the pins and tear away the stabilizer from the back of the block.**

14. **Stitch the blue inner side border strips (C) to the sides of the bird block, as shown in Figure 18-3.**

15. **Stitch the blue inner upper and lower border strips (D) to the top and bottom of the block, as shown in Figure 18-3. Press the seams of both the C and D strips toward the borders.**

16. **Stitch the off-white outer side border strips (E) to the sides of the block. (Refer to Figure 18-3 for placement of these strips.)**

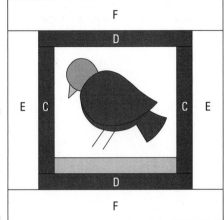

Figure 18-3:
Two borders
frame your
center
appliqué
block.

17. **Stitch the off-white outer upper and lower border strips (F) to the top and bottom of the block. (Refer to Figure 18-3 for placement of these strips.) Press the seams of both the E and F strips toward the blue borders.**

18. **Lay the pillow top facedown on your work surface. Lay the 15- x 15-inch square of batting on top of it, followed by the off-white solid lining piece, and thread or pin baste the layers together.**

19. **Quilt the pillow top as you like.**

20. **Machine stitch very close to the raw edges of the pillow top, and then trim away the excess batting and backing that extends beyond the edges of the appliquéd top.**

21. **Stitch the piping around the edges of the pillow top, clipping at the corners to avoid rounded corners (see Figure 18-4).**

    When you clip the corners of the piping, clip close to but not through the cord.

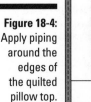

Figure 18-4:
Apply piping
around the
edges of
the quilted
pillow top.

22. **Place the pillow top and the pillow backing right sides together, and stitch around all four sides, leaving an 8-inch opening along the bottom edge for turning (see Figure 18-5).**

Figure 18-5:
Leave an opening to turn the pillow casing and insert the pillow form or stuffing, and clip the corners of the casing so that you get sharp corners.

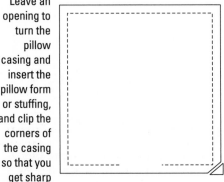

23. **Clip the corners close to, but not through, the stitching (refer to Figure 18-5).**

    Clipping eliminates the bulk in the corners, giving you pointed instead of rounded corners.

24. **Turn the pillow cover right side out.**

25. **Hand stitch one ¾-inch button eye on the bird's head.**

26. **Insert the pillow form or stuffing, and then whip stitch the turning opening closed.**

Appliquéing the place mat

Because you use a premade place mat for this project, the finished size will vary. Follow these steps to appliqué the place mat:

1. **Double the size of the appliqué pattern provided at the end of this project, and trace the four pieces for the large bluebird (head, beak, wing, and body) on the paper side of your fusible webbing.**

2. **Roughly cut out all the shapes.**

   You will cut them neatly after fusing them onto the fabrics.

3. **Fuse the webbing shapes to the wrong sides of their corresponding fabrics:**

   - Beak: Golden yellow fabric
   - Head: Light blue fabric
   - Wing: Medium blue fabric
   - Lower body: Dark blue fabric

   For details on fusible webbing and fusing shapes to fabric, see Chapter 10.

4. **Cut out all the shapes, neatly following the pattern lines on the fusible webbing.**

5. **Using Figure 18-6 as a guide, use a washable pencil to lightly draw the bird and the legs onto the lower-right corner of the place mat (refer to the photo in the color section of this book if necessary).**

   Sketching the bird in this manner gives you a reference point for where to place your fabric pieces.

6. **Remove the paper backings from the four fabric bird parts, and arrange them on the place mat using your markings as a guide.**

   Overlap the pieces slightly so none of the place mat fabric shows between the pieces (refer to Figure 18-6).

7. **Fuse the pieces in place by pressing them with an iron preheated to the cotton setting (or about halfway between medium and high heat).**

8. **Cut a piece of stabilizer just slightly larger than the bird, and pin it to the back (wrong) side of the place mat so that it covers the shape of the bird.**

9. **Machine appliqué the four pieces using a satin stitch and threads that match the pieces.**

   The width of the satin stitch should be about ⅛ inch. For more on the satin stitch, check out Chapter 10.

10. **Using the same width of satin stitch, stitch along the leg markings to machine embroider the legs.**

11. **When you finish with the satin stitch and all the pieces are appliquéd, remove the pins and tear the stabilizer from the back side of the place mat.**

12. **To finish the place mat, hand stitch a ¾-inch button eye on the bird's head.**

Appliquéing the napkin

Because you use a premade napkin for this project, the finished size will vary. Follow these steps to appliqué the napkin:

1. **Using the appliqué pattern provided at the end of this project in its current size (not doubled), trace the four pieces of the bluebird (head, beak, wing, and body) on the paper side of your fusible webbing.**

2. **Roughly cut out all the shapes.**

   You will cut them neatly after fusing them onto the fabrics.

3. **Fuse the webbing shapes to the wrong sides of their corresponding fabrics:**

   • Beak: Golden yellow fabric

   • Head: Light blue fabric

   • Wing: Medium blue fabric

   • Lower body: Dark blue fabric

4. **Cut out all the shapes, neatly following the pattern lines on the fusible webbing.**

5. **Using Figure 18-6 as a guide, use a washable pencil to lightly sketch the bird and the legs onto a corner of the napkin (refer to the photo in the color section of this book if necessary).**

   Sketching the bird in this manner gives you a reference point for where to place your fabric pieces.

6. **Remove the paper backings from the four fabric bird parts, and arrange them on the napkin using your markings as a guide.**

   Overlap the pieces slightly so none of the napkin fabric shows between the pieces (refer to Figure 18-6).

7. **Fuse the pieces in place by pressing them with an iron preheated to the cotton setting (or about halfway between medium and high heat).**

8. **Cut a piece of stabilizer just slightly larger than the bird, and pin it to the back (wrong) side of the napkin so that it covers the shape of the bird.**

9. **Machine appliqué the four pieces using a satin stitch and the threads that match the pieces.**

   The width of the satin stitch should be about ⅛ inch. For more on the satin stitch, check out Chapter 10.

10. Using the same width of satin stitch, stitch along the leg markings to machine embroider the legs.

11. When you finish with the satin stitch and all the pieces are appliquéd, remove the pins and tear the stabilizer from the back side of the napkin.

12. To finish the napkin, hand stitch a ½-inch button eye on the bird's head.

Appliquéing the kitchen towel

Because you use a premade kitchen towel for this project, the finished size will vary. Follow these steps to appliqué the kitchen towel:

1. Using the appliqué pattern provided at the end of this project in its current size (not doubled), trace the four pieces of the bluebird (head, beak, wing, and body) on the paper side of your fusible webbing.

2. Reverse the bluebird pattern, and repeat Step 1 so that you have two birds facing opposite directions.

3. Roughly cut out all the shapes.

   You will cut them neatly after fusing them onto the fabrics.

4. Fuse the webbing shapes to the wrong sides of their corresponding fabrics:

   • Beaks: Golden yellow fabric

   • Heads: Light blue fabric

   • Wings: Medium blue fabric

   • Lower bodies: Dark blue fabric

5. Cut out all the shapes, neatly following the pattern lines on the fusible webbing.

6. Using Figure 18-6 as a guide, use a washable pencil to lightly sketch the birds and their legs onto the center of one end of the kitchen towel.

   The birds should face each other.

7. Remove the paper backings from the eight fabric bird parts, and arrange them on the towel, using your markings as a guide.

   Overlap the pieces slightly so none of the towel shows between them, as shown in Figure 18-6.

8. **Fuse the pieces in place by pressing them with an iron preheated to the cotton setting (or about halfway between medium and high heat).**

9. **For each bird, cut a piece of stabilizer just slightly larger than the bird itself, and pin it to the back (wrong) side of the towel so that it covers the shape of the bird.**

10. **Machine appliqué the eight pieces using a satin stitch and the threads that match the pieces.**

   The width of the satin stitch should be about ⅛ inch. For more on the satin stitch, check out Chapter 10.

11. **Using the same width of satin stitch, stitch along the leg markings to machine embroider the legs.**

12. **When you finish with the satin stitch and all the pieces are appliquéd, remove the pins and tear the stabilizer from the back side of the towel.**

13. **To finish the towel, hand stitch a ½ inch button eye to each bird's head.**

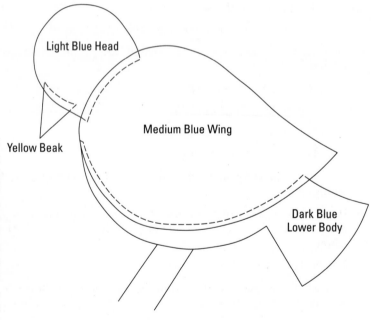

Figure 18-6:
When laying out bluebird shapes, overlap them slightly so that the foundation material isn't visible.

Light Blue Head

Medium Blue Wing

Yellow Beak

Dark Blue Lower Body

Bluebird Template

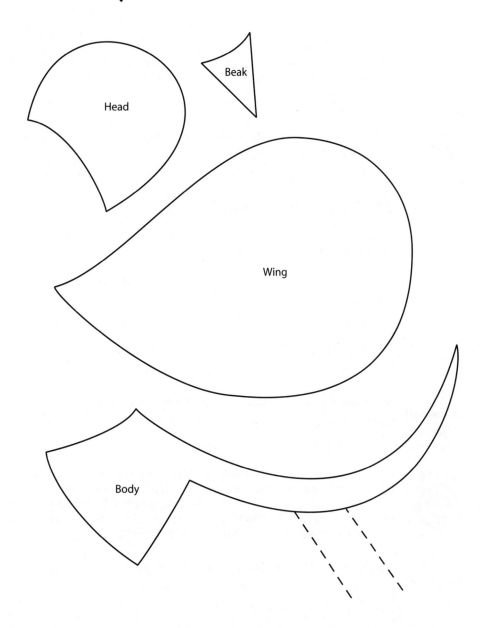

Pink Tulips Breakfast Set

Not all quilt blocks are square! This breakfast set — place mat, hot pad, and napkin — is based on a rectangular, odd-sized block. The floral block in fresh spring pinks and bright greens is perfect whether it's lined up in threes for place mat centers or standing on its own in a hot pad (the napkin is left plain). If pink's not your color, try making the tulip portion of the blocks in yellow, purple, or red — anything goes!

The top area of the block uses a set-in seam, which can be challenging. I guide you through the task in the project instructions, but for more on set-in seams, flip to Chapter 9.

Stashing your materials

The lists in this section tell you what fabrics and notions you need to make two place mats, one hot pad, and two napkins:

- ✔ 1 yard of white print fabric (includes backing fabric)
- ✔ ⅓ yard each of two different pink print fabrics
- ✔ ¼ yard each of two different green fabrics (solids or prints)
- ✔ ¼ yard yellow fabric (solid or print)
- ✔ All-purpose thread in white, pink, and yellow

Additional materials needed for two place mats
- ✔ Two 18- x 24-inch pieces of cotton batting
- ✔ 5 yards of yellow bias binding

If you choose to make your own binding, cut strips of yellow fabric 2½ inches by the width of fabric, and sew the ends together on a 45-degree angle (as described in Chapter 14). Fold the long strip in half lengthwise, and press. When it comes time to apply the binding, you'll just fold the raw edges in and stitch it to your project just like any other binding.

Additional materials needed for one hot pad
- ✔ Two 10- x 12-inch pieces of cotton batting
- ✔ 1¼ yards of yellow piping
- ✔ Scrap of pink ribbon

Always use cotton batting on hot pads, place mats, or anything else that may be subjected to the heat of a warmed dish — polyester batting will melt!

Materials needed for two napkins

✔ Two 19- x 19-inch squares of pink fabric (print or solid, as long as it coordinates)

✔ All-purpose thread in pink

Assembling the quilt blocks

This section explains how to construct the quilt blocks used in the place mats and the hot pad. The finished block size is 4 x 8½ inches.

All seam allowances are ¼ inch and are included in the template patterns.

1. **Using the template patterns provided at the end of this project section, make a template for each piece shown in Figure 18-7. Label each template, and include the grain line markings.**

   In Figure 18-7, "rev." means to reverse the piece. If you need help creating templates, see Chapter 4.

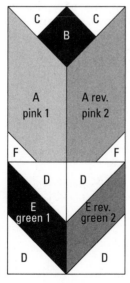

Figure 18-7: The tulip block in detail.

2. **Referring to Table 18-2, trace the templates on the wrong side of the corresponding fabrics, and then cut out the appropriate quantities of each block piece.**

   Because they have set-in seams, be sure to transfer the corner dots on pieces A and B from the templates to the fabrics.

Table 18-2	Cutting Instructions for Quilt Block Pieces	
Piece	*Fabric*	*Quantity*
Flower petal (A)	Pink 1	7
Flower petal (A rev.)	Pink 2	7 reversed
Flower center (B)	Yellow	7
Upper triangles (C)	White	14
Lower triangles (D)	White	28
Leaf (E)	Green 1	7
Leaf (E rev.)	Green 2	7 reversed
Side triangles (F)	White	14

3. **Stitch two white triangles (C) to a yellow square (B) to create a top unit, as shown in Figure 18-8. Repeat to make seven top units. Press seam allowances toward the yellow fabric.**

4. **Stitch one side triangle (F) to the shortest edge of a pink petal piece (A and A rev.) to create a petal unit, as shown in Figure 18-9. Repeat to make seven pink 1 petal units and seven pink 2 petal units. Press the seam allowances toward the pink fabrics.**

Figure 18-8:
Two white triangles and a yellow square create a top unit.

Figure 18-9:
A side triangle and a petal piece create a petal unit.

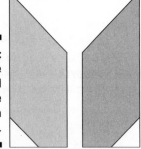

5. **With right sides together, stitch a left petal unit to a right petal unit, as shown in Figure 18-10.**

   Begin your stitching at the dot at the center of the petals so that you can set in the top portion of the block in the next step. This dot is located ¼ inch in from the edges of the pieces.

Figure 18-10: Assemble two petal units to create one piece.

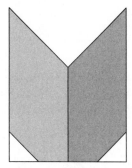

6. **Stitch a top unit (created in Step 3) to the left petal unit, as shown in Figure 18-11. Start stitching at the top-left corner, and stop stitching at the dot. End your stitching, and cut the thread. Then stitch the top unit to the right petal, starting at the dot and ending at the outside tip. Make seven of these flower units.**

Figure 18-11: Stitching a top unit to a petal unit requires a set-in seam.

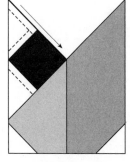
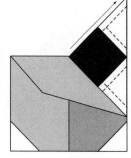
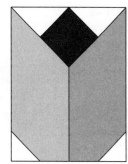

7. **Stitch two white triangles (D) to each green petal piece (E and E rev.), as shown in Figure 18-12. Make seven left leaf sections and seven right leaf sections.**

8. **With right sides together, stitch a left leaf section to a right leaf section to make a leaf unit, as shown in Figure 18-12. Repeat this step until you have seven leaf units.**

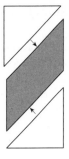

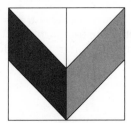

Figure 18-12:
Green leaf
pieces
combine
with lower
triangles
to create
a leaf unit.

9. **With right sides together, stitch one flower unit (created in Steps 3 through 6) to a leaf unit (created in Steps 7 and 8) to create a tulip block, as shown in Figure 18-13. Make seven of these blocks.**

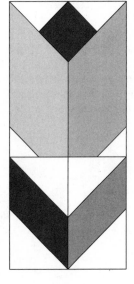
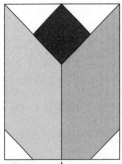
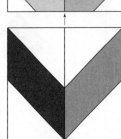

Figure 18-13:
Flower and
leaf units
come
together
to form a
complete
tulip block.

Making the place mats

The finished size of each place mat is 20 x 15½ inches. Follow these steps to create two place mats:

1. **Collect six of the quilt blocks you made in the preceding section. You need three blocks for each place mat.**

2. **Referring to Table 18-3, cut out the borders and backing pieces for each place mat.**

   The letters in Table 18-3 correspond to the labeled pieces in Figure 18-16.

Table 18-3	Cutting Instructions for Place Mat Backing, Borders, and Sashing		
Piece	**Fabric**	**Measurement**	**Quantity**
Backing	White	18" x 24"	2
Sashing (A)	White	1½" x 9"	8
Inner border, upper and lower (B)	White	1½" x 16½"	4
Contrasting upper and lower border (C)	Pink 1	1" x 16½2"	4
Outer border, upper and lower (D)	White	2½" x 16½"	4
Outer border, sides (E)	White	2½" x 16"	4

3. **Alternate four white sashing strips (A) with three quilt blocks, as shown in Figure 18-14, to form a place mat center. Press the seam allowances toward the blocks. Repeat this step to form the other place mat center.**

Figure 18-14:
Three quilt blocks are separated by vertical sashing strips. The place mat center is then bordered by white strips along the top and bottom.

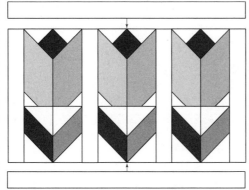

4. **Stitch white inner border strips (B) to the top and bottom of each place mat center, as shown in Figure 18-14. Press seam allowances toward the blocks.**

5. **Stitch pink border strips (C) to the top and bottom of each place mat center, as shown in Figure 18-15. Press the seam allowances toward the pink strips.**

6. **Stitch white outer border strips (D) to the top and bottom of each place mat center, as shown in Figure 18-16. Press the seam allowances toward the white strips.**

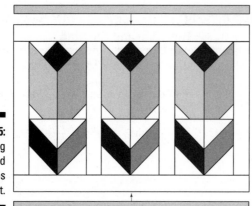

Figure 18-15:
Contrasting
upper and
lower strips
add interest.

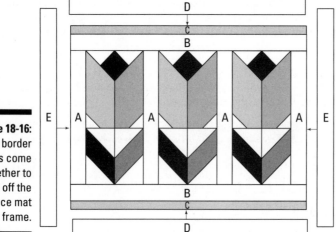

Figure 18-16:
Outer border
strips come
together to
finish off the
place mat
frame.

7. **Stitch white outer border strips (E) to the left and right sides of each place mat center, as shown in Figure 18-16. Press the seam allowances toward the just-added white strips.**

8. **Lay a place mat top facedown on your work surface. Lay an 18- x 24-inch piece of batting on top of it, followed by an 18- x 24-inch piece of white backing fabric, right side up. Thread or pin baste the layers together. Repeat for the second place mat.**

9. **Quilt the place mats as desired.**

10. **Machine stitch very close to the raw edges of the place mats, and trim away the excess batting and backing fabric.**

11. **Bind the place mats with the yellow bias binding.**

Making the hot pad

The pink tulips hot pad consists of one bordered quilt block, and the finished size is 8 x 10½ inches. Follow these steps to create one hot pad:

1. **Lay out one of the quilt blocks you created in the section "Assembling the quilt blocks" earlier in this project section.**

2. **Referring to Table 18-4, cut the backing and border pieces for the hot pad.**

Table 18-4   Cutting Instructions for Hot Pad Backing and Borders

Piece	*Fabric*	*Measurement*	*Quantity*
Backing	White	10" x 12"	1
Border, sides (A)	White	2½" x 9"	2
Border, upper and lower (B)	White	1½" x 8½"	2

3. **Stitch white side border strips (A) to the left and right sides of a flower block. Press seam allowances toward the block.**

4. **Stitch white upper and lower border strips (B) to the top and bottom edges of the flower block, as shown in Figure 18-17a. Press seam allowances toward the block.**

5. **Stitch the yellow piping around the edges of the hot pad top (refer to Figure 18-17b).**

   To apply the piping,

   1. Begin stitching at the center of one side, leaving a 2-inch tail of piping hanging free. When you approach a corner, stop stitching ¼ inch from the corner, and clip into the seam allowance of the piping *close to but not through* the stuffed area. Clipping eliminates the bulk that would otherwise prevent a nice, pointed corner.

   2. Turn the corner, and resume stitching.

   3. When you arrive back at your starting point, overlap the remaining piping and the tail you left at the starting point, and stitch across them. The layers of fabric and batting are a bit bulky, so stitch slowly so that you don't break your needle.

   4. Trim the excess tails of the piping so that they're only about ½ inch long.

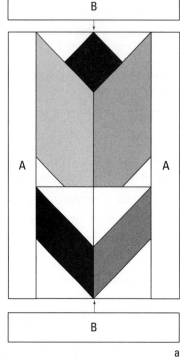
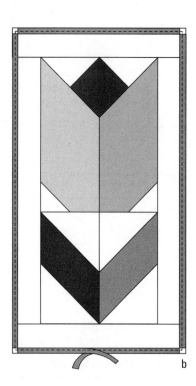

Figure 18-17: Stitch borders to the quilt block (a), and add piping (b) to finish off your hot pad.

a

b

6. Pin the two pieces of batting to the wrong side of the backing fabric.

7. Place the backing piece (with batting) and the hot pad top together, with the right sides of the quilted top and backing facing.

8. With the wrong side of the quilted top facing up, stitch around the edges of the top along the piping stitching lines, leaving a 3-inch opening at the top edge for turning. See Figure 18-18.

9. Remove any pins, trim the excess batting and backing fabric, clip the corners, and turn the hot pad right side out.

10. Fold the scrap of ribbon in half to form a loop.

11. Insert the ends of the ribbon loop in the center of the turning opening to create a hanging loop at the top of the hot pad (see Figure 18-19). Then whip stitch the turning opening closed, catching the ends of the ribbon in your stitching.

12. To finish the project, quilt the hot pad in any manner you choose.

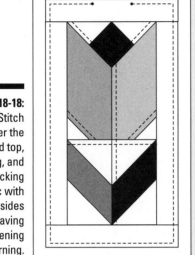

Figure 18-18:
Stitch together the hot pad top, batting, and backing fabric with wrong sides out, leaving an opening for turning.

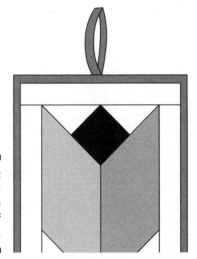

Figure 18-19:
Add a hanging loop to the top of your hot pad.

Making the napkins

These napkins are a breeze to make. Simply hem the two 19-x 19-inch pink fabric squares so that the finished size of each napkin is 18 x 18 inches. To make two napkins, follow these two steps:

1. **For each pink fabric square, fold each edge under ¼ inch and press. Then fold each edge under another ¼ inch and press again.**

Turning under ¼ inch twice on each napkin creates a doubled-hem, which keeps the hem from fraying during laundering.

2. **Stitch the hems in place with pink all-purpose thread, stitching around all four sides a scant ¼ inch from the actual edges of the napkin.**

Pink Tulips Patterns

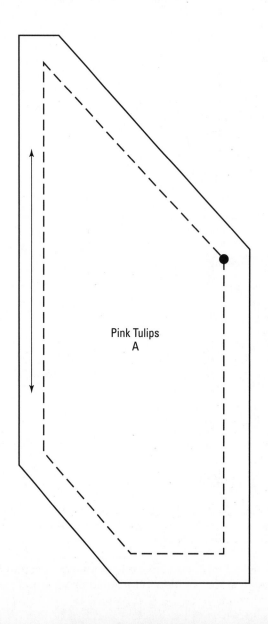

Pink Tulips
A

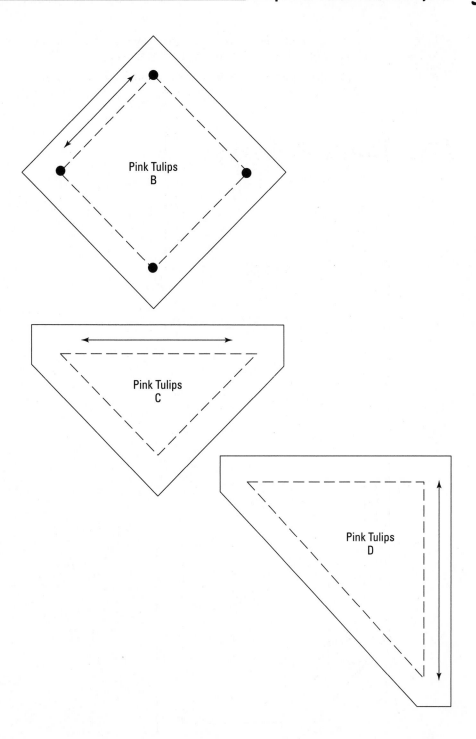

Pink Tulips
B

Pink Tulips
C

Pink Tulips
D

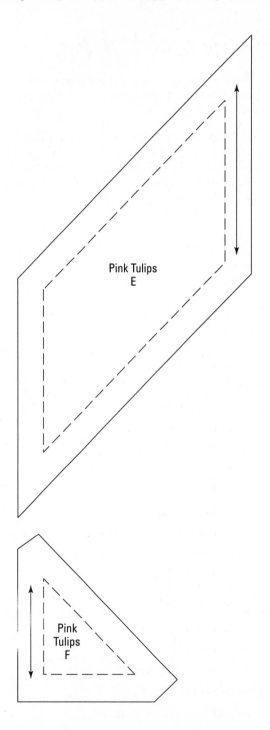

Pink Tulips
E

Pink
Tulips
F

Blue Star Place Mat and Hot Pad

This project is fun as well as versatile. How so? For starters, you can practice your rotary cutting skills and whip out stars in a flash, and the place mat is actually a miniature quilt!

For this project, you get instructions for making just one place mat, one hot pad, and one coordinating napkin. I know many quilters *love* to make mini-quilts, and this place mat is a perfect project for a first-time mini-quilter! To make additional place mats, just increase the materials in the place mat list in the following section. You can make additional hot pads and napkins easily, too.

Stashing your materials

I list the materials that you need to make *one* of each item. Because the place mat fabrics require a *fat quarter,* which is 18 x 22 inches, you can easily figure the yardage needed for additional place mats — ½ yard of fabric makes two place mats, 1 yard makes four place mats, and so on.

Be sure to use cotton batting in this project. Polyester batting often melts when exposed to high temperatures.

All seam allowances are ¼ inch and are included in the given measurements.

Materials for one place mat

- One 18- x 22-inch piece (or fat quarter) of blue print fabric
- One 18- x 22-inch piece (or fat quarter) of tan print fabric
- One 8- x 20-inch piece of blue paisley fabric
- Two 16- x 20-inch pieces of cotton batting
- Two 16- x 20-inch pieces of dark blue solid fabric
- 2 yards of dark blue quilt binding, ½-inch finished width
- All-purpose thread to match the fabrics

Materials for one hot pad

- One 7- x 10-inch piece of blue print fabric
- One 10- x 20-inch piece of tan print fabric
- One 12- x 7-inch strip of blue paisley fabric
- Two 11- x 11-inch pieces of cotton batting
- One 11- x 11-inch piece of dark blue solid fabric
- 1½ yards of dark blue quilt binding, ½-inch finished width
- All-purpose thread to match the fabrics

Materials for one 18-inch napkin

✔ One 19- x 19-inch square of blue paisley fabric

✔ All-purpose thread in blue

Putting together a place mat

The finished size of the place mat is 14 x 18 inches. Follow these steps to create one place mat:

1. **Cut out the pieces for this project, following the measurements listed in Table 18-5.**

Table 18-5	Cutting Instructions for One Place Mat		
Piece	*Fabric*	*Measurement*	*Quantity*
Inner border	Tan	2½" x 14"	4
Star points	Tan	14" x 10"	1
Star corners	Tan	1½" x 1½"	24
Star points	Blue	14" x 10"	1
Center of star	Blue	2½" x 2½"	6
Outer border, upper and lower	Blue paisley	1½" x 14½"	2
Outer border, sides	Blue paisley	1½" x 16½"	2

2. **On the wrong side of the 14- x 10-inch tan piece, use a fabric pencil to mark a grid of 24 1⅛-inch squares. Then draw diagonal lines through all the squares, as shown in Figure 18-20.**

3. **Place the marked tan piece and the 14- x 10-inch blue piece together, right sides facing. Pin them together around the outside edges, placing the pins out of the way of the diagonal stitching lines. Stitch ¼ inch from each side of the diagonal line (see Figure 18-20).**

4. **Cut out the 24 squares by cutting along the solid vertical and horizontal lines you marked in Step 2.**

Figure 18-20:
Mark a grid
of squares
on the large
rectangles,
and then
bisect each
square
diagonally.
Join two
rectangles
together by
stitching on
either side of
the diagonal
lines.

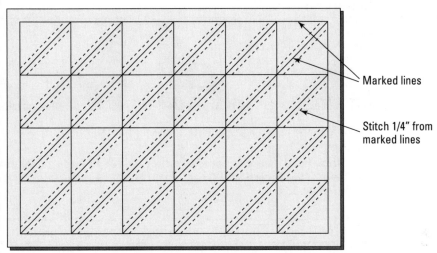

Marked lines

Stitch 1/4" from
marked lines

5. **Remove the pins, and cut the squares in half along the diagonal lines (see Figure 18-21). You should end up with 48 doubled triangles that are half tan and half blue.**

6. **Open each doubled triangle to reveal a two-tone square, as shown in Figure 18-21. Press the squares open, with the seam allowances toward the blue fabric.**

Figure 18-21:
Cut one
square
into two
triangles,
which are
actually
two-tone
squares.

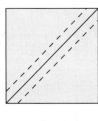

7. **Stitch together two of the two-tone squares so that they're mirror images of each other (see Figure 18-22). Make 24 of these strips.**

Figure 18-22:
Join two squares to form the first points of your star block.

8. Stitch tan 1½-inch squares to either end of 12 two-square units from Step 7 (see Figure 18-23).

Figure 18-23:
Square blocks create the corners of each star block.

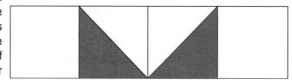

9. Stitch two of the remaining strips made in Step 7 to opposite sides of each of the six 2½-inch blue center squares, as shown in Figure 18-24. Make six of these units.

Figure 18-24:
Sew side strips to the center block.

10. Stitch two of the strips made in Step 8 to the tops and bottoms of the units made in Step 9 (see Figure 18-25). Make six of these star blocks.

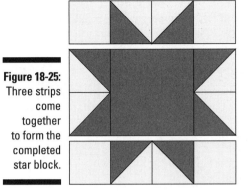
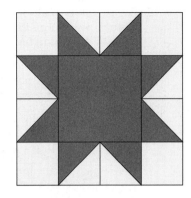

11. **Stitch three star blocks from Step 10 together horizontally to form one row (see Figure 18-26). Make two of these rows.**

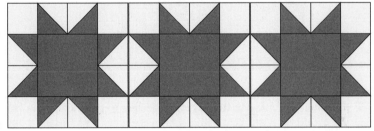

12. **Stitch the two rows together along one long edge to make the place mat center.**

13. **Stitch one 2½- x 14-inch tan strip to each of the two long sides of the place mat center. Trim the ends to align with the edge of the place mat center.**

14. **Stitch the remaining two tan strips to either side of the place mat, and trim the ends to align with the outer edge of the borders from Step 13.**

15. **Stitch the two 1½- x 16½-inch blue paisley strips to the two long sides of the place mat center. Stitch the two 1½- x 14½-inch blue paisley strips to other two sides of the place mat center.**

The tan and blue borders should come together as shown in Figure 18-27.

16. **Lay the place mat top facedown on your work surface. Lay a 16- x 20-inch piece of batting on top of it, followed by a 16- x 20-inch piece of solid dark blue backing fabric.**

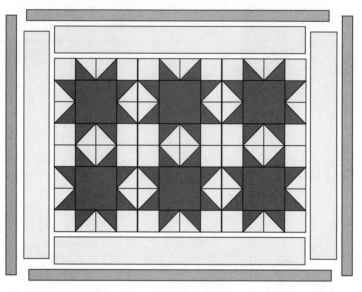

Figure 18-27: Add inner and outer borders to frame the center design of the place mat.

17. **Thread or pin baste the layers together to prepare them for quilting.**

18. **Quilt the place mat as desired.**

    In the place mat pictured in the color section of this book, I machine quilted in-the-ditch around each shape and in a diamond pattern in the tan areas. I used a contrasting thread color just for fun.

19. **Machine stitch very close to the raw edges of the place mat, and trim away the excess batting and backing fabric.**

20. **Bind the place mats with the dark blue binding.**

Assembling a hot pad

The finished size of this hot pad is 10 x 10 inches. The basic construction of the star block with borders is the same as for the place mat (see the preceding section), so if you get stuck on a step, refer to the place mat instructions and figures for assistance.

Follow these steps to make one hot pad:

1. **Cut out the pieces for the hot pad, following the measurements listed in Table 18-6.**

Table 18-6	Cutting Instructions for One Hot Pad		
Piece	*Fabric Color*	*Size in Inches*	*Quantity*
Star points	Tan	7" x 7"	1
Star points	Blue	7" x 7"	1
Inner border, upper and lower	Tan	2½" x 4½"	2
Inner border, sides	Tan	2½" x 8½"	2
Star corners	Tan	1½" x 1½"	4
Center of star	Blue	2½" x 2½"	1
Outer border, upper and lower	Blue paisley	1½" x 8½"	2
Outer border, sides	Blue paisley	1½" x 10½"	2

2. **On the wrong side of the 7- x 7-inch tan square, use a fabric pencil to mark a grid of four 1⅞-inch squares. Draw a diagonal line bisecting each square.**

3. **Place the tan square and the 7- x 7-inch piece of blue print fabric together, right sides facing. Pin them together around the outside edges, placing the pins out of the way of the diagonal stitching lines. Stitch ¼ inch from each side of the diagonal line.**

4. **Cut out the four squares by cutting along the solid vertical and horizontal lines you marked in Step 2. Cut the squares in half along the diagonal lines to form eight doubled triangles that are half tan and half blue.**

5. **Open each doubled triangle to reveal a two-tone square. Press the squares open, with the seam allowances toward the blue fabric.**

6. **Stitch together two of the two-tone squares so that they're mirror images of each other. Make four of these units.**

7. **Stitch tan 1½-inch squares to either end of two of the two-square units made in Step 6.**

8. Stitch the two remaining two-square units made in Step 6 to opposite sides of the 2½-inch blue center square.

9. Stitch two units that you made in Step 7 to the unit made in Step 8 to make one star block.

10. Stitch the two tan 2½- x 4½-inch border strips to opposing sides of the star block, and trim the edges so they align with the block edges.

11. Stitch the two tan 2½- x 8½-inch border strips to the two remaining sides, and trim the edges so they align with the outer edges of the side borders.

12. Repeat Steps 10 and 11 with the blue paisley outer borders, sewing the shorter strips on first followed by the longer strips, to complete the hot pad top.

The borders should come together as shown in Figure 18-28.

Figure 18-28:
Inner and outer borders frame the center design of the hot pad.

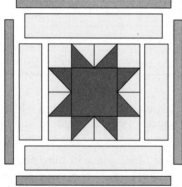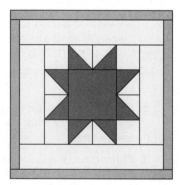

13. Lay the hot pad top facedown on your work surface. On top of it, place both pieces of 11- x 11-inch batting, followed by the backing fabric (wrong side down). Thread or pin baste the layers together.

14. Quilt the hot pad using the same design you used for the place mats, or choose a different design.

15. Machine stitch very close to the raw edges of the hot pad, and trim away the excess batting and backing fabric.

16. Bind the hot pad with the dark blue binding (as you did for the place mats), leaving a 6-inch tail at one corner, as shown in Figure 18-29a.

17. On the end of the binding tail, fold over the raw edge and then fold the tail towards the back of the hot pad to form a loop (see Figure 18-29b). Hand stitch the loop in place to finish the hot pad.

Figure 18-29: Leave a bit of binding (a) to use as a hanging loop (b).

a

b

Making a napkin

The finished size of this napkin is 18 x 18 inches. To make one napkin, follow these instructions:

1. **Take the 19- x 19-inch square of blue paisley fabric and fold each edge under ¼ inch and press. Then fold each edge under another ¼ inch, and press again.**

Turning under ¼ inch twice on the napkin creates a doubled-hem, which keeps the hem from fraying during laundering.

2. **Stitch the hems in place with blue all-purpose thread, stitching around all four sides ¼ inch from the actual edges of the napkin.**

Pastel Nine-Patch Wall Hanging

Here's a project so simple and quick that you can make it in one day — no kidding! It may look complex, but it's actually just simple nine-patch blocks set on point.

Be sure to use a large floral print in this project, and experiment with it. For the quilt that appears in the color insert, I used the heaviest, busiest section of the floral fabric in the center of the quilt top and the least busy areas of the fabric in the sides and corners. This layout is a great way to use a large-scale print effectively because you can balance the visual impact of the quilt, making sure that all the busy areas don't end up on one side while the other side remains plain.

Stashing your materials

To create this nine-patch wall hanging, you need the materials listed here:

- ¼ yard of light yellow solid fabric
- ¼ yard of light blue solid fabric
- ⅓ yard of light pink print fabric
- ⅓ yard of blue large-scale floral print fabric
- One 24- x 24-inch piece of batting
- One 24- x 24-inch piece of coordinating fabric
- All-purpose threads in yellow, blue, and pink to match the fabrics
- 3 yards of light yellow quilt binding

Assembling the quilt top

The finished size of this wall hanging is 21 x 21 inches square. To assemble the top, follow the instructions in this section.

All seam allowances are ¼ inch and are included in all the given measurements.

1. **Cut out the pieces of the quilt per the measurements in Table 18-7.**

   For the best results (nice straight edges), use a rotary cutter to cut all the pieces. You may also use scissors if desired.

TIP

When cutting strips with the rotary cutter, be sure to use the lines on your ruler instead of the ones on the cutting mat! The ruler gives you much more accurate measurements. Only use the lines on the mat when straightening an edge.

Table 18-7	Cutting Instructions for Wall Hanging		
Piece	*Fabric*	*Measurement*	*Quantity*
Nine-patch corner square	Light yellow	2½" x 2½"	16
Nine-patch center square	Light blue	2½" x 2½"	8
Nine-patch outer square	Light pink	2½" x 2½"	16
Border strip	Light pink	2½" x 17½"	4
Corner triangles (A)	Blue floral	5" x 5"	2
Side triangles (B)	Blue floral	9" x 9"	1
Center square (C)	Blue floral	6½" x 6½"	1

2. **To make the nine-patch blocks, stitch one yellow square to one side of a pink square (right sides together), and then stitch another yellow square to the opposite side of the same pink square (right sides together). See Figure 18-30. Press the seam allowances toward the darker fabric.**

   Make eight of these units.

Figure 18-30:
The nine-patch block starts with three squares.

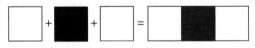

3. **Stitch one pink square to one side of a light blue solid square (right sides together), and then stitch another pink square to the opposite side of the same blue square (right sides together). See Figure 18-31. Press the seam allowances toward the darker fabric.**

   Make four of these units.

Figure 18-31:
Three more
squares
form the
middle row
of the nine-
patch block.

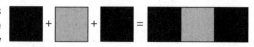

4. **Assemble one nine-patch block by stitching together one of the units created in Step 3 with two of the units made in Step 2, as shown in Figure 18-32. Press the seam allowances away from the center row.**

   Make four of these blocks.

Figure 18-32:
Three three-
block rows
come
together
to form the
nine-patch
design.

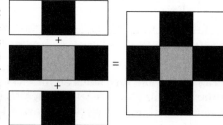

5. **Cut the two 5- x 5-inch blue print squares diagonally in half to form four triangles (A), as shown in Figure 18-33.**

   These are your corner setting triangles.

Figure 18-33:
Cut squares
diagonally
to form the
corner
triangles.

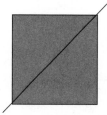 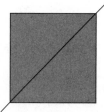

6. **Cut the 9- x 9-inch square twice diagonally into quarters to make four triangles (B), as shown in Figure 18-34.**

   These are the setting triangles for the sides.

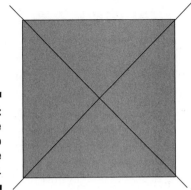

Figure 18-34:
Cut the large square to form the side triangles.

7. Using the A and B triangles as well as the center block (C) and the nine-patch blocks, assemble the quilt center area as shown in Figure 18-35. Start by making rows, and then join the rows together to complete the top. Press seam allowances toward the floral fabric whenever possible.

8. Stitch two of the pink print border strips to the top and bottom edges of the quilt center, as shown in Figure 18-36. Press the seam allowances toward the quilt top.

9. Stitch the four remaining 2½-inch blue squares to the short ends of the two remaining pink print border strips, as shown in Figure 18-36. Stitch these strips to the side edges of the quilt center, and press the seam allowances toward the quilt top.

Figure 18-35:
The elements of the nine-patch quilt are assembled first in rows and then as a whole.

Quilting and completing the project

Follow these steps to complete your quilt:

1. **Lay the quilt top facedown on your work surface. Layer on top of it the batting and the backing fabric, right side up.**

2. **Thread or pin baste the layers together to prepare them for quilting.**

   See Chapter 12 for basting instructions.

3. **Hand or machine quilt as desired.**

   Check out Chapter 11 for quilting design ideas. On the quilt pictured in the color section of this book, I machine quilted ¼ inch from the seam lines with clear nylon monofilament.

4. **Stitch around the quilt top ⅛ inch from the raw edges, and trim the excess batting and backing even with the edges of the quilt top.**

5. **Bind the quilt to finish.**

   For a binding how-to, see Chapter 14.

Figure 18-36:
Border strips and corner medallions finish off this nine-patch quilt.

Part VI
The Part of Tens

The 5th Wave   By Rich Tennant

John Henry was not only a steel-driving man, he was also a needle-driving man.

We'll settle this once and for all. On your mark... get set...

In this part . . .

*W*hen you start quilting, I know you'll get hooked. With that inevitability in mind, this part gives you lists of suggestions (in tens, of course) for how to expand your experience of this uniquely personal, practical, and artistic craft. Develop time-saving techniques with the tips I give you, experiment with new ways to display your quilt art, and even get the inside scoop on what quilt judges look for, in case a quilt show or two is in your future.

Chapter 19

Ten Quilting Timesavers

Throughout this book, I give you timesaving ideas and tips to help make your quilting project progress more quickly and smoothly. In this chapter, I've collected a few more tips I'd like to pass along.

Go For a Wash and Spin

Cutting into unwashed fabric is a quilting taboo. Fabric that hasn't been pre-washed has the potential to bleed, shrink, and ultimately cause major errors in your finished quilt.

I like to wash all new fabrics as soon as I get them in the door, before they even make it into my sewing room. By doing this ahead of time, I know that all the fabric in my stash is ready to use at a moment's notice, whenever a creative whim strikes me.

Keep Your Machine Tiptop

Nothing wastes time better than restitching a seam because your sewing machine needle is skipping, adjusting the tension during a project, or picking lint out of a seam because the machine wasn't cleaned before you started using it. To keep your momentum going and your project error-free, keep your machine clean, oiled, and in top condition, and you'll always be off on the right foot (no pun intended). Check your owner's manual for recommendations on cleaning and servicing. I like to clean and oil my sewing machine once every two months — but I do *a lot* of sewing!

Set Up an Efficient Workspace

To keep your quilt-making adventure running smoothly, you need a well-organized workspace. The "kitchen triangle" that interior designers insist upon works for quilting, too: Instead of a sink-stove-work surface triangle, set up a machine-pressing station-work surface triangle.

Position everything so you only have to take a few steps in between. This layout saves you time and energy when working on large projects that require you to move repeatedly from one task to another.

Stick to Neutral Thread

Sometimes, it seems that threading your machine and bobbin takes more time than actually sewing.

When piecing, choose one neutral thread color that works well with all fabrics. Doing so saves you the hassle of rethreading your machine with a different color for every fabric. Use this same neutral thread in the bobbin, and stitch away! Also, thread several bobbins at one time so you don't have to stop and wind bobbins each time one runs out.

Divide Your Work into Mini-Projects

To make a large or complex project less intimidating and more manageable, divide the work into units that each can be completed in 10 to 15 minutes. With tasks broken down in this manner, you can make great use of small pockets of time, such as when you're waiting for a phone call. For example, you can cut out all the pieces you need for a project at once, chain-piece items for a block in one sitting, cut them apart and press in another sitting, and stitch the units together to make blocks at a later time.

Forego the Iron in Favor of the Finger

When working on small units, *finger-press* the pieces open rather than run to the ironing board each time. Simply run your fingernail over the seam line of the opened unit to press the seam allowance open. You can press the pieces at the ironing board later.

Work Assembly Line–Style

If you've ever had to stuff envelopes, you know that you make faster progress by doing the same task over and over rather than constantly switching gears.

When you're working on a quilting project, you can do several things all at once to save time. For instance, divide your time by cutting out all the pieces of your blocks at once, then stitch all the units together, then assemble all the units into blocks, and finally stitch all the blocks together to create the quilt top.

Save time by chain-piecing whenever possible (see Chapter 9 for instructions). You can cut the units apart later, perhaps while watching television or helping the youngsters with homework. Likewise, trim all thread tails at once, and press in one sitting.

Stitch on the Run

Are you working on a project that requires hand appliqué or hand piecing? Fill a resealable plastic bag with your fabric, thread, extra needles, and a small pair of scissors so you can work on your project just about anywhere. Tote your project with you for endless lobby lounging at the dentist's or doctor's office. Or keep it in the car and work on it while waiting outside the schoolyard on carpool duty.

If you're taking your project on vacation or an overnight visit, pack a 75-watt light bulb so you know you'll always be stitching in good light. Hotels are notorious for using low-wattage light bulbs.

Keep Several Needles Threaded

When doing hand appliqué, piecing, or quilting, it's a great idea to have several needles threaded and waiting at all times. Threading needles is a great job for the kids, especially if your eyesight is a bit weak. (Chocolate or popsicles are wonderful motivators for the kiddies.)

If you're interested in knowing how much thread you put into a quilt, a great time to measure is when you thread your needles. Simply cut enough one-yard lengths of thread for any number of needles (working in tens makes keeping track easier), and keep track of the number of yards cut in a notepad. Thread the needles and place them in a pincushion. Hey, some quilters go in for this stuff!

One way to keep track of threaded needles for hand quilting is to thread a bunch on the spool at one time. As you need a new threaded needle simply push the others back down the spool of thread and, with just one needle on the thread, cut the thread the length you need. Threading multiple needles on one spool means you don't have to thread needles as you work, and it saves your eyesight for just the sewing part. Just remember to push the other needles down the thread or you'll cut them all off at once and undo the threading you were so far ahead on!

Spring for Prepackaged Binding

Save yourself a lot of time and potential frustration by buying prepackaged binding rather than making your own. Binding is usually sold in 2- to 3-yard lengths and is great because all the cutting, folding, and pressing are already done for you. And it's affordable, too, at around $2 per package. The only drawback is its limited color selection. Most of the basics — white, black, navy blue, cream, red — are covered, though, so try to choose a color that compliments your quilt by matching the binding to one of your main fabrics.

Chapter 20

Ten Tips for Displaying Your Art

*Q*uilted items are practical as well as decorative. You may want to show off a quilt as a bedcovering or use smaller pieces as place mats on your table. You can also choose form over function and display your quilting as decorative art.

In this chapter, you can find ten tips and ideas for displaying your masterpieces safely and to their best advantage. Use your imagination to come up with additional ways to show off your quilted art!

Pin Your Quilt to the Wall

To display small quilted items — say, 36 x 36 inches — without leaving major marks on your walls, gather four skinny straight pins — the same kind you use to pin fabric together when sewing. In each upper corner of the quilt, insert a pin in the *backing*, about ½ inch from the corner. (By inserting the pin in the backing, you actually hide the pin *behind* the quilt, and no one's the wiser.) Holding the quilt up to where you want it to hang, push the pins into the wall at an angle upwards about ½ inch. Do the same thing with the lower corners, but angle the head of the pin downwards so that the ends of the quilt don't curl upwards.

This type of display only works for small quilted items. Quilts any bigger than 36 x 36 inches are too heavy for the pins to hold securely.

Use Wooden Quilt Hangers

Wooden quilt hangers are available in many quilt shops and quilting catalogs. However, they're very easy to make, so you may want to enlist your favorite handyperson to make some for you. To support large quilts, you usually need two or three small hangers or one or two long ones. The hangers consist of two pieces of wood that are placed on top of one another, sandwiching the top edge of the quilt between them. This method of display interferes with the top edge of your quilt, somewhat obstructing its appearance. If the obstruction bothers you, consider hand-stitching a *dummy strip* of fabric to the top-back edge of your quilt. Insert this strip into the hangers instead of the binding. (Of course, if you remove the quilt from the hanger to use as a table covering, lap quilt, or bed covering, remove this dummy strip.)

Hang Around with Dowel Sleeves and Rods

Dowel sleeves and rods are used in a popular quilt-hanging method that allows your quilt to hang straight with little distortion. First, you need to make a dowel sleeve and attach it to the upper back side of the quilt:

1. **Measure the top width of the quilt you're making the sleeve for, and add 2 inches.**

   For example, if your quilt is 45 inches wide, your measurement is 47 inches.

2. **From fabric that's the same color as the backing or something different (the choice is yours), cut a strip that's 6 inches wide and as long as your measurement from Step 1.**

3. **Fold the strip in half lengthwise, with the right sides facing. Machine straight stitch ¼ inch from the double raw edge of the strip. Leave the short side ends unstitched so that you end up with a fabric tube, or *sleeve.***

4. **Turn the sleeve right-side-out by pulling it through one open end, and press it flat.**

5. **Pin the sleeve to the back side of the quilt near the top edge, lining up one long edge of the sleeve with the edge of the binding where it meets the backing fabric. Hand stitch both long edges of the sleeve in place using a blind-stitch.**

Hanging large-sized quilts

Because of its weight, a large quilt needs a good amount of support when it's hanging on the wall. To hang a large quilt:

1. **Cut a strip of fabric that's 12 inches wide and as long as your quilt width.**

   For example, if your quilt measures 60 inches across the top, cut your sleeve fabric 12 x 60 inches.

2. **Finish and attach the sleeve as you would for smaller quilts (see the section "Hang Around with Dowel Sleeves and Rods").**

3. **Purchase a length of wood closet rod exactly as long as the quilt is wide.**

4. **Insert a heavy-duty screw eye into each end of the rod, and insert the rod into the sleeve.**

5. **Cut a length of heavy-gauge wire 6 inches longer than the length of the closet rod. Insert one end of wire into one screw eye, and secure it by twisting. Do the same with the other end of the wire and the other screw eye, taking up most of the slack in the wire so that it's just slightly longer than the rod.**

6. **Pound a nail into a wall stud about 1 inch higher than you want the quilt to hang.**

7. **Hang the wire on the nail.**

With the sleeve sewn in place, insert a dowel rod or lath strip into the sleeve. To hang your quilt, attach brackets to your wall to hold the dowel (you can use wood brackets from the home improvement center or curtain rod brackets, depending on the thickness of the dowel). For a decorative look, you can cut the dowel an inch or two longer than the width of the quilt and attach finials to the ends of the dowel. To find out how you can use the dowel and sleeve method with a large quilt, see the sidebar "Hanging large-sized quilts."

Use a Café Curtain Rod

To display small, lightweight projects, purchase a café curtain rod set and mount it to the wall using the accompanying brackets. Draping your quilted items over the mounted rod, sewing a sleeve to the back of the quilt and threading the rod through it, or using clip-on café curtain hooks (no sleeve required!) are great ways to show off an ever-changing display of your work.

Never hang a quilt in sunlight. Even filtered sunlight can cause fading damage to your quilts.

Cover a Table

Use the quilt as a table topper. Smaller quilts are great as table art, especially square ones. Use a quilt as a large doily by placing it at a diagonal in the center of the table. Long, narrow quilts make lovely table runners, and larger quilts can be used in lieu of tablecloths and are especially nice during the holidays, if you have a quilt that coordinates with the season. Some quilts are even small enough to be used as place mats!

Drape the Quilt over Furniture

Draping your quilt over the back of a chair or sofa adds interest to the furniture and allows people to curl up with the quilt when they're chilly. This display method is a great way to show off your creation and get lots of good use out of it as well.

Fold and Stack

For a country casual look, fold several quilts up neatly and stack them in an open cupboard. If you have an antique ladder with lots of character, consider using it as a quilt display as well: Fold your quilts neatly and hang them from the rungs.

Artfully Arrange

Arrange a quilt so that it appears to spill out of a big basket or trunk. This look is very whimsical and relaxed, and it's a great way to display multiple quilts in your collection — simply rotate them often to show off more of your handiwork.

Create seasonal vignettes by arranging a quilt with items relevant to the season. I'm imagining a quilt in fall colors spilling out of a large brown basket, accented with a branch of autumn leaves and a pumpkin or two. . . .

Fold and Place

Fold your quilt and place it at the foot of the bed or on the back of the sofa. This arrangement is another one that's both attractive and practical because you can grab the quilt whenever you need some extra warmth. Even a small quilt that wouldn't normally be large enough to snuggle under can be folded neatly at the foot of the bed, making it look bigger than it really is. Long, narrow quilts or quilts folded into narrow lengths can also be used up in the pillow area in place of decorative shams.

Drape It over the Stair Railing

Quilts look wonderful hanging from railings! In fact, the stair railing is one of those places where you can have an ever-changing display of quilt art for all the world — or at least folks visiting — to see!

Chapter 21

Top Ten Criteria Quilting Judges Use

. . . .

In This Chapter

▶ Mastering the practical craft of quilting

▶ Executing the details with expertise

. . . .

*N*ow that you're on your way to becoming a card-carrying member of the hooked-on-quilting club, you'll no doubt start setting your sights on the big quilting shindig — the quilt show — and the possibility of having one of your very own creations win a prize or two.

Quilt judges are a savvy bunch. They don't scrutinize your quilt up and down to find its faults. Instead, they evaluate your quilt carefully to see what makes it stand apart from the others in a good way. Because they're quilters themselves, judges know all the little tricks and techniques that can make a quilt a knockout or a knock-down. Judges also have to do their very best to put aside their own design and color preferences and view each quilt as a work of art, worthy of being judged on its own merit.

In this chapter, I clue you in on how to get your creation noticed by the judging panel by pointing out the various criteria they have in mind and how to use that knowledge to your advantage.

Design

First impressions do count! The design of your quilt is the first and foremost thing the judges look at. Questions they may ask themselves include: Is the design interesting and eye-catching? Did you show your creativity by creating a new design, or did you adapt a traditional one by resizing, stretching, or styling it differently? Do the colors and patterns create excitement in the quilt, or do they clash worse than pearls at a ballpark?

Unity

Some things just don't go together, and with all the different quilting techniques, patterns, and fabrics available to you, there's plenty of room for error. If the quilt is composed of different elements, such as both pieced and appliquéd blocks, judges consider how the components work together. Is there a harmony to their pairing? For example, pairing a big, clunky nine-patch design stitched from homespun plaids with a well-executed appliqué pattern of tiny trailing vines and pretty flowers may not be such a great idea.

Balance and Layout

Your blocks, sashing, borders, and binding should look like they belong together. Do your chosen borders add another element to your quilt's design, or does an over- or undersized border detract from the overall look of the quilt, causing it to look unbalanced? For example, if the main part of your quilt top is made up of blocks with many intricate pieces in a number of different fabrics, an equally busy border will only distract the eye and fight with the center design rather than complement it.

Neatness

Quilts entered in a competition should always be immaculately clean, free from wrinkles, and completely devoid of "cling-ons" such as thread or fuzz. They should never smell of mildew, tobacco, or your pets.

Also, make sure that any quilting lines or seam allowances that you marked on the quilt are long gone. To remove quilt markings, wash your quilt according to the directions on the batting package or in your washing machine on the gentle cycle using a mild detergent. Many quilt shops carry detergents that are perfect for quilts because they're mild and don't cause fabrics to fade. Most quilts can handle a toss in the dryer, as long as it's on a low setting; when in doubt (and when the weather's nice), place a sheet on a shady patch of your lawn and lay the quilt on top of it to dry.

Stubborn quilting lines can be coaxed out of the quilt by rubbing the edge of a bar of mild soap along the markings and then washing and drying as usual. If the lines still don't disappear, check the package for your marking implement — was it really washable?

Construction

Quilt show judges pay particular attention to the construction of a quilt because it shows your attention to detail and your concern for doing things correctly. If you're considering entering your project in a show, ask yourself these questions first:

✔ **Do all your seams line up and converge on one another properly?** Seams that don't line up indicate that your seam allowances may not have been consistent throughout the project.

✔ **Are your points nice and sharp or cut off at the tip?**

Craftsmanship

In quilt judging, craftsmanship refers to the little stuff: the beginnings and ends of your stitching, the appearance of your stitches, and the overall squareness of your final project. Evaluate your own craftsmanship before the judges do by answering these questions:

✔ **If your quilt features hand blind-stitch appliqué, are your stitches as invisible as possible?**

✔ **If you used a blanket stitch for appliqué, are your stitches consistently spaced?**

✔ **Are your quilting stops and starts obvious or (hopefully) barely noticeable?** Machine quilting can produce the problem of visible starts and stops if you backstitch too often.

✔ **If you hand quilted your project, are your knots hidden?** They should not be seen or felt.

✔ **Is your quilt squared?** A skewed quilt is always marked down because it's noticeably crooked, doesn't hang properly (it favors one side), and just doesn't look "right."

Quilting

Seeing as how quilting is what makes a quilt a quilt (follow that?), it's not surprising that judges pay very close attention to the quality of your quilting work. This criterion involves not only the quilting stitches but also the quilting design. To prepare yourself for the judges' scrutiny, examine your quilt with an objective eye and ask yourself these questions:

- ✔ **If you hand quilted your project, are your stitches evenly sized and spaced?** Your stitches don't have to be itsy-bitsy-teeny-weeny — just consistent in size. Hand quilting that's all over the place in terms of size definitely costs you points.

- ✔ **If you stipple quilted on the machine, are your paths consistently wandering or do they cross one another at odd places?** Crossed paths in any stipple-quilted area are a big no-no and can get you marked down a bit.

- ✔ **If you chose to use a quilting template or fancy design, does it complement the overall style of the quilt?** For example, an Art Deco quilting design isn't the best match for a quilt with an Asian theme. If the quilting design doesn't complement the overall design, it can easily detract from the project's overall appearance in spite of the time and care you took to stitch it.

- ✔ **If you used an allover quilting design to fill large empty areas, does it fill the space without detracting from the more important elements of the quilt?**

- ✔ **Does the color of the chosen thread complement the quilt? Is the thread weight too fine or too heavy for the overall design?**

Finishing

Because it's one of the last elements you work on in your quilting project, the quality of the binding may suffer if you're in a hurry to finally get the project over and done with. However, quilting show judges don't let you off the hook quite so easily when it comes to binding and finishing.

Pay close attention to whether your binding is smooth around all four sides of the quilt. A binding that's too taut can curl the edges of the quilt inwards. Also make sure that your corners are neatly turned and mitered.

Special Features

Judges love extras — anything that makes your quilt stand out from the crowd in a good way is a definite bonus. So if you added any embroidery or other special stitching to the quilt, you should feel confident that it was executed properly.

Overall Appearance

When a quilt's design, colors, fabrics, borders, quilting, workmanship, and finishing all come together, they form the overall appearance (and my favorite "Ah-Ha!" moment). Nothing thrills judges or other quilters more than a truly remarkable quilt that makes them want to look more and more closely and never stop marveling.

Appendix

Resources for Quilters

• •

*Q*uilting opens a whole new world of fabulous fabrics, creative patterns, notions, and other necessities to warm the heart of anyone who once stared starry-eyed at the colorful variety of pencils, tablets, and other goodies arrayed in the school supplies section of the local store.

What follows is a list of my favorite quilting suppliers along with a selection of books and magazines to expand your quilting horizons. These lists are just to start you off — you're sure to develop your own favorites as you proceed. And don't forget to hook up with your local Quilting Guild and fabric stores to develop your quilting style in the best quilting tradition — community.

Shopping for Quilting Supplies

If you need assistance locating supplies for quilting, contact any of the following manufacturers. They can tell you where their products are available in your area or recommend a mail-order source. Many of these manufacturers also support quilting contests and guild activities, provide free patterns or giveaways, or have other resources available to quilters, so be sure to check out their Web sites!

Fabrics

Benartex
1359 Broadway
Suite 1100
New York, New York 10018
Phone: 212-840-3250
Web site: www.benartex.com

Big Horn Quilts
529 Greybull Avenue, PO Box 566
Greybull, WY 82426
Phone: 877-586-9150
Web site: www.bighornquilts.com

Cranston Print Works
2 Worcester Road
Webster, MA 01570
Phone: 800-847-4064
Web site: www.cranstonvillage.com

eQuilter.com
5455 Spine Road, Suite E
Boulder, CO 80301
Phone: 877-322-7423
Web site: www.equilter.com

Kona Bay/Seattle Bay Fabrics
1637 Kahai Street
Honolulu, Hawaii 96819
Phone: 800-531-7913
Web site: www.konabay.com

Marcus Brothers Textiles, Inc.
980 Avenue of the Americas
New York, NY 10018
Phone: 212-354-8700
Web site: www.marcusbrothers.com

RJR Fabrics
2203 Dominguez Street, Building K-3
Torrance, CA 90501
Phone: 800-422-5426
Web site: www.rjrfabrics.com

Robert Kaufman Co., Inc.
P.O. Box 59266, Greenmead Station
Los Angeles, CA 90059
Phone: 800-877-2066
Web site: www.robertkaufman.com

Springs Creative Products Group
P.O. Box 10232
Rock Hill, South Carolina 29731
Phone: 800-572-5771
Web site: www.springscreativeproductsgroup.com/merchant.ihtml

The soft stuff

In this section, I use the following abbreviations to let you know which companies supply which materials: batting (B), stuffing (St), and pillow forms (PF).

Buffalo Batt & Felt
3307 Walden Avenue
Depew, NY 14043
Phone: 716-683-4100
Web site: www.buffalobatt.com
B, St, PF

Fairfield Processing
P.O. Box 1157
Danbury, CT 06813
Phone: 800-980-8000
Web site: www.poly-fil.com
B, St, PF

Hobbs Bonded Fibers
200 South Commerce Drive
Waco, TX 76710
Phone: 800-433-3357
Web site: www.hobbsbondedfibers.com
B

Morning Glory Products
302 Highland Drive
Taylor, TX 76574
Phone: 800-234-9105
Web site: www.carpenter.com/consumer/morning_glory.htm
B, St, PF

Mountain Mist
2551 Crescentville Road
Cincinnati, OH 45241
Phone: 800-345-7150
Web site: www.stearnstextiles.com
B, St, PF, and quilting stencils and patterns

Quilters Dream Batting
589 Central Drive
Virginia Beach, VA 23454
Phone: 888-268-8664
Web site: www.quiltersdreambatting.com
B

Fusible transfer webbing (FW) and stabilizer (Sb)

Pellon Consumer Products
4720A Stone Drive
Tucker, Georgia 30084
Phone: 770-491-8001
Web site: www.pellonideas.com
FW, Sb

Therm-O-Web
770 Glenn Avenue
Wheeling, IL 60090
Phone: 847-520-5200
Web site: www.thermoweb.com/cpd-products.html

Threads

American & Efird, Inc.
P.O. Box 507
24 American St.
Mt. Holly, NC 28120
Phone: 800-438-5868
Web site: www.amefird.com/signature_quilting.htm

Coats & Clark
Consumer Services
P.O. Box 12229
Greenville, SC 29612
Phone: 800-648-1479
Web site: www.coatsandclark.com
All-purpose, rayon, and buttonhole-twist threads as well as needles (both hand and machine), embroidery floss, and readymade bias tape

DMC
www.dmc-usa.com/dmc_products/DMC_Threads/Quilting_Threads

Sulky of America
P.O. Box 494129
Port Charlotte, FL 33949
Phone: 800-874-4115
Web site: www.sulky.com/home.shtml

Quilt frames hoops, display racks, and other items

The Grace Frame Company
P.O. Box 27823
2225 South 3200 West
Salt Lake City, UT 84127
Phone: 800-264-0644
Web site: www.graceframe.com

Hinterberg Design, Inc.
2805 E. Progress Drive
West Bend, WI 53095
Phone: 800-443-5800
Web site: www.hinterberg.com

Jasmine Heirlooms
1308 Water Street
Kerrville, TX 78028
Phone: 800-736-7326
Web site: www.jasmineheirlooms.com

Ulmer Bros.
P.O. Box 6
207 Cherry Street
Otterville, MO 65348
Phone: 888-827-6786
Web site: www.ulmerquilter.com

Quilting software

The Electric Quilt Company
419 Gould Street
Suite 2
Bowling Green, OH 43402
Phone: 800-356-4219
Web site: www.electricquilt.com

Quilt-Pro Systems, Inc.
P.O. Box 560692
The Colony, TX 75056
Phone: 800-884-1511
Web site: www.quiltpro.com

Notions, rotary cutting supplies, and fun stuff

Clover Needlecraft Products
1007 E. Dominguez Street, #L
Carson, CA 90746
Phone: 800-233-1703

Prym Dritz Corporation
P.O. Box 5028
Spartanburg, SC 29304
Phone: 800-845-4948
Web site: www.dritz.com

Wm. Wright Company
85 South Street, P. O. Box 398
West Warren, MA 01092
Phone: 877-597-4448
Web site: www.wrights.com/products/sewing/sewing.htm

Recommended Reading

- *Country Living Country Quilts* by Editors of *Country Living Gardener* (Hearst Books, 2001)

- *Fast, Fun & Fabulous Quilts: 30 Terrific Projects from the Country's Most Creative Designers* by Suzanne Nelson (Rodale Press, 1996)

- *The Joy of Quilting* by Joan Hanson and Mary Hickey (That Patchwork Place, 2000)

- *Judy Martin's Ultimate Rotary Cutting Reference* by Judy Martin (Collector Books, 1997)

- *Quick Classic Quilts* by Marsha McCloskey (Leisure Arts, 1996)

- *Quilter's Complete Guide* by Marianne Fons and Liz Porter (Leisure Arts, 1993)

- *The Quilting Sourcebook: Over 200 Easy-to-Follow Patchwork and Quilting Patterns* by Maggi McCormick Gordon (Trafalgar Square, 2003)

- *Quiltmaking Tips and Techniques: Over 1,000 Creative Ideas To Make Your Quiltmaking Quicker, Easier And A Lot More Fun* by Editors of *Quilter's Newsletter Magazine* (Rodale Books, 1997)

- ✔ *Quilts, Quilts, and More Quilts!* by Diana McClun and Laura Nownes (C&T Publishing, 1993)
- ✔ *Speed Quilting: Projects Using Rotary Cutting & Other Shortcuts* by Cheryl Fall (Sterling Publishing, 1996)
- ✔ *The Thimbleberries Book of Quilts: Quilts of All Sizes Plus Decorative Accessories for Your Home* by Lynette Jensen (Rodale Books, 1998)

Quilting Magazines to Inspire You

Contact these magazines individually for subscription rates, and be sure to check out the Web sites listed — some have free patterns.

- ✔ *American Quilter:* www.americanquilter.com
- ✔ *Better Homes and Gardens American Patchwork & Quilting:* www.meredith.com/publishing/factsheets/quilting.htm
- ✔ *Fons & Porter's Love of Quilting:* www.fonsandporter.com
- ✔ *McCall's Quilting:* www.mccallsquilting.com
- ✔ *The Quilter Magazine:* www.thequiltermag.com
- ✔ *Quilter's Newsletter Magazine:* qnm.com
- ✔ *Quilter's World:* www.quilters-world.com
- ✔ *Quilt Magazine:* www.quiltmag.com
- ✔ *Quiltmaker:* www.quiltmaker.com

Fun Reads Based on Quilting

Do you want to know more about the lives of quilters past? Maybe you just like a good read. Here are a few lists of quilt-related titles I recommend.

Historical studies

- ✔ *Elizabeth Roseberry Mitchell's Graveyard Quilt: An American Pioneer Saga* by Linda Otto Lipsett (Halstead & Meadows, 1995)
- ✔ *Gatherings: America's Quilt Heritage* by Paul D. Pilgrim, Gerald E. Roy, Kathlyn F. Sullivan, and Katy Christopherson (American Quilters Society, 1995)

- ✔ *New Recipes from Quilt Country: More Food & Folkways from the Amish & Mennonites* by Marcia Adams (Clarkson Potter, 1997)

- ✔ *A Quilt of Words: Women's Diaries, Letters, and Original Accounts of Life in the Southwest, 1860-1960* by Sharon Niederman (Johnson Books, 1988)

Fiction and poetry

- ✔ *Buried in Quilts* by Sara Hoskinson Frommer (Worldwide Publications, 1996)

- ✔ *Death on the Drunkard's Path: An Iris House Mystery* by Jean Hagar (Avon, 1996)

- ✔ *Dove in the Window: A Benni Harper Mystery* by Earlene Fowler (Berkley Publishing Group, 1999)

- ✔ *How to Make an American Quilt* by Whitney Otto (Ballantine Books, 1992)

- ✔ *The Persian Pickle Club* by Sandra Dallas (St. Martin's Press, 1996)

- ✔ *A Piece of Justice: An Imogen Quy Mystery* by Jill Paton Walsh (St. Martin's Press, 2001)

- ✔ *Quilt of Many Colors: A Collage of Prose and Poetry* by Grayce Confer (Beacon Hill Press, 1990)

- ✔ *Silent Friends: A Quaker Quilt* by Margaret Lacey (Stormline Press, 1995)

- ✔ *Twelve Golden Threads: Lessons for Successful Living from Grama's Quilt* by Aliske Webb (Perennial, 1997)

- ✔ *Words & Quilts: A Selection of Quilt Poems* by Felicia Mitchell (Quilt Digest, 1995)

Children's books

- ✔ *No Dragons on My Quilt* by Jean Ray Laury (Collector Books, 2000)

- ✔ *Sweet Clara and the Freedom Quilt* by Deborah Hopkinson (Dragonfly Books, 1995)

Index

• *Q* •

BUSINESS, CAREERS & PERSONAL FINANCE

0-7645-5307-0

0-7645-5331-3 *†

Also available:
- Accounting For Dummies †
  0-7645-5314-3
- Business Plans Kit For Dummies †
  0-7645-5365-8
- Cover Letters For Dummies
  0-7645-5224-4
- Frugal Living For Dummies
  0-7645-5403-4
- Leadership For Dummies
  0-7645-5176-0
- Managing For Dummies
  0-7645-1771-6

- Marketing For Dummies
  0-7645-5600-2
- Personal Finance For Dummies *
  0-7645-2590-5
- Project Management For Dummies
  0-7645-5283-X
- Resumes For Dummies †
  0-7645-5471-9
- Selling For Dummies
  0-7645-5363-1
- Small Business Kit For Dummies *†
  0-7645-5093-4

HOME & BUSINESS COMPUTER BASICS

0-7645-4074-2

0-7645-3758-X

Also available:
- ACT! 6 For Dummies
  0-7645-2645-6
- iLife '04 All-in-One Desk Reference
  For Dummies
  0-7645-7347-0
- iPAQ For Dummies
  0-7645-6769-1
- Mac OS X Panther Timesaving
  Techniques For Dummies
  0-7645-5812-9
- Macs For Dummies
  0-7645-5656-8

- Microsoft Money 2004 For Dummies
  0-7645-4195-1
- Office 2003 All-in-One Desk Reference
  For Dummies
  0-7645-3883-7
- Outlook 2003 For Dummies
  0-7645-3759-8
- PCs For Dummies
  0-7645-4074-2
- TiVo For Dummies
  0-7645-6923-6
- Upgrading and Fixing PCs For Dummies
  0-7645-1665-5
- Windows XP Timesaving Techniques
  For Dummies
  0-7645-3748-2

FOOD, HOME, GARDEN, HOBBIES, MUSIC & PETS

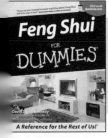

0-7645-5295-3

0-7645-5232-5

Also available:
- Bass Guitar For Dummies
  0-7645-2487-9
- Diabetes Cookbook For Dummies
  0-7645-5230-9
- Gardening For Dummies *
  0-7645-5130-2
- Guitar For Dummies
  0-7645-5106-X
- Holiday Decorating For Dummies
  0-7645-2570-0
- Home Improvement All-in-One
  For Dummies
  0-7645-5680-0

- Knitting For Dummies
  0-7645-5395-X
- Piano For Dummies
  0-7645-5105-1
- Puppies For Dummies
  0-7645-5255-4
- Scrapbooking For Dummies
  0-7645-7208-3
- Senior Dogs For Dummies
  0-7645-5818-8
- Singing For Dummies
  0-7645-2475-5
- 30-Minute Meals For Dummies
  0-7645-2589-1

INTERNET & DIGITAL MEDIA

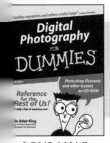

0-7645-1664-7

0-7645-6924-4

Also available:
- 2005 Online Shopping Directory
  For Dummies
  0-7645-7495-7
- CD & DVD Recording For Dummies
  0-7645-5956-7
- eBay For Dummies
  0-7645-5654-1
- Fighting Spam For Dummies
  0-7645-5965-6
- Genealogy Online For Dummies
  0-7645-5964-8
- Google For Dummies
  0-7645-4420-9

- Home Recording For Musicians
  For Dummies
  0-7645-1634-5
- The Internet For Dummies
  0-7645-4173-0
- iPod & iTunes For Dummies
  0-7645-7772-7
- Preventing Identity Theft For Dummies
  0-7645-7336-5
- Pro Tools All-in-One Desk Reference
  For Dummies
  0-7645-5714-9
- Roxio Easy Media Creator For Dummies
  0-7645-7131-1

* Separate Canadian edition also available
† Separate U.K. edition also available

Available wherever books are sold. For more information or to order direct: U.S. customers visit www.dummies.com or call 1-877-762-2974. U.K. customers visit www.wileyeurope.com or call 0800 243407. Canadian customers visit www.wiley.ca or call 1-800-567-4797.

SPORTS, FITNESS, PARENTING, RELIGION & SPIRITUALITY

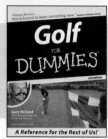

0-7645-5146-9

0-7645-5418-2

Also available:

- Adoption For Dummies
  0-7645-5488-3
- Basketball For Dummies
  0-7645-5248-1
- The Bible For Dummies
  0-7645-5296-1
- Buddhism For Dummies
  0-7645-5359-3
- Catholicism For Dummies
  0-7645-5391-7
- Hockey For Dummies
  0-7645-5228-7

- Judaism For Dummies
  0-7645-5299-6
- Martial Arts For Dummies
  0-7645-5358-5
- Pilates For Dummies
  0-7645-5397-6
- Religion For Dummies
  0-7645-5264-3
- Teaching Kids to Read For Dummies
  0-7645-4043-2
- Weight Training For Dummies
  0-7645-5168-X
- Yoga For Dummies
  0-7645-5117-5

TRAVEL

0-7645-5438-7

0-7645-5453-0

Also available:

- Alaska For Dummies
  0-7645-1761-9
- Arizona For Dummies
  0-7645-6938-4
- Cancún and the Yucatán For Dummies
  0-7645-2437-2
- Cruise Vacations For Dummies
  0-7645-6941-4
- Europe For Dummies
  0-7645-5456-5
- Ireland For Dummies
  0-7645-5455-7

- Las Vegas For Dummies
  0-7645-5448-4
- London For Dummies
  0-7645-4277-X
- New York City For Dummies
  0-7645-6945-7
- Paris For Dummies
  0-7645-5494-8
- RV Vacations For Dummies
  0-7645-5443-3
- Walt Disney World & Orlando For Dummies
  0-7645-6943-0

GRAPHICS, DESIGN & WEB DEVELOPMENT

0-7645-4345-8

0-7645-5589-8

Also available:

- Adobe Acrobat 6 PDF For Dummies
  0-7645-3760-1
- Building a Web Site For Dummies
  0-7645-7144-3
- Dreamweaver MX 2004 For Dummies
  0-7645-4342-3
- FrontPage 2003 For Dummies
  0-7645-3882-9
- HTML 4 For Dummies
  0-7645-1995-6
- Illustrator CS For Dummies
  0-7645-4084-X

- Macromedia Flash MX 2004 For Dummies
  0-7645-4358-X
- Photoshop 7 All-in-One Desk Reference For Dummies
  0-7645-1667-1
- Photoshop CS Timesaving Techniques For Dummies
  0-7645-6782-9
- PHP 5 For Dummies
  0-7645-4166-8
- PowerPoint 2003 For Dummies
  0-7645-3908-6
- QuarkXPress 6 For Dummies
  0-7645-2593-X

NETWORKING, SECURITY, PROGRAMMING & DATABASES

0-7645-6852-3

0-7645-5784-X

Also available:

- A+ Certification For Dummies
  0-7645-4187-0
- Access 2003 All-in-One Desk Reference For Dummies
  0-7645-3988-4
- Beginning Programming For Dummies
  0-7645-4997-9
- C For Dummies
  0-7645-7068-4
- Firewalls For Dummies
  0-7645-4048-3
- Home Networking For Dummies
  0-7645-42796

- Network Security For Dummies
  0-7645-1679-5
- Networking For Dummies
  0-7645-1677-9
- TCP/IP For Dummies
  0-7645-1760-0
- VBA For Dummies
  0-7645-3989-2
- Wireless All In-One Desk Reference For Dummies
  0-7645-7496-5
- Wireless Home Networking For Dummies
  0-7645-3910-8